International Developments
in Large-scale Assessment

International Developments in Large-scale Assessment

Proceedings of the Symposium on Large-scale Assessment in an International Perspective, 16–18 June 1988, Deidesheim, West Germany

Edited by Walter H. Schreiber and Karlheinz Ingenkamp

The Symposium was sponsored by the Stiftung Volkswagenwerk

NFER-NELSON

Published by The NFER-NELSON Publishing Company Ltd.,
Darville House, 2 Oxford Road East,
Windsor, Berkshire SL4 1DF, England.

First published 1990
© *1990. Walter H. Schreiber and Karlheinz Ingenkamp*
© *for individual papers remains with the contributors*

British Library Cataloguing in Publication Data
Symposium on Large-Scale Assessments in International Perspective (1988: Diedesheim, Germany).
International developments in large-scale assessment: proceedings of the symposium on Large-Scale Assessment in an International Perspective 16–18 June 1988, Diedesheim, West Germany.
1. Education. Assessment
I. Title II. Schreiber, Walter H. III. Ingenkamp, Karlheinz
379.1'54

ISBN 0-7005-1247-0

Printed by Billing & Sons Ltd, Worcester
Phototypeset by David John Services Ltd., Slough, Berks.

The Symposium upon which this book is based was sponsored by the Stiftung Volkswagenwerk.

The German translation of this work is published by Deutscher Studien Verlag under the title 'Was wissen unsere Schüler? Überregionale Lernerfolgsmessung aus internationaler Sicht'.

ISBN 0 7005 1247 0
Code 8340 02 4

Contents

List of Tables

List of Figures

Opening address at the Symposium on Large-scale Assessment at Deidesheim, West Germany, 16–18 June 1988

Karlheinz Ingenkamp

It is my honour and pleasure to deliver the Opening Address for the Symposium on Large-scale Assessment. We are very proud that we could bring together such an outstanding group of competent researchers and educators. We hope our sessions will bring to each one new perspectives, new ideas, and we expect stimulating effects particulary for Germany.

But first of all, I have to thank the Volkswagen Foundation, which gave us the opportunity to meet. I hope we shall convince Dr Englert, who is with us as an officer of the Foundation, that they spent their money to good purpose. I would also like to thank Mr Schmitz from the Ministry of Education in Rhineland-Palatinate, who was a great help in contacting other ministries during the preparation. And I thank all those who are going to share their experiences with us. Last but not least, I have to thank Walter H. Schreiber for his invaluable work in preparing all the details of the conference organization. He has the abbreviation 'H' for his middle name, and I think it stands for helpful. Before you go, I am sure you will value his help as much as I do.

When I welcome our guests to Germany, I welcome them to one of the three European countries where the roots of assessment, in a scientific way, were established. I remind you not only of Wilhelm Wundt, but even more of Ebbinghaus and his breakthrough in mental assessment in 1885, with his studies on memory and in 1897 with his clozure-test. We should remember also Erich Meumann and William Stern, who developed a high standard of educational measurement to improve instruction shortly after the turn of the century. They used the term 'experimental proof' more often than the word 'test', but in 1916–17 we had promising studies to identify students from the lower classes for higher education. In the mid-1920s the standard of test methods was as high as anywhere else, even if tests were not often used within schools. But in Germany the philosophy of education and psychology was shifting away from experiments and measurements. The so called 'Geisteswissenschaftliche Psychologie und Pädagogik' was focused on insights by way of intuition, introspection, holistic interpretation, etc. The idea that one can measure certain aspects of human learning and human intelligence with experimental methods was condemned by the majority years before Hitler's government declared tests as methods of the Jewish analytical mind, foreign to the holistic German character. And as far as the level of *practice in education* is concerned, we are still below the level of the mid-1920s. I am now spending some of my time in studying the history of experimental pedagogics and educational measurement in Germany; on studies by Bobertag, Hylla and Laemmermann on student selection, for example, and who are still landmarks in design and results, but completely forgotten in today's German education.

I do not mention this just as a historical curiosity, but to call the attention of our colleagues from other countries to the fact that we have a different philosophy and practice of assessment in Germany. We have a widespread attitude against mental measurement. We have the common belief that measurement can touch only the surface of the human mind, only the less important outcomes of teaching. While I was preparing the first international conference on educational measurement in 1967 in Berlin, I compared by means of expenditure, numbers of copies, etc. the frequencies of testing in American and German schools and arrived at the assumption that in US schools tests are 30–50 times more used in relation to students. Today our test frequency is even smaller. Testing in Germany is a very different reality as compared to the UK, the USA, the Netherlands, and so on.

Let me mention just a few consequences of our different background. If our American or British colleagues speak of the necessity of qualitative data in educational measurement, of performance-, essay-type questions, of teachers' ratings, it means that they need such information in addition to the hard data they already possess. In Germany it means that we want these data instead of hard data – or, in other words, the same demand develops into an excuse not to measure in the sense of reliable information.

In addition, according to law and jurisdiction, teachers' subjective marks are not an issue for court decisions in West Germany. If some formal requirements, such as amount of classwork, participation, etc. are fulfilled, no German court questions the validity of teachers' judgements. But if promotion in school depends on objective testing, it may indeed become the subject of court decisions. The basic philosophy here is roughly: everybody knows that subjective marks have low reliability and validity; there is no real basis for overruling such decisions. But if the assessment should become more reliable, more valid, it could then well become the subject of court decisions. Such a case, however, is not a significant motivation in changing the attitudes of the administration in favour of objective measurement.

And let me touch on one other point to remind you how difficult is the transfer of educational measures from one background to another. In almost every paper of the first two days school administration is assigned an important role in the process of large-scale assessment. But like testing, 'administration' is a very different reality in different countries. We should know how much real co-operation exists between teachers, parents and school boards. Are parents' councils only a kind of decoration, without any power at all, or are they partners in important decisions? Do teachers think of the administration as a source of additional advice and support, or as Orwellian 'big brother'?

We have in our discussions the opportunity to clarify the meaning of the variables we are talking about. Let us make use of these chances, with such outstanding experts in our audience. And may we learn from each other.

Social and Political Aspects

1 Testing in the USA: political and social aspects

Archie E. Lapointe

When I sent the original outline of my paper to Professor Dichanz, he court-
eously phoned me and later wrote some thoughtful criticisms. He reminded me
of those attitudes and opinions that many of you have about testing, as practised
in the USA. He further called to my attention the increasing number of critics in
my own country, namely Allan Bloom, Ernie Boyer, John Goodlad and many
others, who consistently remind us of the weaknesses and shortcomings of testing, especially of multiple-choice tests. I work for an organization, the Educational Testing Service (ETS), that preaches against the abuses of too much
testing; that recommends against over-reliance on its own tests; and actually
forbids the use of its tests in certain situations. In most of the presentations I
make, I acknowledge that there is too much testing going on in most US
schools. It is duplicative and wasteful and often misuses student and teacher
time, as well as distorting the curricula in many schools. Studies consistently
show that test results are often misused and, more often, not used at all.

As tests are increasingly being mandated for a whole variety of purposes,
teachers, school administrators and policy-makers are beginning to observe
their limited value and their weaknesses. This is healthy and the questions that
flow from this recognition will undoubtedly lead to better school evaluation.
We will, I am sure, look to more developed cultures like your own for answers
to these questions that for centuries have been with us all.

Personally, I am a product of the French classical system and well remember
the trauma of preparing for my 'bachot'. Our secondary school curriculum was
not only impacted by the exam, it was minutely defined by its content. We studied books on how to prepare for the exam and how to take it. Recently, I have
had conversations with people from the Ministries of Education in England,
France, Italy and Spain and they all described their disappointment over their
own situation, especially over the lack of any systematic, reliable data on school
performance over time; they are examining US approaches in search of models
to emulate. I am optimistic that a mutual sharing of all our experiences will help
each of our countries improve upon its practice, and I am grateful for Dr Dichanz's candour in reacting to my outline. I hope that the changes I have made
in my presentation, in response to his suggestions, will make my comments
more useful to this meeting.

It was suggested that I provide a complete picture of how school evaluation
takes place in the USA. You should be aware that in a system as large and as
diverse as ours, there is something of everything going on. John Goodlad's
classroom observations are well known and highly regarded. Ted Sizer's

experiments with the collection of student portfolios is being widely replicated. In many schools good teachers are discarding test results and developing profound and fruitful relationships with young people. Bad teachers are misreading all kinds of student data, and most teachers are probably doing a good job with a mix of human intuition and professional experience.

Rather than boast about our innovations since they reflect such a small percentage of our total environment, and are described fully in the literature, I thought I would concentrate on the testing phenomenon which dominates our scene, both locally and nationally, and promises to be with us for the foreseeable future.

There is a growing sensitivity in our country that education is what happens only at the micro level, between one student and one teacher, and an increasing respect for the need for a greater degree of professionalism on the part of the teacher. Providing the tools for these professionals – books, aids, tests – is what we are most impatient about. This haste and impatience makes us somewhat clumsy and may account, in part, for the paradox of a growing concern for the development of individual boys and girls and, at the same time, the generation of reams of macro statistics.

With all their acknowledged weaknesses, why does American education, each year, invest over $200 million for the use of tests to evaluate the performance of its 40 million students in grades 1 through 12? Let me describe to you:

• what our motivations are;
• what our current practice is;
• what issues we are discovering.

First, it must be recognized again that all US educators and policy-makers would acknowledge that Socrates probably had it right! A wise teacher, sitting quietly in an aesthetic environment similar to that of the Athenian Forum, measures his disciples' knowledge and understanding through a series of carefully tailored questions and adjusts his instruction accordingly. In addition to imparting knowledge and facts, he is developing a set of values and ethics, a sense of responsibility and a respect for cultural traditions. A list of the objectives of any US school would include the same elements. No one disputes the elegance of the model, nor the desirability of replicating it.

Motivation

But in the USA it has been decided to educate *all* of the citizens, so that each can have the opportunity to:

• enjoy a learning-filled and quality life;
• contribute to an improving society.

The problems may be presented as follows:

to educate 40,000,000 students (grades 1–12)

we need 2,500,000 good teachers

and 105,000 schools.

We could decide to educate only half of our children, or each child for fewer years. But as a society, we consistently move in the opposite direction by continually raising the school-leaving age and persistently attacking the dropout problem. And I am proud that we do so. We have opted *both* for equality of *and* a quality education. A difficult challenge!

Mortimer Adler, the American philosopher, has suggested in his book *The Paideia Principle* that we have achieved only half our goal by providing access to education to all American children; next we must provide each and every one of them with an equally good education. He is right.

Why is the American taxpayer willing and indeed insistent upon paying $300,000,000,000 each year to educate our young citizens? The answers to this question are complex, but probably they relate to the fact that 300 years of consistently improving prosperity coincide with 300 years of more education for more of our citizens. There is a conviction among American voters that education can help improve our lives and ensure our economic well-being. Large businesses and corporations share this view and encourage and support education, and indeed often provide it for their own employees.

All of the candidates currently running for the office of the Presidency are stressing as a first priority, the education issue. Over 40 of the governors of the 50 states have publicly affirmed a priority for education, support for higher educational standards and support for increased funding for education. Increasingly state legislatures are passing new laws intended to raise standards and strengthen the school curriculum.

As in many other countries, there is no strong federal or national governance of education in the USA. Our Secretary of Education has only recently become a Cabinet-level official, and only about six per cent of the financial support for US schools comes from federal tax revenues. The burden for support of the schools is on the 50 state governments and on about 15,000 school districts, all managed locally by elected officials.

This emphasis on the value and need for an educated population has created some anxiety on the part of the American public about how well the schools are doing. In the face of decreasing college entrance test scores, poor performance on international competitive studies and concern over the requirements of the increasingly technological environment of the future, American taxpayers want an accounting. This means that the administrators of these 15,000 school districts, the directors of our 105,000 school buildings, and the country's 2.5 million elementary and secondary school teachers are being asked to report on their stewardship of the nation's children and on how they are utilizing the resources placed at their disposal. One of the ways to do this is to administer tests and report their results.

Current practice

All of these political and administrative levels are seeking data and information to address their concerns about education's performance, to measure the achievement of students and schools, to determine the competence of teachers, and to monitor current and future performance as new laws and regulations are enacted. They seek these data from the results of existing testing programmes, or they impose new tests to collect additional information.

Since this current reform movement began in the early 1980s, over 40 of the 50 states have legislated some form of state-wide testing programme. Usually these are commercially produced, multiple-choice tests administered to all students at certain grade levels. In some states they are tests (similar in content and format to the commercial tests) created by teachers and psychometricians for that particular state. The tests may be designed to measure student achievement, to certify the acquisition of minimum competencies or to qualify students for promotion or graduation. Some states have all three types of testing programme. In addition to the multiple-choice tests, more and more states are imposing essay examinations as well. They are doing this because of a growing concern over the poor quality of student writing and because of the recognition that if writing is measured, it will be taught more systematically.

In addition to these tests, there are, of course, the two major college admissions tests; the Scholastic Aptitude Test (SAT) and the American College Test (ACT), which are administered to about one-third of the 11th and 12th graders. Finally, there is the National Assessment of Educational Progress, (NAEP) which tests nationally only a small sample of students (about 100,000) every two years in order to get a picture of the performance of all students at ages nine, 13 and 17 years. Also NAEP asks students, teachers and school principals questions about their attitudes about schooling and the various curriculum subjects, how they are taught, what levels of training teachers have had, etc.

Reports of the results of the tests described above are presented to students, parents, teachers, school administrators, policy-makers and through the media to legislators and the general public. Because of the limitations of the tests themselves, taxpayers are often provided incomplete information that can be misleading or too complex to interpret. For example, schools in a community are often compared to one another based on average performance, without explanation of the differences of their student populations.

This confusion is the result of a complex of factors. Policy-makers and political leaders are often looking for quick, simple answers to complex questions, and in their haste, they inappropriately use test results. An example of this is the use by the Secretary of Education of the SAT and ACT scores to rank-order the educational performance of the 50 states. These test results reflect the performance of only the top half of American students at the 12th grade and are completely inappropriate for state comparative purposes.

Another factor has to do with a failure to recognize the important objectives of schooling that cannot be measured – e.g. developing human values, good citizenship, a positive attitude about learning itself, etc. When schools are measured on only part of their objectives, these elements of the programme take on exaggerated importance and disproportionate amounts of time are devoted to them.

A federal law was enacted in May 1988 that will pay for the use of the NAEP tests by any state that wishes to compare the performance of its students to that of any other state, or to the national statistics, this in spite of the recognition of the limitations and shortcomings mentioned earlier and increasingly recognized by all consumers of these data.

Why do we do it?

1. We know tests are imperfect. They *cannot* measure certain intangible and perhaps even the most important outcomes of education.

But what they can tell us about what students know and can do is also important and their results, though limited, are enlightening. As a society, we are determined to improve the educational achievement of our young people and we need data to determine our progress.

In this instance, a major effort has been made by national committees of educators and policy-makers to guard against the misinterpretation of results and the misuse of data. All of the states were involved in this attempt to learn from past mistakes.

2. Multiple-choice tests are reliable. The ETS probably scores more essay examinations each year than any other organization in the world; the ETS has conducted much research on the comparative reliability of multiple-choice measures compared to essays. We understand the strengths and weaknesses of both approaches. Most of the ETS's tests – NAEP included – use a combination of multiple-choice and essay questions.

The results of multiple-choice tests, though limited in the kinds of information they yield, are generally more reliable than essay examinations.

3. Multiple-choice tests make *efficient* use of student time. Intrusion on instruction is minimized – i.e. students can answer many more questions in a given period of time than if they are asked to write essays. They are also forced to display what they do not know, as well as what they do.

4. Multiple-choice testing is *cost-effective*. It costs about 5 cents to scan and score an answer sheet that can record 100 or more student answers. It costs about $3.00 – 60 times more – to read and score a single essay.

Scoring 100,000 answer sheets will cost about $5,000. The same number of essay papers would cost about $300,000 to correct. If we were to rely on essay examinations to monitor the progress of our 40,000,000 students each year, we simply could not afford to do so.

So the demand for data for accountability is increasing, and the response seems to be to insist on more testing. As we test more, we are becoming increasingly aware of the characteristics and the value of the data it can provide, as well as of the issues surrounding the testing phenomenon.

Issues

There are a set of issues surrounding the use of tests and of evaluation generally that must be kept in mind as accountability is considered and as test results are interpreted.

1. The use across schools and school districts of **common tests** assumes common sets of objectives and shared sets of values. The US school system is pluralistic, decentralized, fiercely independent, and the student bodies are made up of the children of religious fundamentalists, political liberals, scientists, humanists and every imaginable combination of beliefs. Local schools are traditionally responsible to local parents and taxpayers. Identifying common curriculum objectives and values that are valid across states and regions of the country is extremely difficult, except for the most basic skills of reading, writing and arithmetic that tend to reflect the least common denominators.

2. **Validity** has always been an important issue in measurement. Does a test question actually measure the objective it was designed to assess, or does it really measure a reading skill or some subtle, unrecognized process? With attempts being made to assess higher-order skills in addition to knowledge about facts, test validity becomes of even greater concern.

3. **Cultural bias** – as our population becomes increasingly diverse, the impact of context and vocabulary as well as the sensitivities of students with various ethnic, religious and cultural backgrounds are of serious concern.

4. **Comparability of results** – since there are no national standards for achievement in any of the curriculum areas in the USA, and since our culture is accustomed to the notion of competition, there is always the tendency to compare the results of one school against those of other schools, and now the results of one state against those of the 49 other states. There are many reasons why this can be misleading, including the following:

- diverse populations;
- diverse educational objectives;
- diverse social emphases of citizens of certain states.

5. **Misleading data** – are bad data better than no data at all? The answer is *No!* It is absolutely true, however, that if the limitations of data are understood and respected, and they reflect what is happening in important aspects of schooling, they are useful in measuring performance. This is especially true if viewed over time and in perspective.

If the characteristics of the tests are kept constant over the years, or careful equating of the various forms has been done, then changes in student performance can be most instructive and trends can be observed. As long as these trends are interpreted within a complete context, they can be helpful in setting good educational policy.

There are other technical and psychometric issues that have to do with sampling, standardized administration procedures and monitoring of testing procedures that are being aggressively explored. Recent and current experiences of

NAEP have generated some major and important methodological break-throughs.

These problems can argue attractively – especially to the research community – that we should wait and study further before proceeding on any large-scale measurement using any of these techniques. Unfortunately (or fortunately?), we are used to dealing with an imperfect world, and the social and political pressures do not offer us the luxury of time. There are demands for improvements *now* and insistence on the identification of baseline data and systems for monitoring progress.

The pressures on educator and policy-maker alike to address questions of stewardship and effectiveness are too insistent to be pushed aside by statements concerning our inability to measure accurately how well we are doing. We must do the best we can with the tools at our disposal, and if we are careful, attentive and creative, then we can improve and refine the results that we present to the American public over time.

The dangers to guard against are the over-dependence on these limited measures or the over-interpretation of their results on the assumption that they reflect all of the objectives of education.

The future

The pressure to monitor progress over time will continue, even as our educational system becomes more diverse in terms of its student population and more ambitious in terms of its objectives. It is also safe to predict that we will learn from the successes and failures of current evaluation practice and that we will use improved measurement systems in the future that will involve much less formal testing in the schools. Probable characteristics of assessment programmes for the initial years of the next century include:

1. The use of a sampling of students rather than census-type testing.

2. More precise definitions of subject domains and greater specificity of objectives and questions.

3. Increased probing of student background and attitude characteristics.

4. Increased probing of teaching and learning techniques and their relationships to achievement.

5. More refined and accurate national and regional or state 'norms' that districts and states can compare themselves to.

6. Greater interest in monitoring changes in performance and student characteristics over time to identify the effects of past policies and predict future trends.

7. An insistence upon 'equating' test forms from year to year, so that comparability of data can be assured and results can be reliably related to a solid anchor or baseline.

8. Reporting procedures that will be understandable by students, parents, teachers and policy-makers, as well as by professional psychologists and measurement experts.

9. The administration to sub-samples of the student population of essays and 'hands-on', performance-type exercises in order the better to measure higher-order thinking skills in all curriculum areas.

10. Greater reliance on teachers, as professionals, to evaluate individual students in relation to the group performance data supplied by testing and evaluation programmes.

Finally, the interest in comparing our performance to the achievement of educational systems all over the world will probably continue. To this end, it is reasonable to assume an enriched participation in the activities of the IEA and other international projects.

Of one thing I am absolutely convinced, that the American reporter at a similar conference in the year 2010 will be disclosing the multiple shortcomings of this new, improved system and be as optimistic as I that the situation will in fact be on the verge of improvement.

2 Large-scale Assessment and Local Accountability

Roy H. Forbes

The purpose of this paper is to suggest appropriate relationships between **large-scale assessments** and **local accountability systems**. First, we shall examine local factors that affect potential relationships between large-scale assessment and local accountability systems in the USA. 'Large scale ' is defined as a national assessment, and 'local' refers to individual school districts or schools. Next we shall provide historical descriptions of educational programme evaluation development, the evolving development of educational personnel evaluation, and we suggest how these experiences will ultimately affect student outcome evaluation. In the final section we shall offer seven recommendations for enhancing the relationship between large-scale assessments and local accountability systems.

Factors affecting local accountability systems

Many local accountability systems in the USA include multiple measures of how well students are being served. The assessment of student academic performance is only one part of these systems. Examples of other measures that often are included are student attendance; participation rates in available learning opportunities; discipline-related factors; attitudes; and the number and percentage of students successfully completing their schooling.

Local accountability systems vary throughout the USA. There are many reasons for this variation, but three prominent factors that influence the design of local accountability systems are: (1) the amount of control that state departments of education have over local education agencies; (2) regional historical values placed on education; and (3) the impact of the current educational reform movement.

The degree of control that state departments of education have over local educational agencies varies widely. Some states have virtually total control over both programme and fiscal factors, while others have virtually no control over either.

Some design and operational characteristics affected by state control are class size, teacher certification, salaries, textbook selection, course-of-study specifications, graduation requirements and promotion standards.

There is a high correlation between the source of funds for financing local schools and state control. If the financing of schools is primarily a local responsibility, then state control is usually minimal, but in states where a majority of the fiscal resources come from the state there is a large degree of state control. North Carolina and Texas are examples of states with extensive control; and North Dakota and New Hampshire are states with minimum control.

States with strong control usually have mandatory state-wide testing programmes, while states with weak control have either very limited programmes or no state-wide programmes. The designs of local accountability systems in strong control states are greatly influenced by the designs of state accountability systems, while just the opposite is true for local systems in weak control states.

Regional historical values placed on education is another reason local accountability systems vary. If a local community places a high value on education, this is usually reflected through high expectations. People are interested in knowing how well students are being served and test scores are viewed as important indicators.

In the USA the value placed on education historically has varied by regions of the country. For example, states in the north-east and upper plains areas historically have placed a high value on education, while states in the south-east had a history of using education as a way to guarantee a cheap source of labour. During the period of slavery blacks were denied the opportunity to learn to read and write. Slave-owners recognized the links between education, information, and power. Illiteracy was used as a controlling factor. Following the Civil War, this attitude was carried forward in southern states through 'separate but equal' segregated schools. These schools were anything but equal. Education provided for blacks was minimal.

The economy of the southern states historically depended upon agriculture and textiles. Both required a cheap labour pool. High dropout rates and low levels of academic achievement were very acceptable. This is reflected today in the statistics that show lower levels of schooling in the south-east than in the rest of the country.

The use of education as an economic control mechanism required a two-level schooling programme. Expectations for most students were low, this ensured the cheap labour pool. Expectations for the 'advantaged' students were higher, but *'higher'* was in comparison to the extremely low expectations for others. This resulted in overall low levels of expectations in the southern states.

The database for the above observations is composed of qualitative descriptive information and quantitative student outcome data. Others may interpret the data differently, but there should be agreement on two points: (1) historically, learning opportunities for blacks, economically disadvantaged whites and advantaged whites varied greatly in the south-east, and (2) southerners were not as well educated as people from other regions of the USA.

This history has placed southern schools in a *catch-up* position. The region is now realizing the link between economic growth and education. Some are beginning to address the problems that have been created because of the historically low level of educational expectations. This need to close the gap is being reflected in accountability programmes now in operation and those being planned for the future.

There is a direct link between how well a community believes its educational system is meeting expectations and expressed desires for improved accountability. *Accountability* is not a big issue for local systems who historically have placed high value on education, and who have met expectations, but it is a driving issue where systems are not meeting current expectations and goals.

The third reason for the variation in state and local accountability programmes is the impact that the current reform movement is having on education. The history of education can be viewed as a series of reform movements. These have usually occurred during periods of economic uncertainty. The current reform movement is no exception. The economic leadership role of the USA is in question. This has created an environment in which business leaders have become more concerned about educational outcomes. They understand the links between strong educational systems, a well-educated workforce, and an expanding and competitive economy. Members of the business community are expressing their concerns by participating in reform discussions by providing verbal support for increased educational resources and by calling for increased accountability. An example of business community support for reform efforts was the full-page newspaper advertisement paid for by the leading businesses in South Carolina urging the state legislators to approve a massive and expensive school reform package.

The reform movement of the 1960s and early 1970s and the current reform movement have had an impact on local and state education agencies. More is expected of teachers, students and administrators. Education is being expected to assume responsibilities once viewed as the sole responsibility of families and the church. With increased responsibilities comes an expectation of the system being more accountable. For example, states and local education agencies are beginning to move towards programmes that combine child care and early childhood education for three- and four-year-old children. This movement brings an additional component for accountability systems. How to best evaluate early childhood programmes is a question for which the answers are only beginning to evolve.

In states which had strong central control the latest reform efforts have had the effect of expanding this control and a predictable response is beginning to surface. Some educators are calling for more local autonomy in making decisions. Business leaders who recognize the power of participatory management techniques are providing support to this call for allowing teachers to be more involved in the educational decision-making process. At the same time, there is wide support for increased resources. The business community balances the rationale supporting participatory management techniques with support for increased resources by calling for increased accountability. This movement towards more local autonomy and stronger accountability systems has a great potential impact on the relationship between large-scale assessments and local accountability systems. An example of what is happening in one strong central control state, North Carolina, should help to explain the importance of this movement.

The General Assembly of North Carolina has granted six schools total flexibility in the use of resources, exemptions from state guidelines and mandates, and the right to make strategic and operational decisions. With the granting of this flexibility came an expectation of increased accountability. The six sites are required to provide the State Board of Education and the General Assembly with periodic reports that describe how well students are being served.

Each school in this pilot programme has developed an accountability model based on the school's need for information. Information needs were identified by teachers, counsellors and others who serve students. The question asked in identifying information needs was: 'what data is needed to make decisions about how to better serve students'. Information requirements for policy decisions at the local district and state levels were not an initial consideration.

No attempt was made to make the models uniform across the six sites, but the models do have commonalities. Each model contains contextual, demographic information. Each model includes programme descriptive and operational data. Each model addresses the measurement of student outcomes. Outcome information goes well beyond traditional testing practices. For example, two of the elementary schools in the programme have included the identification of potential *at-risk* students (those who have a high probability of not graduating from high school) as part of their accountability programmes. These students receive special attention during their attendance at the elementary schools. These services are monitored and student success is documented. An objective of the schools is to reduce the number of at-risk students.

Each accountability model was developed by a team of teachers and administrators with technical assistance provided by the organization responsible for the administration of the total pilot programme. The teams responsible for the accountability models express high levels of ownership in their accountability systems.

During the spring of 1988 an interesting situation developed within the pilot schools. A random sample of approx. 20 per cent of the teachers in each school was interviewed to determine attitudes and feelings about the success of the programme. One of the questions pertained to the accountability model that had been developed for their school. The initial response was that they knew that there was an accountability team, but they did not know very much about what the team had been doing. Probing questions indicated that teachers were very familiar with activities that had been implemented by the team, but they had not tagged these as accountability activities. Instead they were viewed as efforts to obtain information for making decisions about how well students were being served and how to improve these services.

A hypothesis that can be generated from these data is that teachers view accountability as something that is done to them and it has a negative connotation. They do not view the collection, analysis and use of data for the purpose of making better decisions for students as accountability. These activities are viewed as appropriate and worthwhile instructional related processes and not as checks on how well they are doing their jobs.

The level of state control, the historical value placed on education and the impact of current reform efforts all play important roles in determining the characteristics of local accountability systems. The link between these factors and large-scale assessment efforts are discussed in the final part of this paper.

Evaluation theory affects on local accountability systems

Educational evaluation can be categorized by three types: programme, personnel and student outcome. Each of these has its own developmental history. Programme evaluation has evolved into a widely accepted set of procedures and standards. Personnel evaluation is currently evolving in ways similar to the evolution of programme evaluation. An understanding of how programme evaluation developed and how personnel evaluation is evolving is useful for projecting what may happen in the area of student outcome evaluation. This understanding is essential for considering the relationship between large-scale assessment and local accountability.

The terms used to differentiate between the two distinct functions of programme evaluation are formative and summative. Some writers use process and product to describe these functions. Formative evaluation provides information necessary to make *mid-course* corrections, while summative evaluation provides information necessary to judge the overall worth of an effort.

Prior to 1967, many evaluation designs attempted to include both functions as aspects of the same system. Few efforts that tried to serve both formative and summative purposes were successful. There were several reasons why this combination did not work, but only one is discussed. It is extremely difficult for an evaluator involved in formative evaluation not to develop ownership in the programme as recommendations resulting from the formative process are implemented. The formative evaluator needs to be a member of the design and implementation team for the purposes of formative evaluations. It is difficult for the formative evaluator to remain totally objective, hence it is difficult for the formative evaluator to also serve as the summative evaluator and to expect the summative data to be perceived as valid and reliable.

In 1967 clear distinctions were made between these two functions of programme evaluation. These distinctions were quickly adopted by the evaluation community. Today no evaluator familiar with appropriate practices and standards would attempt to mix formative and summative programme evaluation unless the design has two distinct sub-systems.

Personnel evaluation currently suffers from the same conditions that plagued programme evaluation prior to 1967. Systems try to accomplish multiple purposes with little success. For the purpose of this discussion, any data used in making personnel decisions pertaining to hiring, dismissal, promotion, reassignment and compensation are considered as summative.

Educational personnel evaluation systems that attempt to serve both formative and summative purposes are extremely fragile. The success of these systems depends on high levels of trust between teachers and administrators. If the persons being evaluated perceive that information collected for formative purposes has been misused in making summative decisions, the formative component of the personnel evaluation system will almost immediately become dysfunctional.

Some writers are now calling for the same clear distinction of purposes of personnel evaluation systems that were developed for programme evaluation. There is a growing body of evidence that for personnel evaluation systems to be effective, there need to be separate evaluators involved in the formative and summative process. Systems are being designed, implemented and evaluated that provide clear distinctions between formative and summative personnel evaluation. It appears that 1987 may have the same significance for personnel evaluation as 1967 had for programme evaluation.

The primary reason for failure of programme evaluations that mixed summative and formative purposes was the perceived inability of the formative evaluator to remain objective as a summative evaluator. The primary reason for failure of personnel evaluations that mix summative and formative purposes is the lack of trust the persons being evaluated have in evaluators who have both of these responsibilities. Both of these reasons pertain to interpersonal relationships and provide a strong case for separating formative and summative evaluation activities.

The interpersonal relationship aspect of the need to separate formative and summative activities in programme and personnel evaluation probably provides a sufficient reason to explore the need to make the same clear distinction in student outcome evaluation efforts, but the need to separate formative and summative student outcome evaluations has not received much attention.

For the purposes of discussing the formative and summative evaluation of student outcomes, **summative** is defined to include processes that result in the assignment of officially recorded grades or test scores used in making promotion, retention assignment and credentialing decisions. For example, a score on a group-administered, norm-referenced test is considered summative when used to screen students for required summer school attendance. Other summative examples are grades assigned by teachers at the end of courses or at the end of a specified period of study. **Formative** is defined to include diagnostic processes. Examples of formative data include suggestions provided by teachers for students to consider in rewriting a theme, critiques of projects that are in the process of being developed and oral responses to students.

Teachers can be and often are the formative and summative evaluators of students for most educational programmes. Formative evaluation occurs during instruction through discussions, oral questions, probing and the observation of non-verbal cues, for example, the most effective teachers watch for the 'light-bulbs' to turn on as new concepts are being developed. Teachers also use *pop quizzes* and other interim tests to assess progress. Many teachers also use some of these results in calculating a summative grade. If the data are used in a summative process, then the data are summative. The primary summative evaluation responsibilities of teachers are the assignment of end-of-course and end-of-term grades.

Standardized tests, either purchased commercially or developed by the state or a local education agency, that are administered to students for the purposes of screening, sorting, *gatekeeping* or judging, are summative measurement instruments. Teachers often participate in the administration of these tests, but the assignment of scores and grades is not the responsibility of teachers. In these cases, teachers are participants of a summative process but they are not the summative evaluators. However, this has created the general perception that, unlike persons responsible for programme and personnel evaluation, teachers have been performing successfully the dual roles of formative and summative evaluators. Is this perception accurate?

During the late 1970s many states implemented minimum competency testing programmes that required high school students to achieve a minimum score as a condition for high school graduation. This occurred as a reaction to criticism that students were graduating from high school without having obtained a minimal level of basic skills. Up to that point, most high school graduation requirements were based on students successfully completing a specified number of courses. Successful completion, in most cases, was determined by teachers. Hence the public's support for minimal competency testing can be viewed as a lack of faith in public opinion about course grades assigned by teachers.

In North Carolina standardized norm-referenced test scores are used as part of an elaborate system for determining students' eligibility for promotion from grades 3, 6 and 8. The principal has the ultimate decision-making authority, but only after certain standardized measures have been used. The role of the teacher as summative evaluator is limited. Grades can be assigned but promotion decisions are made by other persons. This is another reflection of the lack of faith placed in teachers as summative evaluators. The current movement towards end-of-course testing is another illustration of the questions that the public has about the validity of teacher-assigned summative evaluation results. These examples provide a basis for questioning if teachers are being viewed as having been successful in playing the dual role of formative and summative evaluator.

Are there any advantages to separating formative and summative evaluation at the student outcome level? The answer to this question may be contained in recalling the reasons why mixing formative and summative evaluation does not work for programme and personnel evaluation. For programme evaluation, mixing does not work well because the formative evaluator usually becomes too involved with the programme to remain an objective summative evaluator. The formative evaluator develops ownership in changes that result from the formative process. This makes it difficult for the evaluator to draw summative conclusions. For personnel evaluation, the primary reason for failure is the trust factor. It is difficult to develop and maintain a high trust level between evaluators and persons being evaluated when the sharing of information necessary for a successful formative process can become the source of information for a negative summative decision.

Both objectivity and trust are important concepts for successful teacher–student relationships. Both are important factors associated with effective teaching. To check these statements, ask a group of individuals to provide one-word descriptors for teachers who had the most impact on their lives. Most will respond with words like 'caring', 'loving', 'sensitive', 'sincere', 'fair', 'personable', 'trustworthy', 'encourager', 'motivator' and 'dedicated'. Few will use words like 'smart', 'knowledgeable' and 'intellectual'. The implication is not that these latter descriptors are not important, rather they tend to be secondary to characteristics used to describe concepts related to interpersonal relationships.

Does the dual evaluator role create problems? The knowledge base does not contain a ready answer, but the potential for problems associated with objectivity and trust is suggested by the previous discussion. What is clear is the public's perception that current outcome accountability methods do not work very well and the call for more stringent accountability methods is becoming very strong. Few successful businesses allow employees to be responsible for producing products or delivering services and to be responsible for judging the quality of those products and services. *Borrowing* from business practices by separating formative and summative student outcome evaluation activities may prove to be an effective approach for responding to the perception issue.

Are there problems associated with assigning the teacher the role of the formative evaluator and letting other mechanisms be used for summative purposes? There are at leat three. First, the teacher will not have the same control over curriculum content coverage in cases where summative evaluation is outside the responsibility of the teacher, and this may be viewed as an infringement on academic freedom. Secondly, teachers may be prone to teach to the test by making sure that the content tested will be covered during the course of study. Finally, teachers may view the limiting of their roles as summative evaluators as a lack of trust in their ability.

The concern associated with academic freedom can be responded to by providing teachers with opportunities to participate in curriculum design activities. The concern related to teaching to the test objectives becomes minor if the test is an accurate reflection of what students are expected to learn. The only valid concern related to limiting the teacher to formative student outcome evaluation appears to be the one associated with the trust issue. This concern can be alleviated by discussing the potential positive effects on student–teacher interpersonal relationships associated with separating summative and formative evaluation.

The following points support the separation of formative and summative student outcome evaluation:

- there are publicly perceived problems with the validity of teacher-assigned summative measures;

- effective teaching is associated with good student–teacher relationships and the dual role of summative and formative evaluator can potentially endanger effective student–teacher relationships;

- the potential negatives associated with separating summative and formative roles are minimum.

Evaluation theory has and is affecting local accountability systems. Most local systems reflect good practices in programme evaluation, but personnel evaluation suffers from the same deficiencies that are found at the state level because many administrators and policy-makers have not *discovered* the need for separating formative and summative personnel evaluation activities. Currently, people do not even think in summative and formative terms when discussing student outcome evaluation. These three separate stages in the development of programme personnel and student outcome evaluation reflect the status of evaluation theory in the USA.

Relationships between large-scale assessments and local accountability

In the first section of this paper we reviewed some of the political, organizational and social factors that affect local accountability systems, and in the second section we examined the relationship between evaluation theory and local systems. In this section we shall discuss how the information presented in the previous sections could affect the relationship between large-scale assessments and local accountability systems. But first, it is helpful to consider the following characteristics associated with assessment data generated by effective local accountability systems.

For data to be useful to local-level decision-makers, from the school board member to the classroom teacher, it should have the following characteristics:

- Performance data must be directly related to either individual students or groups of students served by the local school.

- Local users of the data must have ownership in some aspects of the need for the data, the process used in obtaining the data or the ways in which the data are used.

- The data must be valid and reliable.

There must be a high alignment among standards and expectations, instructional objectives, curriculum materials and techniques, and assessment items.

- Test data for individual students must have a high diagnostic value.

- Test data for samples of students must be perceived by the public as accurate measures of how well students are performing in comparison with students from other schools, district and states.

The following recommendations flow directly from the information contained in the two previous sections and reflect the above set of characteristics. The primary point of the first section was that educational perceptions and needs vary across the USA. The level of state control, historical values and the extensiveness and approach to educational reform differ across geographical regions. This suggests a need for local options within the context of a national assessment. The recommendations reflect this need.

The primary point advanced in the second section, above, was that student outcome evaluation will probably evolve along the same path followed by programme evaluation and being followed by personnel evaluation. This suggests a need for local summative evaluation options within the context of a national assessment.

Recommendation 1: The organization responsible for the national assessment should provide state and local agencies with options to participate in a variety of assessment programmes each year.

This recommendation goes beyond what is currently available in the USA. It extends the assessment services provided by the organization responsible for the large-scale assessment. Each year state and local agencies could enter into an agreement with the responsible organization for the administration of an assessment of one or more key learning areas. For example, states or local agencies could contract with the large-scale assessor on an annual basis for the assessment of reading and mathematics.

This does not imply a national large-scale assessment of key learning areas each year. The national applicability of the data collected through this recommendation would be determined by the number and variety of state and local agencies requesting assessment services.

Recommendation 2: Large-scale instrumentation development procedures should provide for the inclusion of state and locally specified items in designated sections of the assessment forms.

This recommendation calls for the tailoring of instruments for use in state and local agencies. State and local agencies, participating in the large-scale assessment either as part of the national sample or by special contractual agreements, should be provided by the option to select or develop up to 10 per cent of the total items included in the assessment. The items selected or developed for this purpose would not be replacement items within the national sample, instead they would be additional items administered at the same time as the national assessment.

Recommendation 3: Optional sampling, analysis and reporting procedures which link the large-scale effort with state and local efforts need to be provided. The organization responsible for the large-scale effort should be prepared to enter into discussion with state and local agencies to determine the feasibility of providing state or locally specified analyses and reports. When financially and technically feasible, analyses should be completed for requesting state and local agencies and reports provided.

This recommendation would provide participating states and local agencies with the option of specifying items to be included in an analysis for their purposes. This option would ensure curriculum and assessment alignment, hence enhancing the usefulness of the assessment data for state and local decision-making.

This recommendation would also provide participating states and local agencies with the option of expanding upon the sample selected for national purposes, so that the numbers of students assessed would meet state or local information needs.

Recommendation 4: The organization responsible for the national assessment should provide local districts and states with the option to contract for criterion-referenced tests composed of national, state and local items.

The local districts and states should participate in the selection and development of items to be included. The tests could be administered to individuals for the purpose of summative student outcome evaluation, as well as meeting the need for national-level comparative information.

Current national procedures use a form of item sampling that results in each student, who participates in the assessment, responding to only a sample of the total items, hence individual student results are limited to specific item level analysis. This recommended option would provide districts and schools with the opportunity to collect and analyse student responses to a full-coverage, criterion-referenced test.

Recommendation 5: The data-collection processes used in obtaining large-scale assessment data should avoid violating local testing and assessment principles.

For example, if students with special instructional needs are not included in local testing efforts, then the national effort should not require the inclusion of these students. If conforming to local principles should make the data invalid for national purposes, then the local agencies should be excluded from the national sample.

The first five recommendations pertain to links between large-scale assessment and local accountability efforts. The following recommendations address the use of large-scale assessment information as part of summative evaluation systems, both at the programme and student outcome levels.

Recommendation 6: When the content coverage and student sample is sufficient to draw conclusions about specific states, districts or schools, the information collected, analysed and reported through the large-scale assessment should become part of the summative evaluation systems for the programmes being assessed. In most cases, the large-scale effort should be the only summative process required for obtaining student performance information for the overall programme evaluation.

Recommendation 7: Local districts and schools that use the optional service described in recommendation 4, above, should use the resulting criterion-referenced test information as a summative student outcome measure.

These last two recommendations, if implemented, would move the national assessment in the USA towards becoming a national test of minimal competencies. If a critical mass of states and local districts opted to enter into agreements to obtain services associated with recommendations 1, 2, 3 or 4, and if the states and local districts accepted recommendations 6 and 7, then the USA would have a *de facto* national test.

Would this be bad for education? It would not be if the safeguards of allowing states and local districts to participate in item selection and development are left in place. This would ensure variety in instructional programmes. The large-scale assessment while affecting the core curriculum would not be the determining factor of the total curriculum. Hence state and local autonomy would be maintained.

Procedures required to implement these recommendations are complex. They introduce additional design requirements for large-scale assessments. They expand the purposes of large-scale assessment systems.

Prior to discarding these recommendations as being too costly, complex, or inappropriate, recall the purposes of educational systems. The systems are here to serve individuals and it is only at the local level that individuals are served. National and state-level efforts may enable things to happen, but the *things* that happen only take place in schools. All assessment activities should have the same primary goal: the generation of information that can be used to determine how well students are being served.

References

STUFFLEBEAM, D., FOLEY, W., GEPHART, W., GUBA, E., HAMMOND, R., MERRIMAN, H. and PROVUS, M. (1971). *Educational Evaluation and Decision Making*. Itasca, Il.: Peacock.

BARBER, L. (1985). 'Improving teacher performance'. In: *Formative Evaluation*. Bloomington, Ind.: Phi Delta Kappa.

JOINT COMMITTEE ON STANDARDS FOR EDUCATION EVALUATION (1981). *Standards for Evaluation of Educational Programs, Projects, and Materials*. New York: McGraw-Hill.

FORBES, R., PANDEY, T., CARLSON, D. and HADLEY, C. (1986). 'Überregionale Testprogramme im Bildungswesen der USA'. In: INGENKAMP, K., HORN, R. and JÄGER, R. (Eds) *Tests und Trends 5*. Weinheim: Beltz, pp. 118–65.

3 Consensus-building in Planning and Developing an Assessment

Ramsay W. Selden

Why consensus-building is needed

My purpose in speaking to you is to describe what we have learned from the consensus-building processes that are undertaken to develop large-scale assessment programmes in the USA. State and local education agencies in the USA routinely carry out such consensus planning when they select or develop an assessment programme, and recently we have gone through this process on a national scale for the first time. This has revealed much about consensus planning for assessment that could be of value to many educators in other situations.

I must open my remarks by discussing one difference between the US and German educational systems. This difference is important in order for you to understand the nature of, and rationale for, the consensus-building processes we go through in the USA.

Large-scale assessment is prevalent in the USA, whereas it is largely not present in the Federal Republic of Germany. In addition to the tests and other evaluation procedures developed and used by teachers in our country, which are probably similar to those used by teachers in your country, we have large-scale administration of standardized tests by local, state and national agencies and organizations. For example, local school districts may use a commercially purchased, standardized test to monitor achievement and to evaluate instructional programmes. They also may use a criterion-referenced test developed specifically to measure local curriculum objectives instead of, or in addition to, such a norm-referenced test. Next the state may administer a different, standardized test on a large scale, usually to all students in selected grade levels, also to monitor achievement and evaluate programmes, and the state may administer a criterion-referenced test to measure instructional objectives, in addition, but usually in different grades. Tests to certify proficiency for graduation or promotion from level to level may be used by states and localities. Finally, the federal government supports testing to monitor achievement nationally and to study specific aspects of education in samples of students.

In one analysis it was found that, in a school district in Connecticut, 12 different, standardized tests were administered for various purposes (Pecheone, 1986). None of the students took all 12 tests, but some students could easily be taking three, four or five of the tests each year.

The presence of large-scale testing in the USA may be shown in Table 3.1. The presence and acceptance of large-scale assessment in the USA is a major difference between our systems, and a fact that you must understand in order to place the rest of my comments in proper context.

Table 3.1: Testing in US schools

Level in system	Type of testing	Students tested
Teacher	Teacher-made tests	All
	Tests provided with materials	All
School	None	
District	Standardized achievement tests	All, selected grades and programmes
	Criterion-referenced tests	All students, selected grades
	Proficiency (graduation) tests	All students, selected grades
State	Standardized achievement tests	All students or sample, selected grades
	Criterion-referenced tests	All students or sample, selected grades
	Proficiency (graduation) tests	All students, selected grades
Nation	Standardized achievement tests	Sampled grades and programmes

Why consensus is needed (1) : there are philosophical differences in the content and emphasis of education in decentralized systems.

In decentralized systems authority for education is delegated to levels lower in the governmental system, and this is presumed to result in differences in emphasis and content among those systems. In our constitution we delegate authority for all aspects of education other than equality of access to the states who, in turn, delegate it to local school districts. Further, local school systems are presumed to leave considerable control over instruction up to local teachers, especially at the secondary-school level.

To the extent that this delegation of authority results in real differences in content, sequence or emphasis, some sort of consensus must be identified before students can be tested on a large scale across systems using the same instrument. Tests must correspond to the content of instruction to be valid and for comparisons and other conclusions to be sound. Thus some sort of consensus must be reached on the content to be tested.

Why consensus is needed (2) : there are philosophical and political differences in approaches to assessment in decentralized systems.

States in the USA vary greatly on a dimension we term 'local control'. This is the extent to which the history, culture and political situation in the state have left local school districts or the state relatively responsible for education. In the American West and in New England a tradition of political individualism and particular historical and economic conditions have left the states largely uninvolved in social institutions, such as education, and have created a situation of strong local responsibility for schooling. In the South and the industrial northeast inverse conditions have created a situation of strong state responsibility for schooling. In other areas the political relationship falls somewhere in between. States like Florida, South Carolina, New York and California represent relatively strong state control, while in Montana, New Hampshire and Nebraska the state has relatively less of a role in education. It is important to note, however, that in *every* state, including Hawaii, which is a state-wide school system, local control is still an issue; it is just that some states have been asked to do more and have been able to do more than others.

The effect of the political phenomenon of local control on testing programmes is quite clear. The Rocky Mountain and mid-western states tend to have no state-wide testing, to delegate testing to local districts, or to have statewide testing programmes that pose no direct threat to local autonomy – the testing programmes tend to have no direct implications on the authority or livelihood of local school systems. In the south-east and north-east states typically have two or three different testing programmes for different purposes, most of which have direct implications for students or local school systems (CCSSO, 1987).

In addition to this political dynamic, different professional positions have built up around testing. There is one group that values traditional, norm-referenced achievement testing, another that advocates criterion-referenced testing, a third that feels that each type has its merits and that both should be used, and a fourth camp that feels that standardized, large-scale testing should not be used at all because of its potentially negative consequences on instruction. These positions are reflected in the opinions of testing professionals working in state and local school systems, and they are represented in the administrators and policymakers who oversee these systems.

These two dimensions – the political environment of the state, and the professional position of educators in state and local school systems – result in differences that also must be addressed in developing an assessment programme, in addition to differences in content and emphasis. To what extent will the testing programme reflect relatively strong central management over the school system – that is, how much will it provide state or national leaders with information about the performance of local systems and schools that can be used to affect the operation of those local systems and schools? What models of testing will the programme reflect – that is a relatively traditional, norm-referenced model, a criterion-referenced approach, or some combination or third alternative? These are questions that must be addressed in developing an assessment programme.

Why consensus is needed (3) : Differences in the features and procedures of testing programmes evolve over time in decentralized systems.

Also entering into planning an assessment programme and requiring consensus is that any new testing in the USA will bump into existing testing programmes. Not only will local, state and federal staff resist any new testing that could detract from existing programmes that serve important purposes, but those staff will tend to desire that any new programme have features that make it as compatible as possible with ongoing programmes. Any proposal for a new programme that conflicts or interferes with existing programmes will tend to be regarded as 'impossible' by staff of those existing programmes.

Features that vary among existing state testing programmes are the instruments used, grade levels tested, whether students are sampled or whole schools or classes are tested, whether students are tested in the fall or spring, what subjects are tested and whether the test is put to some special purpose such as certifying competency for graduation. Local testing programmes also vary, of course, on these dimensions.

Plans for a new, large-scale assessment programme may be viewed as convenient or not, in terms of how they fit with these characteristics. Often the compatibility of a new programme as perceived by local or state testing officials cannot be predicted. One state or district may see a new programme where a sample of students are to be tested in the spring as advantageous – a relatively convenient add-on to its programme which tests in the spring, but another state may fear that more testing in the spring will overload students, and they would prefer testing in the new programme at a different time of year.

Thus, in a decentralized educational system in which testing is already prevalent, three types of consensus must be reached. These follow in *descending* order of social or philosophical importance, but they are probably listed in *ascending* order in terms of the difficulty of reaching them, as I will discuss later. First, consensus must be reached about the content to be tested. Secondly, consensus must be reached about the form or type of testing to be done. Thirdly, consensus must be reached about specific procedural details the testing programme will assume.

These arguments as to why consensus-building is necessary are based on two premises or assumptions. The first is that large-scale assessment is desirable. The second is that consensus is feasible to attain. In the USA, we have concluded that large-scale assessment is not only desirable, but necessary. In the 1960s and 1970s we instituted broadly basic-skills testing (reading and mathematics) because it was perceived that schools were not developing even basic or minimal skills in some students by the time they left secondary schools. Indeed, these testing programmes revealed that, in large cities such as New York, Washington or Detroit, the *average* percentile rank of students was below 30 – i.e. the average student scored at about the 30th national percentile. Also in these school systems and in many states the difference between performance by whites and blacks or hispanics was 30 percentile points or more. Egregious learning problems had gone largely undetected and ignored when we relied mainly on teachers' reports to monitor the quality of learning. With the information from these testing programmes, we have been able to direct resources to improving urban schools and improving performance by disadvantaged students, so in the USA we accept large-scale assessment as a useful (really a necessary) source of information.

Also we have come to believe that consensus about testing is achievable, even in a system as decentralized as is ours. As I will discuss later, decentralization is a complex continuum, not a simple dichotomy. With delegation of authority for determining content, considerable commonality can and does remain, and it is this commonality that can serve as the common ground of an assessment.

Political challenges to consensus

In this section, I would like to outline briefly four ways in which consensus-building for assessment can become a political process. Of course, consensus-building is the essence of the political process, and nowhere in education can it be seen better than in designing a testing programme.

First, the largest political force opposing consensus development and the development of assessment programmes is the tendency to preserve the status quo. As an institution, education is a complex set of balancing forces, representing many decisions that have been arrived at through compromise to meet the specific needs of a local situation. Those who administer schools, and those who operate testing programmes, are custodians of these decisions; not only are they not necessarily inclined to change the order of things, but they are not necessarily *free* to change things, even if they agree with the changes.

Secondly, assessment programmes that attempt to become ideal will be compromised as they are negotiated to be implemented at the local level. Thus features of an assessment programme conceived in the abstract that have strong technical merit may conflict with current practices or may encounter local constraints. For example, it may be desirable for testing to include open-ended performance items, or for it to measure higher-order thinking skills. The performance items will be compromised because of lack of time, resources and practical ways of grading them. Higher-order thinking may be scrapped as a target of assessment because local educators, though agreeing it is important to teach these skills, may know that they have not been teaching them.

Thirdly, the technical features of a newly conceived assessment programme may actually exacerbate political problems. For example, policy-makers in a state may want a new assessment programme to capitalize on the ability of testing to produce comparative results on schools and districts. While this is possibly to do with fairness and efficiency using contemporary sampling designs and analytical models, it is not necessarily feasible politically. Or a new testing programme may be conceived as using sampling to provide school and district-level results; but if the prior system tested all students, at least in certain grade levels, local educators may have come to rely on it to provide diagnostic information on individual students.

Finally, but on an upbeat note, technically desirable features may actually be supported by powerful political constituencies, making it possible to implement them, whereas they would have been impossible without these political actors. In the USA state governors and powerful business lobbies desire comparative achievement data on the state's school systems, to permit state, district and school comparisons. This is making it possible to implement comparative testing programmes, whereas 20 years ago it was politically inconceivable.

Politically successful strategies for achieving consensus

Over the past three years, we have been engaged in an effort to arrive at consensus for the national assessment programme that will provide comparative information on the overall achievement level of students in each state. Prior to that, of course, we worked towards consensus for national assessments with less at stake for states and others, and states and localities in the USA have been working for years to develop consensus on the content and approach of their own state or local large-scale assessment programmes. State-wide, comprehensive achievement assessment dates back at least 30 years, and the New York regents testing programme is over 100 years old.

What have we learned from this experience that could be useful, generally? There are four elements to a successful consensus-planning process for developing a large-scale assessment programme that I would like to put forth and illustrate.

Establish commitment to common rules for the consensus planning process

The first precept is to establish at the outset a commitment to a commonly understood goal for the consensus process. This is to make sure all parties participating in the process have a common understanding of the ground rules. There are several dimensions along which a consensus process may vary, and about which participants' perceptions may vary if they are not agreed upon at the outset. One dimension might be how long the group will attempt to achieve consensus. Another might be what constitutes 'consensus' – i.e. unanimity, or a majority? A dimension we discovered in planning large-scale assessments is how ambitious the goal of the consensus should be. Concerning the content to be tested, one can attempt to get everyone to agree to a minimal set of content that runs through all of their curricula for the subject, but nothing more – what we termed a 'least common denominator'. Or one can attempt to move beyond this to agreement on a broader, more inclusive, ambitious and educationally meaningful statement of the subject-matter that should be learned and, hence, tested.

In planning for state-by-state assessment in the USA, we queried states as we set out to ask them where on this continuum we should place the goal. Almost universally, states agreed that the goal should be the full, ambitious, inclusive notion of subject-matter, even if that went beyond some of their own, current curricular policies. They felt that it would be bad public policy to key the assessment to a minimal common denominator. But it was essential, as we proceeded, to have had a commitment and common understanding at the beginning because we were able to remind people along the way of the scope to which they had agreed.

Base planning on sound knowledge about differences among constituents

The second precept is not to proceed without thorough and specific knowledge about what those from whom you desire consensus are already doing. The consensus planning process will be set back if planners proceed in the dark, making proposals that encounter 'surprises': differences or incompatibilities in current testing programmes. These setbacks are worsened if they are not anticipated because they put consensus-builders off balance and on the defensive.

What do I mean by this? Suppose a new, national assessment programme has been conceived that has as one of its features testing mildly handicapped students. In a meeting the plan is presented to state testing directors. When it is explained that learning disabled and educably retarded students are to be tested, one state director interrupts, saying that they cannot test such students in their state. 'As a matter of fact', he says, 'we have a state law that prohibits testing them.' Another test director says, 'Our law *requires* that we test them!' The meeting dissolves at this impasse.

In two recent experiences in the USA we have avoided this by carefully assembling precise information on states' current practices, and then designing features of a testing or statistical programme, knowing which states will have which problems with the design, and handling the design to avoid these foreseeable problems as much as possible without compromising quality.

One example was our effort to standardize basic educational statistics, including national counts of public schools and school enrolments. We surveyed the states as to the definitions and procedures they used to collect these statistics and report them to the government (CCSSO, 1986). We found 11 different definitions of public schools, depending on whether states counted night programmes or alternative high-school programmes, for example, as separate schools. Ten per cent of the schools counted by one state would not have been counted under the definitions used by a neighbouring state.

In the other instance, we were attempting to arrive at a statement of the subject-matter in mathematics to be tested in 1990, when we will do our first state-comparative test of educational achievement. We commissioned a content analysis of the curriculum policies of the 40 states that had such policies, and of a representation of 15 local school districts (EPIE, 1988). Using a computerized system for analysing the degree of overlap or alignment among curriculum objectives, we assessed the relative commonality among the curriculum policies and could pinpoint how each state's policies departed.

In each case, we then proceeded to a discussion of possible ways of standardizing the statistics or of defining the curriculum to be tested. By knowing where states' practices varied, we could anticipate points of resistance or opposition. Perhaps more important, we could keep the discussion on the *facts* of each state's practice or policy, and not be dependent upon the state's assertion of where they differed and how important or insurmountable their differences were.

This step is important and can be done whether one is trying to arrive at consensus among existing testing programmes, or whether one is contemplating a large-scale assessment programme for the first time. The focus of the pre-planning task simply varies. In the former case, consensus-building might be aimed at reconciling the features of current testing programmes. In the latter case, it might be aimed at reconciling teachers' descriptions of their curricula or lesson plans, or at other evidence of the content of instruction and its diversity.

A very important feature of this pre-planning step is that it allows those planning an assessment programme to determine early in the process how feasible it is to attempt to arrive at consensus. We have realized, based on our experience, that one must acknowledge in any effort to plan an assessment programme the possibility that no genuine consensus exists. An attempt which proceeds on the premise that *some* sort of consensus will be reached and accepted is false and misguided. At least it is founded on the assumption that conceptual compromises will be made that may be very great. It is preferable to acknowledge the possibility that no consensus exists, and that none therefore may be found and not maintain the pressure to discover one and base an assessment programme on a consensus that is forced.

Include genuine opportunities for review and comment

The third precept is to provide points at which the views of constituents are sincerely sought and reflected in plans.

Many participants entering a consensus planning process for a sensitive or controversial programme will assume or, at least, suspect that the process is a sham – that the programme has already been designed, the decisions made, and the consensus process is intended only to rubber-stamp endorsement of what has already been decided on high.

This perception is difficult to overcome because it has often been correct in the past, and educators and testing directors are as astute and realistic as anyone else in their perceptions of how organizations operate. There are two keys to convincing participants that the consensus process is genuine (or to deceiving them, if it is not!).

The first is to provide participants genuine opportunities to contribute to plans and to comment on them as they emerge. In planning state-by-state assessment in the USA, we convened one entirely open meeting to which all states were invited to send a testing programme specialist and an instructional programme administrator. About 40 of the fifty states attended. At that meeting, three major issues of greatest concern to states were laid out for discussion: how to arrive at the content to be assessed; how to design the scaling and other displays as to how states would be compared; and how to achieve uniformity in the administration of testing across states. These issues were presented in a way that conveyed to states that the answers were open and that participants would determine how they would be answered. This meeting was extremely important in establishing faith in the consensus-development process among participants.

As the process proceeded, conscientious solicitation of comment was used to maintain this faith. For example, as a preliminary statement of mathematics subject-matter was prepared, it was presented to states for reactions, and as designs were formulated for the procedures by which the testing would be done, they were also circulated for comment. In each case, comments received were incorporated in the planning reports, and in instances where states' comments conveyed a substantial concern or a major difference of opinion among states, the basis for the decision reflected in the plans was explained in the planning documents. This sent the message back to participants that their concerns were acknowledged and reflected in the decisions that were made.

Build plans through representatives of the groups affected

The final precept is to construct plans as much as possible by using individuals who represent the constituents in the consensus planning process. This involves several related strategies. One is to present planning committees both with differences in current practices and with the need for consensus. If most participants accept that large-scale assessment is desirable (which may be a prerequisite logically for embarking on a consensus process), then they can be asked to develop solutions that ameliorate or resolve differences that currently exist among teachers, schools or states. In our effort to standardize enrolment counts, we found 13 different definitions used by states to report enrolment, resulting in variations among counts that amounted to hundreds of thousands of students. Our planning groups had to acknowledge that these differences seriously affected the validity of the data, and they accepted the need for standardization. Then we could appeal to their professionalism and ask them to conceive definitions and procedures that would be sound technical solutions.

Even beyond this, the better nature of planning committees can be appealed to, inspiring them to endorse solutions that are technically sound and ambitious in terms of the educational uses to which the assessment programmes can be put. For example, our committee for arriving at consensus around the mathematical subject-matter to be assessed among states decided to base their recommendations heavily on a set of objectives developed by our mathematics teachers' association. These were conceived as very forward-looking, long-range goals for the 'ideal' curriculum in mathematics, to be achieved over the next ten years, but the consensus planning committee decided that the content of the assessment was so important and that it would affect instruction so much that it *should* be ambitious and progressive. This value overwhelmed any practical or political resistance by the committee, and the integrity and social utility of the recommendations commanded support as they were presented to the field. Few professionals will entrench themselves publicly in a position of self-interest which conflicts with positive professional values and integrity.

These strategies work only if the planning committees are truly representative of constituents in the consensus-building process. If plans are issued by a group that is perceived as different from the constituencies who are affected and as being out of touch with current practices and concerns, forward-looking solutions may be rejected as idealistic, but if committees are representative, then forward-looking plans will be regarded as leadership on the part of one's peers.

Strategically, there are things one can do to assist these processes. First, in simply managing a committee, they can be steered tactfully away from peculiar, unsound or unpopular positions. In our experience, consensus planning committees go through many evolutions before arriving at final recommendations. If their thinking at points along the way were tapped, it would look very different from their final positions. Those chairing or managing the deliberations of consensus planning committees must sense when the committee is on a peculiar or tangential position and move it along to better thinking.

Tactically, we have found it effective to mix consensus planning committees with three types of participants. First, we make sure the 'old guard' is represented – those who will resist change and raise obstacles – so these views are aired and put on the table early. Next we make sure that the committee includes people, usually technical experts, who can propose workable solutions to technical problems, who can propose a way of doing things that will resolve problems. Thirdly, we include representatives of constituent groups who will probably take a progressive stand and who are respected by their peers as leaders. With these three kinds of participants, we create the opportunity to identify genuine concerns of constituents, we ensure that those most likely to contribute solutions to these concerns are present, and we ensure that constituents who represent a vanguard of technical and programmatic 'progressiveness' are present.

The final tactical consideration is to begin to anticipate the political implications of the recommendations as they emerge from committees. This is not to bias or discourage the committee from these recommendations, but to begin as early as possible to work on the political implementation. What points of opposition can be anticipated? Who must be persuaded? What arguments or trade-offs will be effective in winning support?

Success of consensus planning in the USA

Our recent consensus planning efforts have revealed one surprise and a lesson.

The surprise was that the consensus we thought would be most difficult to reach – agreeing on the subject-matter to be tested to compare states – was quite easy to achieve. We did not encounter entrenchment on the part of teachers, local school districts or states on their curricular decisions and policies. There seemed to be general agreement that a common body of content existed with which most constituents were comfortable. Other, more logistical and procedural issues inspired more controversy and revealed more strongly-felt positions on the part of participants in the process.

Very few political trade-offs had to be made in order to arrive at plans. With fairly lofty goals set for the process, technically advanced, 'idealistic' solutions were adopted, and final plans departed little from the visions and hopes we had going into the process. In retrospect, we were probably too cynical about the potential of the process to be compromised, politically.

The first lesson was that consensus planning can and should be approached systematically. Decisions can be made up front that will help make the process more successful. The key is to approach consensus planning as a genuinely open process. The decisions that should be made up front concern the *process* of planning. The product or outcome of the process should be left open for the participants to determine. This is risky if one wishes to control the outcome of assessment planning, but it is the legitimate way to proceed, and it is intellectually exciting and gratifying. Once this principle of openness is set, then, the method of working toward consensus can be handled thoughtfully to make it more successful.

The other lesson is that consensus planning is only the beginning of the process of developing assessment programmes, and that the real difficulty comes in getting constituents to adopt the programmes once they are planned and agreed-upon. Then, the problem is not one of philosophical difference with the content of the plans, by local constraints that prevent states and localities from implementing the plans. Their resources and political environments prevent them from changing data-collection programmes or adding new ones as quickly as we would like them to, even though they agree in principle with the new plans.

This is our next challenge: how to help states and local districts and schools change over to expanded and standardized testing and statistical procedures, now that we have achieved consensus on the philosophy and content the measures reflect.

References

COUNCIL OF CHIEF STATE SCHOOL OFFICERS (CCSSO) (1986). *Summary: State Collection Practices on Universe Data Files.* Report of the Education Data Improvement Project, Washington, DC: CCSSO.

CCSSO (1987). *Accountability Reporting in the States: Report of a Survey.* Washington, DC: CCSSO.

EDUCATION PRODUCTS INFORMATION EXCHANGE (EPIE) (1988). *Mathematics Core Curriculum Report for Grades K-8.* Produced for the National Assessment Planning Project, Washington, DC: Council of Chief State School Officers.

PECHEONE, R. (1986). Presentation to Connecticut Statewide Testing Conference. Sponsored by Connecticut State Department of Education, April.

4 The Assessment of Performance Unit: From Psychometric Survey to Diagnostic Analysis*

Peter Silvester

In 1974 the British government announced its intention to establish the Assessment of Performance Unit (APU) within the Department of Education and Science (DES). Its terms of reference were to promote the development of methods of assessing and monitoring the achievement of children at school, and to seek to identify the incidence of under-achievement.

The Assessment of Performance Unit (APU)

Origins

Effectively, the APU began to function in 1975 with its work centred on four main tasks:

1. to identify and appraise existing instruments and methods of assessment;

2. to sponsor the creation of new instruments and techniques for assessment, having due regard for statistical and sampling methods;

3. to promote and conduct assessment in co-operation with local education authorities (LEAs) and teachers;

4. to identify significant differences of achievement related to the circumstances in which children learn, including the incidence of under-achievement, and to make the findings available to those concerned with resource allocation within government departments, local education authorities and schools.

Two of the above tasks have since been modified: findings from APU surveys of children's attainments have never been used to identify deficiencies in school resources, nor to justify financial policies for remedying these; and the identification of under-achievement as a specific target has never been adequately de-

* The views expressed in this paper are those of the author and do not reflect government policy.

veloped because of the difficulties in setting absolute upper limits to achievement. A parliamentary committee gave formal recognition of this problem in 1986 when it recommended that 'under-achievement' should be removed from the terms of reference and the investigation of unexplained differences between the performance of groups of children, substituted in its place.

Surveys and reports

The Unit commissions research on behalf of the DES, which currently funds research teams representing five different areas of the schools' curriculum. Since 1978 national surveys have occurred as follows:

1. Mathematics (at ages 11 and 15) – 1978–82, 1987;
2. English language (at ages 11 and 15) – 1979–83, 1988;
3. Science (at ages 11, 13 and 15) – 1980–4, 1989 (at 11), 1990;
4. Foreign languages (at age 13) – 1983–5;
5. Design and technology (at age 15) – 1988.

All surveys are followed by comprehensively written research reports which are distributed to all LEA, educational institutions, education libraries and to ministers in the government. The reports provide a description of pupils' current performance in the various curriculum areas with observations, and trends in performance over time. For example, in the five years between 1979 and 1983, girls have consistently performed better than boys in writing (at a statistically significant level) at ages 11 and 15; and in reading too, but not always to an acceptable level of significance. Their performance in speaking and listening is about the same in the two years (1982 and 1983) when these skills were tested. Significant findings have been reported in the other curriculum areas.

In 1980 a decision was taken to move from annual surveys to a five-year cycle. Surveys are therefore currently being undertaken – during the period 1987 to 1990 – following a five-year break.

In addition to the survey reports, exploratory groups of subject specialists have produced reports which consider the feasibility of assessment in the areas of physical development, aesthetic education and personal and social development. Their inclusion in the APU's early work programme was a reflection of the interest being shown in the whole curriculum at a time when the Unit was establishing its credibility with the education profession. No follow-up surveys have, however, been undertaken in these three areas.

Organization and committees

Since its inception the APU has resided in the branch within the DES which has responsibility for the school curriculum during the statutory years of schooling (5–16 years). In 1987, the APU transferred to one of two Teachers' Branches. The Unit is managed by an Administrative Head and a Professional Head who both work to an under-secretary. Ultimately they all report to the Permanent Secretary, the Head of the DES and to ministers.

The Administrative Head of the Unit gives only a proportion of his time to the APU, while the professional Head of the Unit is one of Her Majesty's Inspectors of Schools (HMI) who works full-time in the Unit. Additional support is given by a part-time HMI.

The involvement of HMI is an important feature of the APU management structure. It ensures that an educational viewpoint deriving from a professional knowledge of schools is available when policies for the Unit are being formulated. A support staff of civil servants service committees and undertake other business, notably in connection with budget control and the scheduling of publications and responding to the many inquiries made of the Unit from all over the world.

An internal management committee comprising the two heads and the Unit's staff meets regularly to consider policy. The two heads maintain contact with the survey research teams through regular meetings and, more formally, through steering group meetings. These groups have an invited membership drawn from teachers, LEA advisers, teacher trainers and academics in the particular field being surveyed. The group discusses such issues with the research teams as the research design, the interpretation of the survey findings for teachers, the content of draft publications and the focus of future surveys.

Two further groups complete the committee structure of the APU. They are the Statistics Advisory Group which gives technical advice on survey design and data processing, and the Consultative Committee which acts as a 'watchdog' on the Unit's activity.

Issues surrounding the establishment of APU: 1975–81

Political attitudes at the time of APU's genesis

Coincidentally with the appearance of the APU in the mid-1970s criticism of the education service and what were seen as its shortcomings in producing well-educated young people began to emerge. The government's attitude was made clear in a speech given by James Callaghan, the then Prime Minister, at Ruskin College, Oxford, in 1976, in which he said that the education service should become more accountable for its product; and the groups outside the service with a vested interest in education, such as industrialists, should be able to comment about its effectiveness. Public meetings organized by the DES provided the platform for concerns to be aired. The Great Debate about education had begun. The announcement to establish the APU in such a climate was deeply disturbing to the national teacher associations who were immediately suspicious of the government's intentions and hostile to the APU, which was thought to be the vehicle for some as yet unknown government policies for controlling the curriculum and the teaching profession.

Areas of conflict

The antipathy of the profession was revealed in four major areas of conflict:

1. teacher accountability;

2. curricular backwash – that the survey findings would determine the content of the curriculum;

3. the frequency of surveys;

4. the collection of information about schools, teachers and pupils' home circumstances.

Accountability

Many teachers believed that a concern for accountability would be translated into a centrally imposed testing regime carried out by the APU for the government, which would not only measure the attainments of individual children, but also the performance of their teachers.

The issue of accountability was responded to swiftly by the APU: light sampling of populations was used and no individual child was expected to take part in the full range of tests in the area being surveyed. Indeed, the improbability of attempting to do so in science, for example, would have required an individual, to be exposed to more than 30 hours of testing. Once schools had been identified randomly and their voluntary co-operation obtained to carry out testing, complete anonymity of schools, teachers and pupils was safeguarded by the Unit.

Curricular backwash

In the 1970s the curriculum was still referred to as the 'secret garden', known only to those who planted the seeds and tilled the soil. It was argued by critics that the APU assessment frameworks, and the tests compiled for the surveys, would reveal in their subsequent analyses omissions in certain areas of the curriculum: and as a corollary, that the Unit would begin to recommend what should be included in the curriculum or where emphases might change. The APU acknowledged this general concern by ensuring that the researchers limited their statements to a description of existing attainment levels without any suggestions as to whether they could be improved, or how the information might be of value to practising teachers. In short, they could say what the surveys revealed about attainments but not what should be done to improve them.

The APU's other strategy of being even-handed in considering all major areas of the curriculum for surveying – although only five were eventually selected – diffused any potential messages about the importance of some subjects over others. A deliberate policy of choosing cross-curricular lines of development (verbal, mathematical, scientific, ethical, physical and aesthetic) in its curricular model was also an attempt to retain a varied and balanced content. It was eventually dropped because it did not totally represent the subject-based curriculum in most secondary schools.

A legacy from the cross-curricular model is seen in some assessment tasks which cross subject boundaries. For example, the language team has used scientific tasks ('Tracks' and 'Damoiselle Fly') and a geography task ('Maps'), while the mathematics team in the 'Class Trip' task made use of timetables and menus for creating a realistic mathematical problem.

Survey frequency

The intensive sampling of pupils at ages 11 and 15 in each year during the early life of the APU, in mathematics, language and science, did make heavy demands on schools and the response rate began to be affected. The APU has always been aware of their dependency on the goodwill of teachers to survey effectively, and this is one of the reasons why the frequency of surveys was changed from annually to once every five years. Despite the considerable demands on their time, schools take part willingly in the assessment programme – generally the co-operation is now in the order of between 85 and 90 per cent of those schools who are asked to participate.

Background variables

Further safeguards were taken to protect the anonymity of children through the decision of the Consultative Committee not to allow information about home background variables to be collected. This decision has imposed a constraint on the survey findings because it limits the number of critical independent variables available for interpreting test scores. As a result of this decision, the APU has never, for example, gathered information about the socio-economic background of the pupils. Nor has it been able to give any pointers to the needs of the educationally disadvantaged, one of its initial tasks. Present policy is in keeping with this earlier decision but the limited background data that are collected are used as a backcloth against which the survey results are interpreted.

Significant factors in opening up new directions for APU's work: 1982–85

No single factor triggered the change of emphasis in the APU's work from 1982 onwards. It was more the result of a cluster of events arising from government policy and the Unit's own appraisal of its needs to change direction that brought it about. The earlier-mentioned criticisms had largely been countered and the teaching profession reassured. However, the self-imposed, independent stance of a government research unit which monitored children's attainments and reported its findings without comment about their educational implications still remained.

Government commentary on educational matters has accelerated since 1976. By 1980 the curriculum had become a focus of attention with the DES publication, *A Framework for the School Curriculum*. A second publication, *The School Curriculum*, resulting from consultation after the publication of *Framework* was published in 1981. Such close government interest in the curriculum, which had never been apparent before, coupled with a statement that 'The Assessment of Performance Unit will [also] continue its programme of monitoring specific aspects of the performance of pupils in schools' began to reverse earlier arguments that the APU should distance itself from curricular matters.

More direct recognition that the APU might have something to say about the curriculum was given prominence in *Mathematics Counts*, a report of a committee set up by the government to review the teaching and learning of mathematics across the whole age and ability range and chaired by Dr W.H. Cockcroft (1982), in recommending that: 'an overall appraisal should be prepared of the educational implications of the [APU] mathematical testing which has been carried out so far.'

That recommendation was accepted by the Secretary of State for Education, who also announced an independent appraisal of the mathematics findings (*New Perspectives on the Mathematics Curriculum 1983–85*): 'The purpose of the appraisal is to make more widely available the information contained in the work of the APU in such a way as to draw on its educational implications.'

Not one but three independent appraisals were eventually commissioned, in mathematics, language and science. They all examined the educational implications of the survey findings and were written by distinguished experts in each of the three fields. The commissioning of the appraisals by the secretary of state was an endorsement of the rich data collected by the APU to be made available for improving pedagogy, as well as for monitoring pupils' attainments.

It was already becoming clear to the APU's management that the survey research reports, although well presented and well received, were not appropriate in their present form to influence everyday classroom practice. Indeed, frustration was openly expressed in a number of reported evaluations of the early survey reports (cf. *Monitoring Children: An Evaluation of the APU*, by C.E. Gipps and H.G. Goldstein; Supplementary Appendices 6–9. University of London Institute of Education, February 1983: see pp. 33, 35 and 52 for examples). The teachers' needs were expressed most succinctly in the plea for 'simpler and shorter reports . . . which would summarise the findings and highlight likely conclusions'. This had a twofold advantage. First, it marked an important change on the part of teachers who now expressed a need for materials from APU to influence their teaching. Secondly, that aspect of the work of APU clearly began to emerge as having more importance than its national monitoring function.

The Unit adopted a new publications policy and commissioned the research teams to produce shorter booklets on restricted topics which would be helpful to teachers. The first booklet to be issued in 1983 was *Science at Age 11*, which drew on the first and second science surveys of pupils aged 11. It included sections on the main findings, the implications of these for classroom practice, examples of test questions and children's responses and a summary of the implications.

Although the interest of the teaching profession generally in the APU's work was spasmodic in 1982, since that time there has been a growing awareness in certain quarters that the survey findings and the assessment frameworks could have application for work in schools. Consequently, requests began to be made for HMI working in the APU and for the research teams to talk about its findings. This activity reached a climax between 1983 and 1985 and was encouraged, in part, by a series of regional conferences for LEA advisers of science, language and mathematics, lecturers in teacher training institutions and wardens of teachers' centres. The purpose of the conferences was to report the main survey findings, to consider their educational implications and to give participants the opportunity of using APU practical test materials. In theory, the participants would then be equipped to go back to their LEAs and pass on the messages in their own provision of in-service training. Unfortunately, the reality was not always as clear-cut as the Unit might have hoped because there were still those who had reservations about APU approaches to assessment and did not consider they had any direct relevance for classroom use. There were other tensions too, relating, for example, to the underlying rationale of teaching, say, spoken English as a living, spontaneous form of communication in contrast to the APU's approach of testing language performance by devising tasks with specific features (summarized in *Speaking and Listening: Assessment at Age 15*) as:

> Different purposes require different types of talk. This implies that no one style or register of speech will be appropriate for all situations. Indeed formal speech will be quite inappropriate to tasks of a semi-formal nature, and vice versa. Therefore, the *appropriateness* of the speech used in a given situation becomes an important criterion of assessment.

A growing source of expertise among teachers trained by the research teams to administer practical tests has helped spread the APU's messages into schools. These assessors were required to handle complex test items in mathematics, science and speaking and listening which required 'on the spot' judgements in a one-to-one test arrangement with the child being assessed. As a result of the training and subsequent experience, many teachers have gained insights into such areas as: the procedural knowledge of pupils attempting to work through practical test items (mathematics at age 11: 'Class Trip', and science age 13: 'Survival'); the gaps revealed in pupils' understanding when clear assessment criteria are applied; and pupils' misunderstandings which are shown by an analysis of errors made in response to specific themes (mathematics at age 11: 'Place Value').

APU's response: 1985

The realization that the APU was accumulating data from its surveys that went beyond the production of simple summative statements about attainment was instrumental in defining new directions for its work.

What were the factors contributing to the richness of the data? Importantly, the research teams had broken new ground in designing tests. Narrowly conceived paper-and-pencil tests, unrelated to the content of the curriculum, were discarded in favour of more relevant tasks: practical assessments in which an assessor worked with one child were introduced into the language, science and mathematics surveys. The benefits arising from this approach were shown through the analysis of the test results, which not only permitted population scores to be calculated, but also resulted in detailed descriptions of performance in, for example, writing, reading and speaking and listening which allowed various levels of performance to be identified for each language task and the features of that level to be made known.

The research teams were not in a position to identify common pupil errors and in later surveys examine the reasons why they were made. Thus, for instance, it was found that there was confusion over the terms 'area' and 'perimeter' both at ages 11 and 15. The way questions were asked affected, to a greater or lesser extent, the success rates in calculating area and perimeter (what is the perimeter, or how far is it right round the edge of the shape?). Similarly, it was found that 30 per cent of children age 11, when asked to compare the size of two angles (of the same size), thought that one was larger because the two lines forming it were longer than those in the other example.

Increasingly, somewhat less emphasis has been placed on comparing mean scores of children's attainments from survey to survey with comment about their relative performances; or on comparisons between sub-groups within samples (boys vs girls). One of the important messages arising from the wider remit now adopted by the APU is that the assessment of learning is complex and requires sophisticated and time-consuming tests to achieve effectively. Their adoption reveals a wealth of important information about pupils' procedural knowledge, gaps in their knowledge and where they are experiencing difficulties in understanding certain concepts.

Since 1985, the APU has made increasingly available some of the essential findings from the surveys which have important practical implications for teachers. In addition, examples of test items have also been made available to illustrate the range of APU assessment strategies. In pursuance of this policy, a practical test kit has been produced containing APU test items and manuals to show how they were used in the surveys, plus video tapes with exemplars of children being tested. Four or five boxes of the kit have been sent to all LEAs to be used for in-service training. The intention is that teachers should have an appreciation of the APU assessment criteria and be able to practise making judgements themselves about the different levels of pupils' performance. Research studies have also been commissioned with a view to developing APU test materials for classroom use. The most significant of these are: the School Curriculum Development Committee (SCDC) Writing Programme which has a member of the APU language research team attached to it; the Modern Languages in Schools Project (MODLS); and Children's Learning in Science Project (CLIS) – a piece of fundamental research examining children's understanding of scientific concepts (and directed by a former APU science team researcher).

With five years of surveys completed in language, mathematics and science (during 1978–84), the research teams have each produced a review which brings together all the important features of the testing programme in one book. They comment on levels of performance such as, in the Language Review, where it is stated that good readers can hold in mind a number of possible lines of development in character and plot which they modify as the story unfolds or, in addition, that they are sensitive to the implications of irony. Similar generalizations about pupils' performance are contained in the Mathematics and Science Reviews.

Some of the time between surveys has been spent on undertaking additional research, part of which has been concerned with cross-disciplinary assessment. Two projects have examined respectively the contribution that discussion in small groups can make to solving mathematical problems; and the kind of language used in science lessons. Workshop packs have also been produced by the research teams for use on in-service courses.

Issues to be resolved in moving on from psychometric surveys to diagnostic analysis

The expectation that APU surveys will produce data about pupils' attainments, as well as information about their progress in learning and their understanding, has required important changes to be made in the design of test times and how the data are to be presented. These will now be considered.

The first issue to be resolved is how are the results from surveys to be used? A psychometric survey allows benchmarks to be set in relation to pupils' attainments from which comparisons can be made. This may be in its simplest form as a pass or fail benchmark, or alternatively, a total score can be provided by adding together all the various components of a test. This information is generally used for providing some kind of grade based on a summative score. At another level of analysis, it is possible to correlate summed scores with background information about the population of pupils taking a psychometric test. Thus, for example, the researcher might wish to comment on the performance of boys and girls, pupils of different ethnic origin or pupils from different socio-economic groupings.

An alternative approach, increasingly used by the APU, is to analyse responses to test items, so that some insight can be gained into pupils' thinking processes and their procedural knowledge in attempting a particular test item. This kind of information reveals as much about the ease and difficulty of learning as it does about the level achieved. Herein lies an important difference between the psychometric approach and this approach which relates more closely to the learning context.

It is a relatively simple matter to create benchmarks by using a small battery of easy-to-mark test items that are marked as having a right or wrong answer; or to use a multi-choice question to which pupils have to select the correct answer. Analysing the detailed responses of pupils or asking them to explain their response cannot be obtained by these methods, however, and requires more complex approaches which are now considered in relation to some of the mathematics findings.

The practical testing of mathematics has demonstrated where certain pupils have difficulty in solving problems. At age 11, children were given a number of plastic chips which equalled a given mass. Many were unable to calculate the weight of one chip because they were unsure as to whether they had to divide the number of chips by the weight or to divide the weight by the number of chips. This kind of inadequate mathematical thinking can best be explored in a practical assessment involving one pupil and an assessor, in which appropriate prompting may reveal the thought processes and subsequent actions. Frequent and recurring errors which are revealed in one survey can often be followed up by carefully designed probes in later surveys, in an attempt to find why some misunderstanding is occurring. Thus it was revealed in one survey that many 15-year-old pupils, as well as 11-year-olds, were having difficulty in understanding decimal-place value. Directed questions revealed the extent of this problem. Pupils aged 15 were asked to write down a decimal greater than 1.6 and less than 1.7. Seventy per cent gave the correct answer, and a further 4 per cent gave '1.6$\frac{1}{2}$'! A second question asking them to identify a number with the greatest value from the following: 0.075, 0.09, 0.1 and 0.089 was answered correctly by 83 per cent of pupils indicating a reasonable grasp of the rules of decimal fractions. Thirteen per cent, however, answered that the last number (0.089) was the largest, perhaps because when ignoring the decimal place and dealing in whole numbers (75, 9, 1, 89), it becomes so. Another question probing the understanding of place value of 15-year-olds asked them which of the following numbers had the smallest value: 0.625, 0.25, 0.125 and 0.5. Thirty-four per cent of responses gave the answer as 0.625 as the smallest number. In a retrospective report by the Mathematics Monitoring Team it was suggested that a widely held misconception of pupils was that the 'largest' decimal was always the 'smallest' value – perhaps a confusion with the denominator value of vulgar fractions where the smallest contain the highest value digits. Thirty-nine per cent gave the correct answer as 0.125, and 20 per cent gave 0.5, presumably because it had the least number of digits.

Another significant finding of the mathematics surveys has revealed that if the question is set in an appropriate and realistic context, children who may not have a full grasp of mathematical concepts will often answer the question correctly. An example of this can be seen from three questions given to 11-year-olds. To the question: 2.7 ÷ 2, 17 per cent gave the correct answer, but a further 21 per cent gave the answer as '1.3 remainder 1'. When the same question was put in the form: '2.7 metres of cloth make two tablecloths. Both tablecloths are the same size. How much cloth is needed to make one tablecloth?', 27 per cent gave the correct answer with 31 per cent giving '1.3$\frac{1}{2}$'. None of these problems arises where the question is framed within the context of 'money: '£2.70 is to be divided equally between two children. How much will each child get?', when the success rate increased to 73 per cent. These examples show how pupils' understanding is dependent upon the context in which the questions are set.

The marking methods will differ depending on whether psychometric testing or diagnostic analysis is being attempted. If benchmarks are required, they can be arrived at relatively easily, for example, by adding together scores from separate test items and agreeing on a score which is to represent the benchmark. When diagnostic qualities are introduced, the marking methods need to reflect this additional purpose. One way of achieving this is to use some kind of analytic framework which allows the various dimensions of the assessment tasks to be examined and observations made about the relative strength or weakness of the dimensions. An example of this can be seen from the approaches taken to assess oracy in the language surveys. A framework was used for analysing tapes of pupils responding to various tasks. Four analytic categories were used: overall organization; the ideas and elements of meaning conveyed in particular tasks; grammar; and vocabulary. Although these categories are general to all oracy tasks, the nature of the task dictates what specific characteristics of each should be used. The organization of a story will be different from a scientific report which, in turn, will differ in its organization from describing an event and so on. Similarly, the particular aspect of meaning associated with each task will vary according to the type of communicative activity being used.

Analytic marking attempts to reveal exactly what is involved in carrying out each task successfully, the reasons why some kinds of spoken communication are more difficult for pupils than others and those specific qualities which distinguish the less successful from the more successful attempts. Using this information from analysis, it is possible to produce descriptions of performance which can be classified as good, average or poor for comparative and diagnostic purposes.

Finally, where population scores are the focus of interest as in psychometric surveys, analytic marking allows for comparisons to be made between various surveys carried out over the years or between sub-groups within any survey population. An interest in diagnosis switches the attention towards sub-groups or individuals and the extent to which they are, or are not, performing well on selected tasks. For example, it is possible to identify the features of performance of, say, the top 20 per cent of pupils in mathematics or how well girls cope with physics. A summary of the respective features is presented below.

Psychometric survey	**Assessment near the context of learning**
Summative	– formative
Population	– sub-group or individual
Overall score	– descriptive analysis
Simple short items	– complex items and often 1:1 interviews
Decontextualized items often less meaningful to pupils	– contextualized items (often appropriate for use as teaching materials) to which pupils can relate more readily

The future

There are two aspects of APU work relating to the future which need to be mentioned in order to complete the picture of the Unit's progress over the past 14 years. They are the survey methodology and analysis to be used in the next surveys and the 'political' future of APU.

In future surveys it could be predicted with a fair amount of certainty that the division of populations into ability bands and the identification of distinguishing features of bands will feature markedly in the analyses of the data. We would expect to see analytic marking of written scripts in language and clear statements about the features of particular ability groups – the top 20 per cent, for example. There will be an increasing emphasis on measuring pupils' responses to complex test items such as their understanding of micro text in language and microcomputers in mathematics. The mathematics team has, in the current round of surveys, included questions probing the circumstances in which pupils use a calculator.

In conclusion, APU research has revealed the task-specific nature of a number of learning difficulties which certain groups of pupils experience. From concern for describing performance, it is possible to reveal where some of the difficulties lie. This kind of information published in the form of APU booklets is already proving helpful to teachers in their every-day classroom practice. One interesting adjunct is that the APU findings may on occasions challenge teachers' expectations. A simple example of this would be the varied kinds of written tasks used in the language surveys which may suggest extending the range of writing experience in some classrooms.

The APU assessment frameworks are already contributing to a broader understanding of assessment within the teaching profession. Again, much of this information has been obtained from booklets but another source of help has come from short, in-service training courses using APU materials. Members of the language research team have contributed to the thinking of national examination boards on the assessment of speaking and listening. As the survey findings continue to reveal learning difficulties as well as the stages of conceptual development of children, follow-up action is sometimes necessary in the form of additional research. The Children's Learning in Science Project is an example of such research which attempts to develop APU materials for direct classroom use.

Proposals for a national curriculum are now being considered by the British government. These include setting attainment targets in various curriculum areas for pupils at ages 7, 11, 14 and 16 and assessing the extent of their achievement. Such a testing regime is likely to mean that the APU will not be required to monitor performance using assessment surveys once the new system is operating. However, the APU currently has an important role to play in a number of ways. There is a great deal of wisdom about assessment vested in the APU research teams which could support the national curriculum initiative. The DES will continue to require to be kept informed about the results of national testing, and it is possible that the APU will have a contribution to make in that respect; there is also a wealth of untapped information available about pupils' performance. The analysis of this existing data, and that obtained from future surveys, could help to guide the selection of the different levels of performance required in the national curriculum. Finally, with such a wealth of information now available, an overall dissemination policy is being implemented specifically targeted towards initial and in-service training. This is an immediate concern which will be given high priority by APU, both as a contribution to professional development and because of the immediate needs of teachers to understand assessment techniques, now that the national curriculum is close at hand.

References

ASSESSMENT OF PERFORMANCE UNIT (1983). *Science at Age 11*. London: APU.

CENTRE FOR THE SCIENCE AND MATHEMATICS EDUCATION (n.d.). *The Children's Learning in Science*. Research Report. Leeds: University of Leeds.

DEPARTMENT OF EDUCATION AND SCIENCE (1980). *A Framework for the School Curriculum*. London: Department of Education and Science.

GIPPS, C.E. and GOLDSTEIN, H.G. (1983). *Monitoring Children: An Evaluation of the APU*. University of London Institute of Education.

Mathematics Counts (Cockcroft Report) (1982). London: HMSO.

New Perspectives of the Mathematics Curriculum 1983–85 (1985). London: HMSO.

Speaking and Listening: Assessment at Age 15 (1987). Windsor: NFER-NELSON.

The School Curriculum (1981). London: HMSO.

5 Reasons for the Initiatives in the Dutch Parliament for an Assessment Programme

Sjaak Sandbergen

In explaining motives for political behaviour to foreigners, the speaker runs the risk that the audience will be bored long before reaching the end. This is one reason to be rather brief in my sketch of the social and political situation which led to the decision that assessment might be fruitful. Another reason is that the process of policy is complex, so one cannot always claim complete understanding of events.

Therefore, my contribution to this symposium is probably not a complete reconstruction. It is possible that some of the finer details are lacking. Your consolation, and mine, may be that trying to achieve an accurate synopsis can be a frustrating, if not impossible task.

Let me start with the logical reason for assessment. It is evident that assessment is considered useful in an educational system, in the situation where one needs information on the level of achievement of the system. That is clearly not necessarily synonymous with political reasons. In the Netherlands, and other countries, policy-makers can live on without such information, even while trying to improve the quality of education by taking various steps. In our country the main reason to take such an initiative was: growing concern about the quality of education, and the impossibility to defend oneself against critical observations by pointing at empirical evidence. This reason (and other implied reasons) are not sufficient for action in a stable situation when everybody seems to be moderately satisfied with the state of education. Therefore, it seems necessary to provide you with some details of the political backgrounds of the Dutch assessment project, as follows·

1. If there are main stages in the construction, then they seem to overlap; in reconstructing events, it is easy to create the impression that the course of the process was more orderly than in reality.

2. The start of our programme cannot be exclusively attributed to political reasons on a parliamentary level.

3. The transition from an extremely suspicious attitude towards a more positive one to assessment took place very gradually; dramatic changes hardly occurred.

4. We cannot claim a brilliant long-term strategy in our project; if there is anything to boast of, it is the fact that we persevered despite setbacks.

But first of all, we should present a few basic facts on the Dutch situation in the world.

A few facts on the Dutch situation

Perhaps the best-known fact about the Netherlands is that it is a small country, which is very flat and lies for the greater part below sea-level. The political system is that of a constitutional monarchy; Parliament consists of two houses; and due to historical tradition, the political and cultural orientation is an international one. International trade and transport are traditional sources of income, so that there are firm economic and political links with other members of the European Community. The country is a critical Nato-member.

The political climate in past decades has been dominated by the usual issues in Western Europe: economic reconstruction after the Second World War; industrialization; and European co-operation. Changing coalitions of Social Democrats, Christian Democrats and Liberals were occupied by the building of a welfare state. A specific factor was the process of decolonization in the late 1940s and early 1950s. Although this period had its traumatic aspects, one cannot say that there are any longer deep scars. Later on, the country had to cope with the effects of the energy crisis and economic vicissitude. As in other countries, this caused reconsideration of political priorities, including that of education.

In the area of education, several major reforms took place, and secondary education underwent a large change. This resulted in an increased enrolment in secondary education of a general academic type and pre-university schools; decreased enrolment in vocational schools also took place. In primary education Kindergarten and primary education were integrated into one sub-system. University and college training were shortened to a formal four-year duration (with some exceptions).

The general demographic dynamics are comparable to other developed countries. Decline in birth rate has had its effect on the maintenance of the education system. Another factor is the influx of migrant workers; especially in larger cities, the numbers of so-called 'allochtoneous children' has increased.

The political basis for assessment: two relevant levels of negotiation

Mention has already been made of three large-scale updatings of the education system in the Netherlands. Changing the system goes together with some tension: the structural reform in secondary education is a case in point. The new structure created a number of new school types, which were clearly attractive to students. Under the reform, the traditional point of selection and allocation to various forms of secondary education shifted to later points in the school career. Nowadays we are all aware that when the social system known as 'education' is aiming at greater equity or 'external democratization' and, at the same time, is attempting to become less selective, then there exists the risk of decreasing levels of achievement. As far as I know, the administration in the early 1970s was aware of this situation; I have the impression that, in this period, the leading political coalition was mainly occupied by a constructive policy in which structures and processes within schools formed the main priority. Aspects such as education outcomes, ascertaining the results of education by measuring instruments, were clearly not so popular. The attitude in Parliament towards reform was ambivalent. The wish for reform was clearly correlated with the more progressive factions; a more 'hardboiled' point of view was easily associated with the more conservative elements in national politics.

It is not surprising therefore that critical remarks and critical statements from the business community, and from certain teacher associations, were not used in an optimal way, nor even rejected as 'reactionary'. Nevertheless, a permanent critical undertone accompanied reform in this area; it even led to a certain escalation, so that the introduction of the comprehensive school, was blocked in Parliament.

In primary education much more support for reform was present; however a comparable ambivalent attitude towards reform certainly existed here too. Especially in discussing the broad goals of education, with the emphasis on creativity and continuous development of the child, the more progressive aspects sometimes came under fire.

At the beginning of this period of innovation, evaluation of projects was very often restricted to 'process evaluation', 'action research' was popular.

In political discussion on education constructing 'something new', in many cases, was more important than evaluation of the policy-inspired programmes. In some cases, evaluation of a specific measure was considered to be the price one had to pay the opposition.

It is hardly surprising, viewed from this perspective, that early proposals to assess the achievement of schools on a national scale were hardly acceptable. Supporters of the position that innovation and evaluation should go hand in hand were almost automatically placed in a conservative corner of the political scene. Early attempts to introduce systematic assessment were ignored by the ministry and the work of the IEA (International Association for the Evaluation of Educational Achievement) did not receive enough support to make a substantial impact.

This situation changed slowly. Some contributions to a more pragmatic stance may be noticed. In the first place, the political coalition changed. Then there were a number of developments during the past decade, signalling that not everything was well in education. The following examples may sound familiar:

1. The realization that programmes which tried to stimulate the school careers of lower socio-economic status (SES-level) students were not very successful.

2. An increasing number of dropouts in secondary education.

3. An increase in the number of students who were referred to special education.

4. Problems in the schooling of children from different cultural and linguistic backgrounds.

5. Disappointment over the fact that structural reform did not guarantee successful implementation in school.

These examples are, of course, relevant for education. Perhaps some external factors were more influential; and concern over public expenditure is worth mentioning. The concept of **accountability** gradually became familiar – no longer was it considered merely as an Americanism.

A second cause for concern was the growing pressure from the society. The business community continued to pinpoint certain malfunctions in the labour market due to an undersupply of skilled and highly trained workers in certain areas, and an oversupply of other students. Criticism was no longer primarily directed at the supposed idealistic and humanistic aspects of reform. It took a more sophisticated form, in the following statement and questions: 'Money is scare, is it well spent and is education functioning optimally?'.

Decisions in education are not exclusively made at the parliamentary level. In the Netherlands policy is also prepared elsewhere. Most of the initiatives of the Department of Education are formally discussed in a central commission for education. This commission has become a formal platform, where policy is discussed by representatives of teacher unions and various associations of school boards.

Representatives consult their rank and file before they give their opinion on issues on the agenda. Sometimes the recommendations of external advisory committees are acted upon; most of the members are in constant relation with Members of Parliament or have associations with political parties. As we live in a small country, there exists a network of people who discuss things.

On this level of policy-making, we have met considerable opposition. The idea of an assessment project was received coolly when we discussed plans informally. The typical answer of an important organization was: 'Let us ask the teachers whether they need such a project', and the implication was clear that the questionnaire was to be sent through the channels of the organization involved.

The initiatives of some people in the ministry to propose an assessment project were based on a few somewhat naïve arguments. As a reminder, it is necessary to collect data on educational output, which we can then use fruitfully in describing the development of education and evaluating the system. These arguments were clearly not sufficient. Objections of influential people and institutions seemed to be rooted in a traditional pedagogical background; and any opinions voiced against assessment were clearly inspired by the well-known American debate on testing. Other objections were inspired by fear of the abuse of results by the government.

An analysis of objections in the Netherlands, and in other countries, produced the following:

1. Theoretical mistrust of testing and evaluation by 'objective' instruments; teachers want to decide on the basis of their own observations.

2. Fear of assessment inspired by possible misuse of results, such as comparisons of students and teachers purely on the basis of achievement, noise in the press and measures taken by the ministry and directed at individual schools.

3. A concern about the possible emphasis on cognitive goals, 'the basic' and easy-to-measure skills.

4. Concern about the workload of schools and the lack of direct applications for schools and classroom teachers.

Needless to say, arguments such as the above are extremely difficult to counter; the history of educational measurement and of educational assessment does show enough examples of abuse of results, naïve applications, and such like. Therefore, my colleague and I concluded that it might be wise to take seriously the negative attitudes, not simply to fight fears and allay concerns by rejecting them as irrational. An element of such a strategy should be to design a model which could show that certain fears were indeed unfounded.

Within the department we received some official support in this project. After a change of administration, a new Minister of Education showed some interest in our plans. Trained as an economist, he proved to be open to arguments as provided by cost-effectiveness and accountability. Most important, perhaps, he realized that he could not defend himself against attacks on his policy and on the decreasing level of achievement because of a lack of empirical evidence. Also significant was that the ministry published a policy statement on quality, in which the necessity of measuring quality was explained. Furthermore, we received some support from an external advisory commission on innovation.

In Parliament a session of the permanent committee of education was dedicated to the problem of quality. Any far-reaching decisions were not produced, but at least some speakers agreed upon the necessity of empirical evidence for a balanced appraisal of the state of education.

Designing assessment: tactical procedures

The work on constructing an assessment programme took approx. nine years. Preliminary activities started in 1977: the regular programme will yield its first results in 1988, but the programme started in 1986. Five stages in the implementation may be distinguished; they also represent a rough chronological order:

1. origins of a naïve notion;
2. technical discussions;
3. feasibility study;
4. construction of a model;
5. final implementation.

Origins of a notion: 1977–9

The need for an empirical indicator of quality in educational policy became evident, when a small working group of which I was a member prepared a statement on the quality of mother-tongue education. This statement had to answer severe criticism, expressed in the press and in Parliament. It proved impossible to find empirical evidence that negative opinions were right or wrong.

In the same period, a small working group in the ministry prepared a statement on quality of education. In this activity we had to confine ourselves to a classification of the many variables which seem to be related to quality. As an ex-researcher, my own conviction grew that a systematic collection of data was necessary to enable me to say something about the development of educational achievement under the influence of innovation, official measures and autonomous development. A few colleagues and I experienced a number of negative reactions until we succeeded in planting some relevant elements in the draft of a policy statement on quality. The official support of the minister prevented some of the more open objections within our department. A visit to several assessment programmes supplied a number of approaches, together with a number of successes and failures. We were lucky, in this stage, that a member of an external advisory committee could accompany us. The products of this stage were: (a) one fat internal report; and (b) an awareness that technical and methodological solutions are necessary but not sufficient.

Technical discussions: 1980

After orientation and reporting, we organized a technical conference with institutions which might share in the responsibility of the programme. We prepared this conference by asking a number of experts both in education and assessment to write some recommendations on a number of questions.

How to make a partition in the curriculum, what kind of taxonomy to use for the measuring instruments, how to proceed in order to observe creativity, and so on. On the basis of our internal report and on the basis of the recommendations, we drafted some proposals for a division of labour between institutions such as the foundation for test development and that for educational research and the inspectorate.

The results of this conference were disappointing. Participants, in general, were rather neutral or even sceptical regarding our ideas. Representatives seemed to adopt a wait-and-see position. The spokesman of the foundation for educational research created four problems for every possible solution, and much of the available time was spent on territorial matters between institutions instead on methodological and technical issues! We inferred from this conference that more political and financial support was needed. The products of this stage were: (a) the careful support of the foundation for test development; (b) after our loss of innocence, a new basis for our strategy; and (c) the feasibility study, 1982–5.

For some time after the technical conference, progress was almost nonexistent. We succeeded in creating a budget, but were unable to spend the money.

An official report by the national foundation of educational research was extremely negative. Meanwhile, within the department we failed to find powerful support. It seemed, then, that the programme was dead because the powers that be considered the programme to be risky.

A new opportunity came on the occasion of the parliamentary discussion of the educational state budget. Questions were asked by a few members as to the progress which was made in the quality policy. It was also a help that the US report, *A Nation at Risk*, attracted attention. Irritation caused by the situation that no progress could be reported in a session on quality by the permanent commission in Parliament was another factor which helped to change the situation. Thus frustration proved to be a powerful political drive. We took our chance and proposed a feasibility study; and we received permission to commission this study.

One of our leading researchers, Dr Hildo Wesdorp, took the risk, together with another prominent researcher, Dr Jan Bos. In record time, we launched a mini-assessment programme for mother-tongue teaching. Here several reasons for choosing the assessment language are relevant.

In the first place, language is complex; it involves several skills, therefore this area is suitable to prove that assessment need not be restricted to simple 'objective' instruments. Another reason is that language testing can be operationalized as a set of functional skills, which have something to do with real-life situations. Additional reasons are rather programmatic. Reports on language achievement attract attention, and there are experts in this field available.

Feasibility study: 1983-5

This mini-assessment was a success; results were rather conclusive:

1. Assessment turned out to be much more acceptable in the field than expected (according to a separate study).

2. Assessment was technically feasible.

3. The level of achievement in using functional language was surprisingly not high.

Reports were summarized in one small volume. The report was circulated among schools and key personalities. The popular report was covered in the national press, following a press presentation by the under-secretary of state. Publication of the first results was a turning-point in the chronicle of the Dutch assessment.

Construction of a model: 1985

In designing the mini-assessment project, we took care to adopt some essential features of the ultimate model which we had in mind. A number of technical, financial and methodological problems were discussed in a series of technical meetings. Apart from those problems, we had to remove a few rather formidable obstacles of a fundamental nature. One problem was that some of the participants in the negotiations held the strong conviction that assessment should be directed primarily at describing the current curriculum in primary education. Output was less important, according to this view. Another problem was that in Parliament the notion had been ventilated that assessment had to be school-based in order to guarantee the independence of schools. These views were of potential importance for the design of the model; we were able to solve the problems by reaching consensus on two points:

1. In the mini-assessment, measurement of output remained the main objective, but both time and energy was to be spent on describing the curricular background and didactical procedures in participating schools.

2. The ultimate assessment model was intended to be flexible as to permit deriving instruments for individual schools. However, this objective would be achieved in a separate project.

Final implementation of assessment: 1985–6

The last stage in the construction of the assessment programme formally took place after publication of the popular report on the pilot study. In reality, designing and implementation of course overlapped. An official policy statement was prepared for discussion in our central commission for education. If this commission would agree on the main features of the model, Parliament would also agree, we expected.

The success of the pilot study, in this period, gave us support within the department and other institutions such as the foundation for educational research. Still, there remained a number of objections, which were ventilated freely by several representatives. Therefore, we arranged a number of informal meetings with a limited number of key people. In these meetings we took care to explain openly what we had in mind, and we also took care to allow ourselves to be convinced by reasonable proposals to change some parts of our statement.

The statement which reached the finishing-pole in this 'hurdle race' included the following main specifications:

1. The government guarantees an independent programme and also an uncensored reporting and interpretation of results.

2. Participation of schools takes place on a voluntary basis.

3. It is intended to extend assessment to secondary education and to special education. It is also intended to explore the feasibility of school-based self-evaluation.

4. No reduction to 'basics' is intended in the assessment programme.

5. Results of individual schools and teachers are to remain anonymous; results of schools will not be a basis for measures directed at individual schools.

6. The assessment programme will be evaluated after all initial assessment cycle of four years.

Everybody involved – including ourselves – was rather satisfied with that agreement. Nowadays, after a few years of actual work on assessment, the main problem is perhaps the fact that persons and institutions sometimes expect too much of assessment.

International Roundtable: Social and Political Aspects of Large-scale Assessment

Chair and Minutes:
Professor Dr K. Ingenkamp, Zentrum für Empirische Pädagogische Forschung der EWH Rheinland-Pfalz, Landau (FRG).

Participants:
Dr W.Ebert, Verband Bildung und Erziehung (FRG).
A. Lapointe, Director of National Assessment of Educational Progress, Princeton, NJ (USA).
Dr S. Sandbergen, Ministry for Education and Science (NL)
Dr R. W. Selden, Director of State Education Assessment Center (USA).
Dr E. Thürmann, Gewerkschaft Erziehung und Wissenschaft (FRG).

The chairman proposed to discuss first the question whether a society needs to assess the outcomes of the school system by objective, valid and comparable methods and not only by teachers' judgements. If some prefer the first option, they should say why and describe the necessary characteristics of the assessment programme. Such in favour of teachers' judgements should explain why they are sufficient.

Dr Thürmann expressed his opinion that the German educational system does not need any additional assessment programme. He believes that Germany has already a system of checks and balances that guarantees the functioning of the school. The Federal Republic has (1) state curricula (altogether about 300,000 pages); (2) a public examination of textbooks; (3) assessment as an important part within the pre-service training of teachers; (4) detailed regulations for classroom assessment and examination (around 100,000 page; and (5) yearly promotions to the next grade on the basis of decisions in teachers' conferences. These are enough safeguards to keep standards. In addition, Germany has an inspection system, a highly developed in-service training for teachers, and there is an awareness of legal and educational consequences of the advancement or non-promotion of individual students. Lastly, comparability of subjects and teaching time within each state are further elements to stabilize the system.

Therefore, at first glance, he would say that Germany does not need an additional assessment system. At second glance, however, he had learned something and he could accept two reasons for new programmes: (1) if assessment could help to find a common ground of facts and arguments to end year-long political fights on school curricula and organizations. But it is hard to believe that politicians would ground their debates on facts, and (2) if assessment could determine which factors are the characteristics of a good school. Some aspects of the Dutch and British system seemed rather promising in this aspect.

Mr Lapointe responded that Dr Thürmann's comments would have been exactly the comments of a representative of the teachers' union or a member of a school board in the USA about seven years ago. But things have changed dramatically. Two of the greatest supporters of large-scale assessments are the presidents of the two largest teachers' unions in the USA. They are members of the governing board of National Assessments of Educational Progress (NAEP). Large-scale assessment needs the support of the teachers. The co-operation with teachers in different committees ensures some basis of realism for the programme. The position of teachers towards testing has changed generally and particularly towards NAEP.

One other thing that turned the American society around was the impression of a crisis within the educational system expressed in the publication *A Nation at Risk*. That is one reason that the nation looks more strongly to educational results than before. Some points, which Dr Thürmann mentioned, such as the number of courses, the textbooks selected, regulations for examinations, etc. are in his opinion **input**. But that a student has studied mathematics four hours a week in no way tell us how much mathematics the student will learn. The only way to find out is to measure the **output**. And as far as the legal implication is concerned, he would argue strongly for anonymity.

Dr Ebert confirmed the view that there are in the Federal Republic of Germany too many assessments, but there is no large-scale assessment. First of all, we have to clarify the differences between assessment by the teacher and within the school and large-scale assessment on the other side. He certainly accepts the necessity of a large-scale assessment as described today. Large-scale assessment, if carefully administered and supported by the public, could be a balance against the misuse of testing and statistics by politicians. The items and objectives must be carefully selected, the implementation must be carefully planned and the limits of the programme should be well known. If, in addition, the data are carefully interpreted, such a programme could be of high value for German schools. A danger could arise if the researchers were not free to report every result. The sponsor – i.e. the state, should not be in a position to influence the reporting of the results.

In Dr Sandbergen's opinion, the crucial points for the discussion are the functions of the assessment programme and the intended uses. Large-scale assessments have very limited, but very useful, functions. They do not go into the rating of individual students by individual teachers. That is a completely different kind of assessment. One should define the characteristics of the programme in order to know what could be achieved.

Many of Dr Thürmann's arguments have been expressed, in the Netherlands, in the same way. During discussions about curricula, regulations for examinations and public control of textbooks he had often the impression that there is a tendency to overload textbooks with objectives and content. Large-scale assessment could show what could be achieved in reality. The feasibility of goals is an often forgotten topic. Curriculum development could use results of large-scale assessment in a meaningful way.

Dr Selden said that he was thinking of the serious burden of responsibility for the teacher, when Dr Thürmann was mentioning that teachers discuss very seriously when they do not promote a student – i.e. if they take away a 'year from his life'. In Dr Selden's opinion, the German systems put a tremendous responsibility on teachers. An external point of reference from an assessment programme might relieve some of this pressure and could provide a way for teachers to get some co-operation and support from the society over the question of how the school system is doing.

The chairman asked permission to add some remarks to the contribution of Dr Thürmann. Even mountains of regulations could not guarantee the outcomes of the school system. According to many research findings, teachers' marks are not comparable between classrooms. Good marks could correspond with good test results in one class and with bad test scores in another. Without standardized tests, teachers have only a system of references limited to their own classroom. Therefore, the real achievement of the best students in one class could equal the achievement of the slowest learners in another, without the evidence of the teachers' marks. If one trusts curricula and regulations for traditional examinations too much, one would immunize the system against critics. Data, which are independent from subjective opinions, are crucial if a process of learning based on the strength and weakness of the system should start. At present, most countries do not have sufficient teachers training in assessment, and one should not believe that a better training without additional instruments could solve the problem. A large-scale assessment programme could provide data that teachers could not gain from other sources. But certainly, large-scale assessment should guarantee the individual's anonymity and should be free from political directions in reporting the results.

Dr Thürmann pointed out that he was not defending the mountains of paper. But the many pages of curricula demonstrate that the eleven German states (*Länder*) did not yet reach a consensus about objectives of teaching. One cannot expect that they will agree on assessment items and systems. For political reasons they need boundaries between the *Länder* in order to keep political differences alive. If assessment would be used as a tool for innovation and reform, it would be a meaningful enterprise. But assessment would have a bad effect if it stabilizes bad teaching. At present, teachers in Germany are more interested in new methods of teaching and are not much objective-minded. If we introduce assessment in a traditional type, we would then stabilize an outdated type of teaching. If assessment policy could stimulate new ways of teaching, he would certainly support it. But, in his opinion, such a stimulating effect could also be achieved by new curricula.

According to Dr Selden's experience an assessment programme could do either one: stabilize a wrong practice or stimulate reforms. It depends on the way the assessment is planned and executed. If assessment is orientated on a narrow range of mechanical skills, teachers will focus their efforts on those skills. But according to experiences in the USA, assessment can also stimulate and drive reforms. In California the State Education Agency (SEA) wanted to have a more sophisticated, high-order, kind of reading taught in schools and, hand in hand with that, they classified the curriculum and built tests. After introducing the new system in reading, teachers for other subjects asked for similar reforms. If one builds new strategies into the tests, the motivation grows to use the new strategies also in teaching. Working on an assessment programme can strengthen the co-operation between teachers and administration.

Dr Ebert pointed out that the marks, given in German classrooms every year, are an important assessment for every student's future but they are based on subjective judgement only. The German schools need another way of assessment: it must be criterion-centred and individualized. That would help the school and teachers. But for school policy, it would be important to have an independent large-scale assessment, and we should do our best to protect it against any political or other misuse.

Going back to US experiences, Mr Lapointe told that NAEP now reports about every four months and repeats its conclusions: poor children do not do as well as children of wealthy parents. Black children do not do as well as white children. It is important to reinforce these messages to the public in order to make the society aware that this situation is not tolerable. To find valid data on such issues, and to make the data public, is an important task for the programme.

In connection with the political questions, Mr Lapointe reported that the federal programme in the USA was developed with funds from foundations, not from the state. The governing board was independent from the government and its members were from the states, teachers' associations and the public. In the future the federal government will nominate the delegates. But there are enough ways against manipulation.

If we decide to measure a curriculum, we first create objectives with the aid of committees. The next step is to construct items; independent from different philosophies looking at the test questions, there is quick agreement.

The chairman raised the question: 'What kind of information does society and school administration need to make large-scale assessment meaningful and successful?' What kind of information is unnecessary and dangerous?

As a representative from a ministry, Dr Sandbergen, recognized a tendency in many European countries towards decentralization of education. Local school organizations got more freedom. The more the government steps back, the more it needs information about the functioning of the decentralized school system. Because on rare occasions of failure one has to know exactly what is going on. In addition, one should know how the money is spent. In the Netherlands the budget on education takes a great proportion; many members of the society should, and would like to, know what education is doing. For large-scale assessment, it is meaningful to keep account of the outcomes and make it public; unnecessary and dangerous, on the other hand, it is to give details about individual teachers and students.

Dr Selden supported the last point of view. To give information about an individual and to make decisions, one needs not only one test, but more sources of information. In his opinion, reporting classroom averages is not meaningful either. The most important data besides the average at nation, state and district level are the outcomes of different groups of students. The results, gained in different groups, could be compared with similar groups in other learning environments. If there are differences in achievement, one could ask for the reasons. That could be often a starting-point for reforms.

Dr Thürmann summarized all informations which, in his opinion, are useful. These are particularly informations on teaching methods, learning attitudes and learning behavior, interdisciplinary activities in school, teacher co-operation extracurricular activities and openness towards community. All these data could lead to the improvement of teaching and to reform strategies. He would not hesitate to add such information to the data about learning outcomes.

Dangerous, on the other hand, is all information which allows the identification of individual teachers and individual schools. It is not necessary to gather obvious information. We know that certain groups of children are underprivileged – e.g. children of migrant workers – and we did spend a lot of money on their education. It seems not necessary to have large-scale assessment for the identification of these groups. The particular outcomes of these assessment procedures are a great help for politicians, but they might not have the same value for teachers in school, unless other things are assessed or evaluated too.

Dr Ebert expressed his agreement with many points, but he objected to the collection of so much additional information at the level of large-scale assessment. Large-scale assessment should given comparable information while not encouraging or stimulating competitiveness.

The chairman asked us to consider the difference between research in teaching and learning – which needs many environmental data, partly very sensitive data. Data protection requires, in such cases, strict limitations over handling. He does not believe that the data protection office would allow the collection of sensitive personal data within the frame of large-scale assessment.

The chairman suggested that we deal with the question of the possible side-effects of large-scale assessment. Dr Ebert said that, in his opinion, large-scale assessment is much better for educational planning than ideology, a political programme or even the subjective experience of individual educators. One must be aware of the limitations of such an assessment; it should be carried out anonymously; and the organisation be as independent as possible, together with safeguards against misinterpretation of data.

In Dr Sandbergen's opinion, the question of side-effects is interesting; but what we rate as positive or negative effects depends very much on the structure of the society, the organization of the educational system, past experience and many other factors. The perception of side-effects is quite subjective and questions more hypothetical.

From the experience of the USA, Mr Lapointe mentioned again the effects on the debate on curricula: in viewing the US assessment results, some people lamented how terrible it is that students know so little; others were quite content about how much students already know. One result of the debate was the reviewing of curricula and textbooks and the search for better teaching methods.

One other example was the statement in a newspaper that 20 per cent of American adults are illiterate. There was a public debate concerning the potential aptitudes of young Americans within the age-group 21–25 who are unable to read. In a careful study only 2 per cent have been identified as being illiterate, some possibly able to read in another language. The facts did show that the young people recognized quite well the importance of reading for their life and that they do something for their own improvement.

Dr Selden identified one positive side-effect from the large-scale assessment programmes in the USA. Looking at the data, one becomes aware of how many aspects could be re-analyzed and re-interpreted. Having the studies replicated, one is able to discern the trends, the gains and losses. Further, one may compare different systems; perhaps the most important aspect of the interpretation is comparison between goals and present achievement, the criterion-referenced interpretation.

The chairman offered a hypothesis, which in his opinion, could be drawn from the several contributions. In some papers one could find as a prerequisite for large-scale assessment the relative independent position of local school authorities. But within states, having a strong central administration with strict and detailed regulation down to the single school, there is no local independence. Could one, then, arrive at the assumption that large-scale assessment corresponds better with a system of some local independence for the school boards? And, on the other hand, that local independence requires some kind of comparison between the local systems? No democratic school system could tolerate serious inequality of chances for transfer to secondary schools, dependent on differences in local standards. Those who want decentralization need large-scale assessment in order to secure some equality in the requirements for students. On the other hand, the dangers in large-scale assessment are greater if a strong, centralized administration can apply immediate pressure on single schools, or even individual teachers, without the limitations which local authorities can secure.

Dr Thürmann emphasized that in order to introduce large-scale assessment in Germany, one should first change the school system. With a centralized school system, assessment would become an additional element towards centralisation. If local autonomy prevails, large-scale assessment would become a convincing supplement of the system. The implementation of large-scale assessments is very difficult to achieve, since all attempts to change the educational system have failed in the past decades.

Another point in favour of large-scale assessment is the possibility of defending the schools against the criticisms of the chambers of commerce. Compared with the poor data arising from the 'pedagogical experts' in the chambers, large-scale assessment would provide an improved basis for discussions. A second positive effect would be that according to the experience both of the UK and West Germany, teachers will gain in competence in evaluation if they are involved in an assessment programme. A negative effect, in his opinion, would be that more money spent on assessment would mean less money spent on teaching.

Referring to that last remark, Mr Lapointe stated that it would seem reasonable to spend one-tenth of 1 per cent for the evaluation of educational projects when a country spends so great a total on education, for example, in the USA an expenditure of $300,000,000,000 a year.

The chairman then drew attention to the question of what to do first in the German situation – i.e. change the school system or introduce large-scale assessment? Dr Ebert pointed out that Germany has centralization only at the level of the eleven *Länder*, a somewhat different situation compared with, say, France. Large-scale assessment could serve centralized systems. But how could we be sure that there is less misuse in decentralized systems? He remembers an example of nepotism in the very decentralized system of Switzerland. And we should not forget that teachers in Germany have independence and social security to a remarkable amount.

Educational and Didactic Aspects

6 The Relevance of Data Gained from Assessing State Schools: The California Example*

Dale Carlson

> We all know how Adam said to Eve: 'My dear, we live in a period of transition.'
>
> (Vida Scudder)

We began assessing the performance of students by using standardized tests in 1962 in the State of California. We have made a number of changes to the programme, which I will briefly touch upon today, and we are now facing a major paradigm shift with implications for all aspects of the programme. I will first describe the California programme as it has evolved over the past 15 years, then I will sketch the basis for and characteristics of the programme that we envision.

Testing in California

Early history

The people of the world, but especially the North Americans, were shocked when Russia put *Sputnik* into the heavens; a shocked cry of 'how can this be?' travelled throughout the world of national education policy. It was assumed that the Western world had the best possible educational system, surely not one surpassed by those behind the Iron Curtain. Books have been written tracing the impact of that single satellite launch. For our purposes today, however, it is sufficient to know that one small impact was the formation of a public committee which recommended that California public school students be tested annually at several grade levels with standardized tests. The alleged purpose was to determine the quality of California education and make recommendations for change. Assessment began in 1962 using commercially developed, norm-referenced standardized tests – virtually the only tests in existence at the time. The tests were purchased and administered by the school districts, and the results were

* I wish to express my appreciation to Gary Konas and Dr Susan Bennett, for their substantial contribution to any coherence this paper may contain, and to Ms Renée Best, for her patient and competent transcription.

sent to the State Department of Education in Sacramento for tabulation and public reporting. At first, the districts were allowed to select the test of their choice from an approved list. That freedom was not long-lived; the system made it impossible to make the kinds of comparison among school systems which legislators believed to be the basis for higher achievement and knew would be of great interest to the public.

Programme evaluation and matrix sampling

In 1972 teachers grew so discontented with the programme that the legislature called for a thorough review. A committee chaired by Professor Lee Cronbach of Stanford, not only reviewed the programme but re-conceptualized it as well. The group determined that the appropriate purpose of California's state-wide assessment programme was to determine the effectiveness of school programmes, not to evaluate the skills and weaknesses of individuals. The new technique, multiple-matrix sampling, proved to be ideally suited to this purpose. The first matrixed test was administered in 1973/4, and since that time, millions of Californian students have taken short, matrixed tests. In the Californian application of multiple-matrix sampling all students are tested, but each student takes only a small portion of a large test pool. All test forms are non-overlapping and are stratified on content, sub-content and item difficulty.

The concerns of the schools touched three issues: first, testing time; secondly, the scope and coverage of the exams; and thirdly, the overall fairness of the reports and general usefulness of the findings. Matrix sampling provided an obvious solution to the first complaint, cutting testing time from approx. four hours down to less than one class period. The second concern, content coverage, was expressed by the complaint that 'These tests don't measure what I am teaching'. The department responded to this complaint by moving from off-the-shelf, pre-developed tests to custom-developed tests, designed to match California's curriculum. Since in fact there was no common state-wide curriculum, matrix sampling served as a perfect way to provide extremely broad curriculum coverage, so that the test seemed to sample whatever any district happened to be teaching. The third complaint, that score reports unfairly represented the performance of a school, was answered by a research agenda beginning with the use of multiple regression to establish 'comparison score bands' for hypothetically similar schools, so that schools with non-comparable groups of students would not be penalized in the media.

Matrix sampling has a number of advantages. Our school achievement estimates are based on responses to 1,000 items per grade level. It is obvious that a test of 1,000 items for a grade level yields great power in covering the scope of instruction, so that testing does not narrow the curriculum; and secondly, that very coverage means that the results can be reported for a great variety of sub-skills (but more about the advantages and disadvantages of this later). The third advantage deals with the credibility of the scores, that is the ability of the test to resist artificial gains by teachers who might be tempted to teach to the test – not that such teaching cannot have spurious effects, but at least one can feel a sense of relief that if a thousand items are taught to students, they will, first, be focused on what is viewed to be the best curriculum and, moreover, if their scores are higher, one can feel that some learning has certainly taken place. Fourthly, students are foiled from looking upon one another's papers as a source of 'extra help' because not all students receive the same set of test items. Fifthly, and most important, it was assumed when matrix sampling was adopted in 1972 that the scores would only suffer slightly from a reliability standpoint. Since that time we have learned and reported that (although school administrators facing an angry press still have difficulty believing what I am about to say) the results in terms of school-level stability are approximately twice as reliable as the results of the previous longer, common instruments. This is true, despite the fact that tests taken by each student are approx. one-tenth as long as the previous instruments. In the world of educational research where replicable statistical differences are rare, it is stunning to find a method effect that yields differences exceeding an order of magnitude!

Application of item response theory

The next major application of technology to the new assessment programme was based on the work of Professor Darrell Bock of the University of Chicago. He saw the power of combining matrix sampling and item response theory for programme evaluation. Subsequently he customized Bilog, his two-parameter logistic programme, to scale the results for schools as units. The scale was set at an origin of 250 and stabilized at that point to provide for comparisons across years and, with qualifications, across grade levels and content areas. Underlying these scales and the conditions necessary for their delineation was the concept of 'indivisible curricular units', or 'elements' to use Professor Bock's phrases. Since the scaling is best done at the smallest curricular/ability unit, the test outline was delineated to the point where each sub-skill is likely to be unidimensional. The advantages of this method of scaling at the lowest level, then aggregating sub-scales into skills and those skills into higher level skills, are described in Bock and Mislevy (1981, 1987).

The current testing programme

FORM AND ITEM CONFIGURATION

The culmination of 15 years of research and development has led to the array of tests, forms and items as enumerated in Table 6.1. This table also shows the type of background and related self-report information that is collected at the time of testing. One can see that for the latest year, we have administered 5,530 multiple-choice test questions to over 1,200,000 students. Missing from this chart is a description of our writing assessment programme which merits at least a short description here.

The direct writing assessment is based on the theory that writing is not a unidimensional endeavour, but rather there are many types and modes of writing for different purposes and occasions. Anyone familiar with the research on

Table 6.1: CAP test overview

	Grade 3	Grade 6	Grade 8	Grade 12	Total CAP
First administered	**1980**	**1982**	**1984**	**1987**	
Content areas tested					
English language arts				X*	
Reading	X	X	X	X	
Written expression	X	X	X		
Direct writing assessment			1,987	1,988	
Mathematics	X	X	X	X	
History-social science			1,985		
Science			1,986		
Number of forms	30	40	36	30	136
Items per form	34	31	70	25**	135
Total items	1,020	1,240	2,520	750	5,530
Number of skill scores					
Reading	27	54	48	13	142
Written expression	34	39	54		127
Direct writing assessment			12		12
Mathematics	29	50	40	9	128
History-social science			41		41
Science			40		40
Total skill scores	90	143	235	22	490
Supplementary information					
Sex	X	X	X	X	
Mobility	X	X	X	X	
English language fluency	X	X	X	X	
Other language spoken	X	X	X	X	
SES–parent occupation	X	X			
SES–parent education			X	X	
Special programme participation	X	X	X		
Time reading		X	X	X	
Time watching TV		X	X	X	
Time on homework		X	X	X	
Writing assignments		X	X	X	
Attitude towards subjects	X	X			
Ethnic background	X	X	X	X	
Courses completed				X	
Extracurricular activities				X	
Grades repeated	X				
Special maths questions		X	X	X	
Post high school activities				X	

*   At grade 12, reading and editing are combined into English language arts.
** 24 maths items per form, plus one computation item per supplement (30).

writing assessment knows that the ways of classifying writing nearly equal the number of classifiers! We have reached a compromise position that there are approx. eight types of writing that merit special school attention, and therefore deserve to be assessed and reported separately back to school personnel. We have implemented such a programme at grade 8 and will add grade 12 next year. In this programme consistent with the matrix sampling used in the objective testing part of the programme, students are randomly assigned a topic from a pool of approx. five 'prompts' for each type of writing. Scoring is based on a three-part system, the first being 'rhetorical effectiveness', the degree to which a piece of writing meets the essential conditions and characteristics of that type of writing. The second is a 'feature' score that focuses on a supplementary aspect of each type of writing, for example, elaboration or coherence, and the third is 'conventions' which includes punctuation, capitalization and grammatical usage. All essays are scored once on a one-to-six scale for each of the three scores, and scores are aggregated across students as in the matrix sampling of multiple-choice items.

REPORTING

We rely upon the scaled scores as our chief vehicle of reporting data. These scores are compared with the scores for similar schools and districts through regression and are broken out in full detail in the part of the report known as the Program Diagnostic Display (PDD) (see Figure 6.1). The PDD has been the showpiece of our programme. We also provide information to schools and districts about the performance of sub-populations such as boys and girls and students who have been in the schools for a lesser or greater period of time. Our state report primarily presents an analysis of strengths and weaknesses in curriculum areas and skill topics. We try to weave this information into holistic themes, so that the report will provide local personnel with a backdrop for interpreting their own results.

USE OF TEST RESULTS

Local uses. This section will briefly summarize the chief uses of the assessment results. They will be discussed from the viewpoints of local uses of school and district results and state-wide uses and impacts. The chief intended use of the test results – after satisfying natural curiosity of how one school compares with all schools or similar schools – is to study the strengths and weaknesses of the programme as revealed on the PDD. Since the press looks forward annually to doing lengthy stories on the latest trends in educational achievement testing, there is considerable motivation for school personnel to say they have studied the report. Increasingly, school system task forces actually do so and report to their publics that, 'Yes, there are certain weaknesses, but we have studied them, analysed the characteristics of our instructional programmes, and are initiating the following programmes to deal with these deficiencies'. We are ambivalent about this: we are glad to see they are using the results, but are also becoming

Figure 6.1: Survey of basic skills – grade 6 (CAP): 1982 (Program Diagnostic Display)

School WATSON ELMENTARY
District CALWEST UNIFIED
County SACRAMENTO

WRITTEN LANGUAGE

The total written language score which was shown on page 1 reflects student achievement on a wide range of skills. Scores for the skill areas are shown here numerically and graphically to help educators identify possible ways to improve their written language programmes. This display highlights relative strengths and weaknesses within a school. It does not show any comparisons to other schools. For a complete explanation of the Program Diagnostic Display, see page 3.

The program diagnostic display for written language reflects two areas of concern expressed in the *English Language Framework* by providing an analysis of (1) writing process skills which deal primarily with matters of judgment in writing; and (2) supporting skills dealing primarily with matters of correctness in the conventions of writing.

Interpretive example:

Our total Written language score of 263 is expressed below as a bold vertical line, and each skill area score is displayed as a shaded bar. Your score in Sentence Recognition is identified as neither a relative strength nor a weakness because the shaded bar overlaps the vertical line.

See Part IV for an illustrative description of the Written Language skill areas tested.

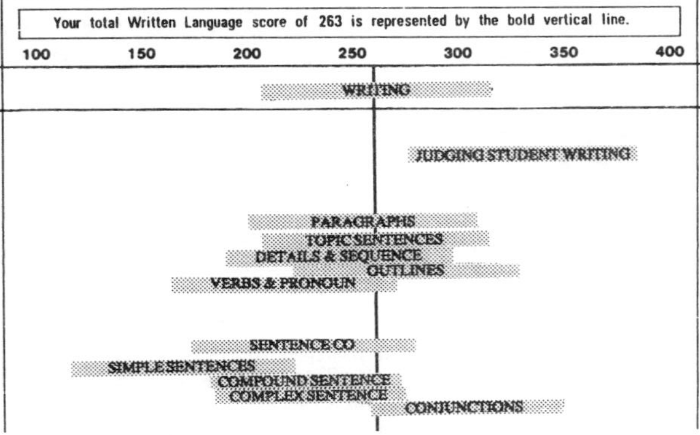

Written language skill areas	Scaled score and standard error	Your total Written Language score of 263 is represented by the bold vertical line.	Relative strength/ weakness
Writing process skills	263 ±11	WRITING	
Judging student writing	331 ±41	JUDGING STUDENT WRITING	RS
Paragraphs	253 ±19	PARAGRAPHS	
Topic sentences	266 ±41	TOPIC SENTENCES	
Details and sequence	245 ±35	DETAILS & SEQUENCE	
Outlines for organization	280 ±41	OUTLINES	
Consistency of verbs & pronouns	221 ±28	VERBS & PRONOUN	RW
Sentence combining	227 ±19	SENTENCE CO	RW
Simple sentences with modifications	172 ±43	SIMPLE SENTENCES	RW
Compound sentences & sentence parts	222 ±31	COMPOUND SENTENCE	RW
Complex sentences	273 ±30	COMPLEX SENTENCE	RW
Conjunctions	302 ±49	CONJUNCTIONS	

Graph scale: 100   150   200   250   300   350   400

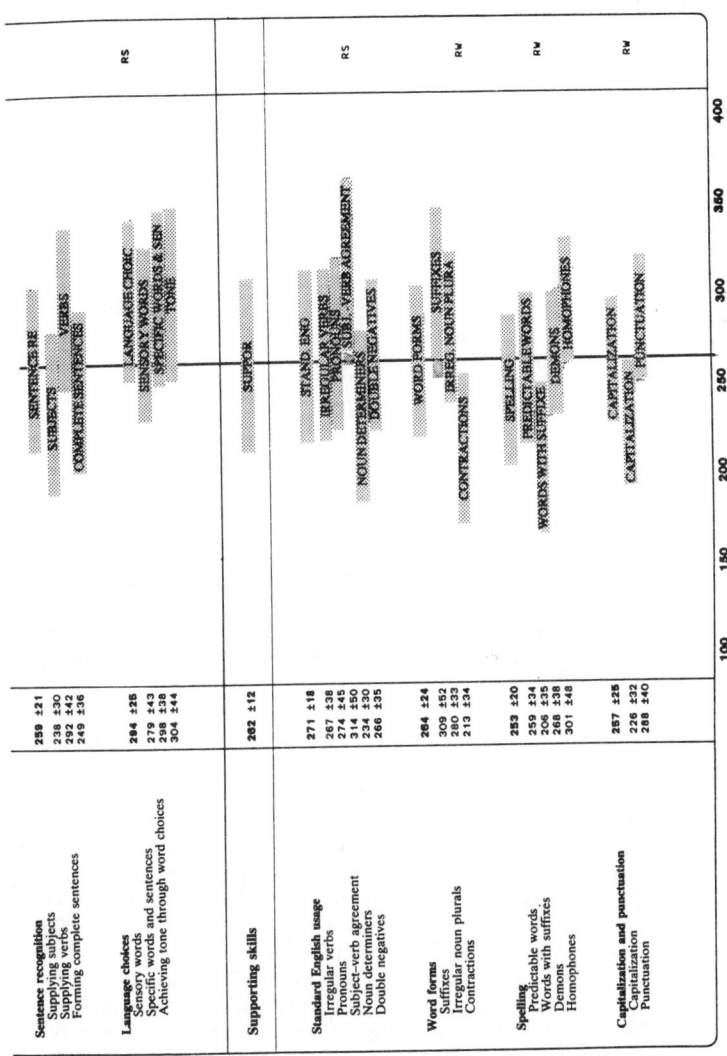

quite uneasy. Our concern is with the specific steps that districts take, especially the short-term, overly specific teaching of narrow skill elements. We are concerned about worksheets and remedial lessons that are prepared to teach students specific skills and to give them superficial refresher courses in all of the skills. Not that review is not a good thing, but the question is whether the valuable instructional time devoted to these review activities is an efficient expenditure of class time when weighed against the students' lost opportunities to continue their regular course of study.

State uses
(a) *Informing curriculum change.* I have already stressed the value of broad information yielded by hundreds of test questions in helping determine the specific patterns of growth across the state. While we present these results in our state-wide report and discuss them at state-wide professional conferences, we are never certain how they are used in a given district other than to alert district personnel to potential areas of concern. However, we have seen how this type of state-wide information can be used to inform state-wide curriculum leaders. For example, we believe that the mathematics advisory committee's persistent call for renewed emphasis on problem-solving has had an impact in effecting a large shift in that direction in the new California curriculum documents.
(b) *Resource allocation.* Over the years several state-wide programmes have used the California Assessment Program (CAP) results as a basis for specific resource allocation schemes. The first set of programmes incorporates a need-based mechanism, whereby the schools with the largest number of students having problems in reading or mathematics got the greatest share of special funds. We have also had two programmes that rewarded schools financially for outstanding achievement. Both of these programmes have now been terminated.
(c) *Identifying successful schools.* The new curriculum movement is energized by the re-emphasis on motivational incentives related to public recognition. A variety of programmes use CAP results to identify schools for official public recognition.
(d) *Identifying schools needing assistance.* Over the years, several efforts have used test results to identify schools needing assistance and to focus the efforts of task forces appointed to improve programmes in those schools. These efforts have met with limited success since outside 'experts' are limited in what they can accomplish.
(e) *A research base.* Over the years, a variety of school effectiveness studies have relied on CAP data as the chief criterion for determining which schools are achieving above expectations. In one of the first studies done in the USA, the California state department staff identified what has now become known as *the* formula for increasing school effectiveness. That formula is now being reconsidered in the light of the current curriculum reform movement.
(f) *School performance reports.* The chief vehicle for providing accountability by reporting to the public on the effectiveness of Californian public education relies on CAP scores. The performance reports are produced annually and sent to all schools. They are also publicized widely through the media. The results represent efforts at broadening the scope of outcomes as far beyond CAP results

as possible. To date, the effort has had only limited success because limited data exist or can be readily collected.

The turning-point

All of US education has been influenced by pressure for greater academic rigor over the five years since the report *A Nation at Risk* was released by the US Department of Education. Much of the recent emphasis on testing, even in California, is a result of the movement that produced the report. The movement is best characterized by its quantitative outcomes; school districts have made the policy changes to increase the length of school day, amount of testing and a variety of other schooling traits that can be changed by law or regulation. More important, the movement recognized the need to focus curriculum on higher goals and to raise students' expectations of meeting those goals. In the testing arena this has often been translated as a need for greater emphasis on testing higher-level thinking skills, critical thinking and problem-solving. It is this impetus that has led us to upgrade considerably the CAP tests over the past four years. Several examples come to mind: the critical skills component of the our history/social science test; the emphasis on underlying process in our new science test; the emphasis on drawing inferences in our new reading tests; the move towards problem-solving and away from mere applications of algorithms in developing new mathematics tests; and the direct writing assessment.

Towards a re-conceptualized assessment programme

Cracks in the foundations

A variety of factors have caused us to question our assumptions and methods of testing in CAP. When we hear from top educators, who are trying to implement the latest curriculum, that there is a conflict between their efforts to implement that curriculum and scoring well on the state tests, we are led to believe something is wrong. When we hear that funds slated for library improvement are siphoned off to pay for 'test prep' materials, we know it is time to take a realistic look at the actual impact of the test. In many schools testing may not be assisting teachers; in fact it may actually be retarding the process.

We subjected CAP to an 'existential audit', and three large concerns emerged. First, while we do have considerable capacity for broad assessment of instructional programmes we wonder if this may not also have disadvantages. Since the test has no single specific curriculum focus, the results reported back to schools could very easily lead teachers to believe that the best way to look good on the test, if not to serve children, is to cover as much of the curriculum as possible, regardless of how shallow instruction must necessarily be to do so. We may be accidentally reinforcing one of the most insidious blocks to a good instructional programme that the teachers face, that is the feeling that everything in the book or in the curriculum syllabus – and now on the test – must be covered, regardless of what the students are learning in any depth. Our second great apprehension about CAP's current approach is that the sheer sub-division of curriculum goals into such a multitude of sub-content skills and sub-skills may lead to fragmented instruction. We show the number of skills displayed in Figure 1, and have already discussed our fear of misuse. Our third concern is that CAP, like other assessment programmes in the Western world, relies on multiple-choice examinations that can be scored quickly and easily by electronic devices. The limitations of paper-and-pencil testing in representing the scope of the intended curriculum is severe, and we have exacerbated the situation by focusing only on those skills that can be measured in fixed, pre-structured ways where students respond by blackening bubbles on a sheet of paper. We now take a closer look at this US phenomenon.

How we outsmarted ourselves with technology

Once upon a time, the oral–aural tradition ruled supreme in education. Students learned by listening to the instructor, and they consolidated that learning by engaging in oral recitation, which was as much a learning device as an evaluation exercise. Lunsford (1986) points out that this eighteenth-century system of oral writing assessment had several positive features: (1) it was strongly interdisciplinary, bringing reading, writing and speaking together to deal with issues of public concern; (2) it unified theory and practice; and (3) it reflected a dynamic, collaborative learning model.

Little by little, graphic modes of communication entered education. Although we see evidence of writing going back hundreds of years in China, the history of writing in the Western world is much more recent. We begin by noting the writing that took place with the slate and chalk. This was writing in the most elementary sense since the friction of the chalk on the slate made the process extremely cumbersome. Progress can be traced through the centuries: the early Greeks wrote with a stylus of bone or ivory, and the quill pen, first mentioned in the writings of St Isador of Seville in the seventh century, was widely used for hundreds of years. It is amusing to note the application of technology to quills. In 1809, Joseph Bramah developed a machine for cutting quills into lengths. The short lengths were then inserted into a wooden holder, which made it possible to change points quickly. This led to other inventions and experimentation with holders made of diverse materials such as horn, ivory and tortoise shell (Travers, 1983).

Real progress did not appear until the invention of the modern pencil several hundred years later. Until the end of the eighteenth century, the pencil was a primitive instrument. Then a method evolved for mixing graphite and clay to achieve a consistency that allowed the material to be drawn out into sticks placed into wood holders. Pencils were developed in Europe in the early part of the nineteenth century, but the production of the cheap pencil, available for use by mass educational systems, was not developed until the late nineteenth century. The pen has a similar history. Although the metal pointed pen was used in Europe by the middle of the nineteenth century, its use was limited until technology made it possible to mass produce steel pens that could carry sufficient ink inside the barrel to write continuously over long periods of time. Once this new medium was developed, written examinations soon became the substitute for oral examinations.

By the early part of the twentieth century we had two powerful modes for learning and for assessing that learning: speaking, and the technology of writing. The significance of this technology must not be underestimated. Writing was not just a tool for assessing learning; it changed the course of that very learning itself, providing for written discourse and the power of that discourse for thinking and the acquisition of knowledge.

Strangely enough, the development of writing instruments coincided with the development of 'new-type examinations' which didn't require any writing! These assessment methods, chiefly multiple choice, became extremely widespread during the examinations used during the First World War, then spread quickly throughout the schools as part of the scientific movement in education. A happy, but unfortunate, marriage occurred between the new type of examination, which required a mere mark on a sheet of paper and the technology that made it possible for machines to read those marks. As scoring technology progressed from rather primitive magnetic devices to today's extremely sophisticated high-speed optical scanners, the use of assessment based on oral and writing exercises in the USA was all but eliminated – a sad state of affairs. The convenience and low cost of gathering information on hundreds of thousands of students made the use of such technology irresistible to programmes like CAP. We have now reached the point where oral exercises are limited almost specifically to certain courses called 'speech' or 'drama', and speaking is often considered a mode of low-level social intercourse and discouraged in classrooms. Simultaneously, writing is associated with courses in English, and occasionally to other courses, but the burden on teachers to read students' written work is profound and is not accounted for in salary or adjustments in class loads.

What must be done? This direction must be reversed. We know that the mode of assessment affects the mode of instruction. It shouldn't be true, but we believe the casual link is strong enough to mandate changing assessment to directly promote the best instruction. We must go in three directions simultaneously. First, we must reclaim our past heritage, rediscovering the power and social relevance of speaking in a world which emphasizes the spoken word so highly. Secondly, we must exploit the simpler forms of technology, using the pens and pencils at our disposal to draw upon students' ability to compose, in the broadest sense of that term. We must increase the use of written exercises, drawing upon the advantages now explicated clearly by linguists and psychologists. Thirdly, we must look to the more complex forms of technology in the form of word processors that can change the shape of students' writing and teachers' reading. We must invest resources in applying the latest in optical scanning and other relevant technology to 'reading' students' free and extended responses to novel and creative questions. This can range from scanning complex figures and graphs to expert systems for natural language processing of short phrases and eventually, we must believe, extended responses.

In the next two sections we discuss two significant shifts in educational thinking: the need for major curriculum reforms, and a new understanding of knowledge and learning. These carry profound implications for an assessment programme.

Instituting a worthwhile curriculum

The need for a new curriculum is widely recognized in the USA. The impetus behind that curriculum is the fundamental belief that all students are capable of learning, and it is imperative that they do so to become contributing members of society. The new curriculum presupposes not only that high expectations are essential to high outcomes, but that students entering the twenty-first century face considerably higher literacy demands than those faced by previous generations. To meet the needs of today's students, the new curriculum must provide interdisciplinary opportunities for students to blend their learning and apply it to life. It also re-emphasizes the unique value of the essential knowledge at the core of each discipline. This curriculum is frequently called a 'thinking' curriculum, an indication that students are required to understand what they are doing and not merely parrot well-rehearsed responses. In this conception, thinking is unique to and heavily dependent upon the structure of knowledge in a given discipline. The curriculum that embodies this conception of thinking calls for an active, hands-on, experiential, co-operative approach to learning. Students will be encouraged to argue, to persuade, to produce, to create and to compose – not merely to discriminate among proposed alternatives or presented works. The first paragraph of California's *English Language Arts Framework* puts it as follows:

> We are in the midst of a revolution – a quiet, intellectual revolution spinning out dramatic insights into how the brain works, how we acquire language, and how we construct meaning in our lives. Psycholinguistics, language acquisition theory, and research in composition and literacy unite to present new challenges for students and teachers of English-language arts and to suggest the need for a fresh look at literature, the core of the discipline, and at strategies for teaching listening, speaking, reading and writing.

What then would this curriculum look like for the major areas being assessed? The main thrusts as paraphrased from the newest California curriculum documents are:

History/social science
1) Emphasizing the importance of history as a story well told.
2) Emphasizing the importance of the use of literature of the period and literature about the period.
3) Emphasizing the importance of studying major historical events and periods in depth.
4) Encouraging teachers to present controversial issues honestly.

Science
1) Science must be taught as an integrated subject; integrated among the science disciplines (earth, life and physical sciences) and integrated with other subject areas, especially mathematics, the arts and language skills.

English language/arts
  1) A literature-based programme that encourages reading and exposes all students to significant literary works.
  2) Instructional programmes that emphasize the integration of listening, speaking, reading and writing and the teaching of language skills in meaningful context.

Mathematics
  1) Emphasizing problem-solving: using knowledge and experience when encountering new and unexpected situations to solve problems.

The new curriculum is not limited to these 'basics'. In fact the term 'basics' can no longer be used to refer only to the 'skills' subjects, reading and mathematics, but must focus on learning and thinking in the contexts of literature, science and history. It will take time to put a curriculum of such scope in place; massive training efforts will be needed to help a largely new teaching staff move from awareness to commitment to expertise.

New conceptions of knowing, learning and the learner: from the mechanistic to the organic

Picture a diptych. The left half shows a gloomy picture associated with US behaviourism and the psychometric tradition. The right side, by contrast, shows an emerging conception drawing upon the thinking of the enlightenment through modern cognitive psychology.

The view on the dark side

First the bad news. It is hard to overemphasize the impact of behaviourism on education in the USA. It is only a slight exaggeration to trace the current situation back to B. F. Skinner and his search for the smallest possible, bite-size chunks of behaviour that could serve as operants. Schedules of reinforcement could then be developed to ensure the behaviour's near certain automatic appearance and to ensure its appearance in a chain of behaviour 'shaped' by the teacher/trainer.

We are all familiar with Skinner's experiments with pigeons and other organisms, but only occasionally are we made aware of the massive and unprecedented application of the principles of operant conditioning to military training or their impact on US education. We can see the thread running through programmed instruction and objective-based testing. Scores of publishers of education materials proudly advertise the virtually guaranteed effectiveness of their programmes on the basis that they have analysed all the tasks and behaviours underlying success in their reading or mathematics programmes. The theory states that students need to learn small skills, and that they need to chain these together to form larger, (eventually) meaningful chunks of behaviour. It is held that the process of reading, for example, goes from phonemes, to letters, to words, to phrases, to sentences, to paragraphs, to larger chunks of connected prose. Throughout the 1960s and 1970s, and unfortunately well into the 1980s, US students were subjected to reading programmes founded on this sequential principle; it held that if students would learn the small bits, they would eventually come together and take on meaning. Even today, one can visit classrooms in the USA and see students filling in bubbles or drawing lines to connect elements on worksheets. Fortunately, students are pliable and resilient as well as docile; they not only tolerate such meaningless and trivial exercises, they manage to learn in spite of the process.

Behaviourism had the full help of the psychometric tradition in the USA. The belief that all complex behaviour could be analysed into its constituent parts was irresistible when combined with the assertion that the intellect consisted of a finite number of separate abilities that could be linked, albeit unevenly, to the tasks. The impact of such theories on education and on assessment is unmistakable. In assessment we found it professionally justifiable to focus exclusively on the component and *en route* skills – the minute pieces of knowledge or subskills that seemed to be linearly and hierarchically linked to the execution of important school-related tasks. In mathematics we have been satisfied to measure the execution of algorithms with minimum allowance for their proper application. Reading assessment in the USA has moved away from its emphasis on decoding in the last 20 years, but the comprehension tasks now in use are still relatively one-dimensional; they allow students virtually no opportunities to construct their own response to show the nature and depth of their comprehension. The most laughable example of this phenomenon (if it were not so tragic) is that there actually has been debate about the degree to which multiple-choice exercises focusing on grammar, punctuation, spelling and/or recognizing the best way of stating a sentence can be used legitimately to assess writing proficiency. We know that the correlation between actual writing skills and the multiple-choice assessment of related skills is relatively high.

Given the cost and relative reliability of objective assessments, objective test items may be justifiable for use in selecting students for training programmes or perhaps even for identifying those students needing additional work in composition. For assessment programmes that purport to measure the outcomes of education, however, it is unconscionable that we have even considered the use of such exercises. We have seen the impact of such testing; teachers, not to mention educational publishers, focus on the sub-skills, the *en route* skills and the easy-to-measure skills because these skills are measured by the test. Because the test results are made public, educators face an unhappy dilemma of how to balance the instructional time allocated to sub-skills that are tested and the more general educational outcomes that are valued but not tested. California is only one of many states facing this problem, but it has at least begun to recognize and take major steps to rectify the error of its ways. The reason for our misgivings about reporting a multitude of sub-scores should now be obvious.

The new view

Moving to the other side, we view a holistic, organic scene. These two descriptors characterize what is now considered a more proper and accurate view of the way students learn. Other key terms are dynamic, meaning-centred, purposive, contextual, active and authentic. The older, behavioural approach would not admit to being static and inorganic; it considered the conditions of dynamism and organicity as constructive and even helpful – but not central or crucial. In truth, learning and learners vary, and much learning does take place according to the rules of behaviourism. The field is open to a wealth of research possibilities and interpretations. The point is that most learning in school should be meaningful, verbal learning of symbol systems. Children are meaning-seeking, sense-making creatures. They scan, classify and organize stimuli that bombard their senses constantly as they struggle to match what they are receiving – on a nanosecond basis – with what they have already stored away. Clearly, learning can only be meaningful if there is a proper relationship between the instructional setting, the student's knowledge and new information; behaviour that seems to be proof of learning falls away quickly if it cannot be integrated or if it doesn't make sense. Learning comes about as a function of purpose. Children see that purpose when they observe adults engaging in dialogue, solving problems and using language to communicate. While, in the past, instruction intentionally focused on separate elements – e.g. word pronunciation, spelling or linguistic analyses – we now realize that context is the key.

I have searched for the proper analogy or metaphor to illustrate the organicity of the learning process. In my struggle to understand the nature of the sub-skills in the reading process, for example, I have been vexed with the task of classifying these skills as real; artefactual; real but inseparable; real but not teachable; or a variety of other possibilities. In CAP we report skill areas in considerable detail at the group level, and we need to know whether it is useful to foster such division through deliberate instructional practices or whether these practices are only confusing and destructive. The following analogy may be useful. In the mechanical world systems have separate components; for example, cylinders and camshafts exist in the world of internal combustion engines. These are legitimate parts that exist separate from, and in combination with, other parts of a functioning engine. The whole is greater than the sum of the parts, yet the parts exist in their full existential splendour prior to the existence of the whole, and in fact they can be taken apart and replaced. On the other hand, consider the leaves, stem, flowers or roots of a plant. Such 'parts' are not really parts, they are aspects of the whole; they do not exist before the whole. Other things being equal, they cannot be replaced, nor can they exist in any meaningful sense when separated from the whole. Reading, like a plant, is a viable process that cannot survive disassembly the way an engine can.

In truth, teachers really don't teach anything to a given student, in the sense that they can design an instructional experience that is certain to achieve any given end. Rather the teacher is responsible for providing such a wealth of stimuli and experiences that each student can choose those that are relevant to him or her, merge them with existing structures to forge new meanings and, hence, form new knowledge. Receiving information is not obtaining knowledge;

information must be processed, considered, questioned, catalogued and understood before it can be considered knowledge. Although students learn in and from groups, forming knowledge is still an individual affair. To believe that a teacher can provide a precise instructional strategy by sequencing the subordinate tasks is as ludicrous as expecting a physician to walk into a crowded waiting-room and write out a common prescription to solve the various ills of ten patients.

The new conception of learning and the learner is based on a dynamic view of knowledge; learning is itself a process of making meaning as new information is blended into existing structures. The classical view held that knowledge is formed, transmitted and received *Holus bolus* by the learner from some superior source. In contrast, the new view holds that knowledge is unique to the learner; common meanings emerge within a culture through a process of testing perceptions and checking for similarities in responses to propositions and events. The new rhetoric, based on recent discourse theory, holds that the mind is active, constantly striving to make sense, to understand and to know. The role of language, in this process, is nearly impossible to exaggerate; it is the very currency of the mind. Using words and sentences to forge connections between events and stimuli, the mind asserts those connections that lead to new understandings and, hence, to new knowledge.

The idea that discourse plays a central and generative role in the production of knowledge goes back at least to Descartes, who rebelled against the proposition that knowledge was given by the gods, proposing instead that it was dynamically formed in the process of interacting with and organizing/interpreting data. Locke followed in this tradition. In his view, words and ideas were inseparable; knowing was the process of shaping sets of these words into 'texts' and discourses. From this perspective we can say that discourse actually makes knowledge, and knowledge is discourse – a creative open-ended process based on repeated formulation and revision of internal text, with rules that emerge in the process of structuring new information and making new meanings. Linguistic acts are attempts to know, to form arguments about the significance of experiences and language is the very essence of mind. It develops from early childhood with structures that are extremely plastic – not 'mechanical pieces bolted together in the minds' (to use the phrase of Knoblauch and Brannon, 1984).

Discourse, like language itself, is meaning-making – first, last and always. Once we see that meaning simultaneously guides and results from discourse, we can begin to understand Kant's phrase, 'Experience is without doubt the first product which our understanding brings forth'. Our knowledge and understanding are not shaped to fit reality, but rather determine reality for us. This approach draws upon the work of Cassirer and Langer, who hold that discourse defines the world and constitutes the very substance of experience. We can subdivide the act of composing and thinking into several parts: receiving information, making assertions and connecting assertions to form lines of reasoning. Together, these three parts lead us to construct knowledge as a pattern of connections that cohere. Through the very process of making discourse, we discover these connections and link them to create new knowledge.

Back on track

So, why is this considered *a new conceptualization of knowing and learning* if these opinions represent a near-consensus of learning in the Western world? Because education and psychology in the USA – the forces that account for the current shape of assessment – took a wide detour between the 1920s and 1970s. The detour, marked by behaviourism and expediency, took us over a considerable stretch of rough road, and left us at a spot far from our destination. The conception of knowing described in the preceding paragraphs was temporarily shelved while we took the detour through this American tunnel. We can now look back quickly at how it happened, and more important, see how we returned to the main route guided by cognitive theory and research.

The enlightenment that led to the view of mind we have been discussing continued through the end of the nineteenth century when such giants as Wundt and Titchner were struggling with the mysteries of the mind, hoping to map out the territory using sensory processes. By the 1920s the scene had changed in US psychology. J. B. Watson had decreed that it was unnecessary, indeed unscientific (a phrase used considerably by behaviourists to reify their point of view), to expect to understand the workings of the mind by introspective techniques. B. F. Skinner stepped on to the stage with his *Analysis of Behavior* in 1953, followed by *Verbal Behavior* in 1957, 'scientific' treatises that based complete explanations of behaviour on the function of operants and reinforcements. These ideas retarded progress in US psychology and, unfortunately, led to an inappropriate application of psychology to education and educational assessment. They closed the door to legitimate discussion about the role of the person in the learning and thinking process, leaving no room for discussion of self-choice, decision-making, intentions or plans. It took a young upstart, Noam Chomsky, who studied with Bruner and Miller at Harvard, to publish a devastating critique of Skinner's *Verbal Behavior* (Chomsky, 1959). Chomsky asserted that Skinner's explanations relied on such vague definitions of key terms like 'reinforcement', that they were as unscientific as those of the mentalists he criticized. Furthermore, Chomsky argued, Skinner did not bother to provide the evidence for his 'scientific' paradigm.

Chomsky literally turned the study of language learning upside down, putting American researchers back again on the path of studying the whole person. He argued that it was logically impossible to account for language proficiency in terms of stimulus–response chains. Meaning, he proposed, operates as an overarching, seemingly magical, system rather than appearing as a function of the consolidation of streams of operants. Comprehension is driven not just be processing incoming information from the bottom up, but conceptually by top-down assimilation to mental and relational structures. From this perspective it is obvious that a person's information processing strategies go far beyond merely obtaining meaning from each word or sentence, adjusting it and then storing it. In fact the storage of units, such as words and sentences, hardly occurs at all, rather memory processes function on the basis of meaning. It is said we have a bad memory for words, but a good memory for meaning.

A science of cognition

So a new cognitive science has now come to the fore. What is this science, and what impact does it have on our thinking and research? It is hard to articulate a clear consensual definition, other than to say that it is interdisciplinary, and that its focus is cognition/mind/thinking/intelligence. The new cognitive science could even be called a return to introspectionism, for it follows in the traditions of William James and Alfred Binet. One can see its roots in Gestalt psychology with its emphasis on such mental phenomena as memory and forgetting. The emphasis on problem-solving efforts by psychologists of the '30s and '40s are also a part of its heritage. Another of its ancestors is information theory, an outgrowth of Claude Shannon's 1948 demonstration that information could be quantitatively measured. In 1956, George Miller proposed the idea of chunking, as part of a theory of how the mind processes information in patterns rather than individual units. Research continues on many fronts, ranging from verbal learning, to human and communications engineering, to artificial intelligence.

One hears a whole new language associated with cognitive psychology and an alphabet soup of acronyms. One hears about neural nets, scripts, general knowledge structures and a variety of labels. A key topic is that of metacognition, a concept foreshadowed by Vygotsky when he described the two phases in the development of knowledge: (1) the automatic unconscious acquisition of knowledge, and (2) the gradual active increase in the conscious control of language. This topic symbolizes the essence of the move away from traditional behaviourism in which the individual plays virtually no conscious role; metacognition focuses upon the voluntary conscious role of the learner.

Perhaps the central concept in the whole movement is that of the schema. In 1922 a German psychologist, Franz Wulf, attempted to 'schematize' the details of what we remember about pictures and events. Later, in 1932, Bartlett, claiming to dislike the term, informally defined it as the way in which new information was actively incorporated into a set of organized cognitive structures. They are considered to include the ways that the mind guides the storage and retrieval of knowledge, the generation and interpretation of ideas and even the initiation and regulation of actions. Schemata are discrete, abstract knowledge structures that represent past actions or experiences. Their two chief functions are: (1) structuring knowledge in retrievable form, and (2) organizing it in more and more efficient ways. Whether we are speaking of the processes of comprehension, perception or interpretation, new input and existing knowledge interact constantly as schemata are developed and continually refined and restructured.

So why all this attention to schemata? They are based upon knowledge and are largely responsible for the acquisition, organization and retrieval of all new knowledge. The relationship of schemata to instruction is not yet clear. It does seem, though, that instruction should be related to the generation, modification and instantiation of schemata. We know that their nature is dynamic. In fact schematic change is the *sine qua non* of acquiring knowledge, as opposed to merely aggregating information. The implications for instruction (and for assessment) are not too difficult to divine. Instruction in support of knowledge ought to focus on the structure of each discipline and of its knowledge base; it ought to help students find connections among concepts and principles; it ought to emphasize meaningful links and relations, and it ought to provide opportunities for individuals to discover and refine their understandings. Assessment in the service of such instruction should focus on the structure and complexity of students' schemata more than on their aggregated information.

The controversy about knowledge vs skills is relevant to instruction and assessment. Although schemata are knowledge structures, they are also the bases for what we have previously thought of as skills, that is independent abilities. American educators now generally concede that they have paid too much attention to the development of skills, independent of the knowledge structures upon which they operate. Californian educators have moved to restore content in the new curriculum, reacting against the move towards empty, content-free formalism. Research findings on the differences between 'novices' and 'experts' have supported this insight. In the USA they have led one scholar (Hirsch, 1986) to form the concept of cultural literacy. Hirsch proposes, based on schema theory, that many of the differences among individuals and groups of different socioeconomic strata can be accounted for by the differential knowledge bases and differential access students have had to the general knowledge in the culture. Other writers take a less extreme view, focusing more on the complex and fully interactive, symbiotic relationship between knowledge and abilities. Messick, for example, focuses on the dual and simultaneous growth and restructuring. In his words, 'developed abilities influence the structuring and restructuring of knowledge while developed knowledge structures influence the organization and application of abilities, leading to increasingly more complex structures of each as well as to increasingly more complex, knowledge-dependent combined structures of both' (Messick, 1984). We hold the view that thinking should be studied and taught within the context of each discipline. This is demanded by our understanding of schemata and of their role in thinking. In any mental activity, especially the complex ones that schools should foster, the boundaries of knowledge and skills interact and are inseparable, or as Yeats puts it,

> O body swayed to music, O brightening glance
> How can we know the dancer from the dance?

Mind over machine

What about this new cognitive science; have we now found the golden touchstone – the key that unlocks the mystery of the mind and promises to usher in the new millennium? Or should we be cautious, realizing that this is another attempt to explain the incomparably complex and mysterious workings of the essence of the human mind? We do not want to fall into another trap, over-believing in a theory unit: 'it can be shown to predict human behaviour and provide a guide to its development. The title for this section, 'Mind over machine', taken from a readable, pungent little volume by Dreyfus and Dreyfus (1986), is meant to highlight the inadequacies of current theory and research. We must be careful lest we succumb to those aspects of the theory that seem to reduce mental activity to definable elements – chiefly rules and processes that fit the Procrustean bed of information-processing theory. The purpose of this section is to remind us that the finest hour of the human mind is not that associated with rules, facts, procedures and certified algorithms, but rather those leaps of intuition and unexplainable acts – not just those of recognized creative geniuses, but those that we all perform many times daily. We do not want to be guilty of substituting algorithms and schemata for operands.

If cognition is a science, it ought to be able to help us not only predict behaviour, but also produce human-like behaviour in the absence of humans, that is using artificial intelligence to develop 'expert systems'. The history of the field of artificial intelligence is a fascinating one. Dreyfus and Dreyfus (*ibid.*) chronicle this history from early attempts through grandiose predictions to more recent efforts. In 1965, Herbert Simon of Carnegie-Mellon University projected that 'Machines will be capable, within 20 years, of doing any work that a man can do'. Not only did that prediction fail to materialize but the high hopes of the general scientific approach also proved to be disappointing. Some think that the decline of the superiority of American management coincides too obviously with the often overzealous introduction of scientific management' – the application of decision theory with its emphasis on rules and procedures, unfortunately causing a decreasing faith in the wisdom and judgement of the manager borne of ideas of experience. Long-range and strategic planning is in a similar state of disillusionment. Once considered *de rigueur* for any forward-thinking business, the planning departments of American businesses, like that of General Electric where it all began, have been all but abandoned and are considered to be archaic. The most highly touted aspects of the application of artificial intelligence (i.e. expert systems) have failed. The inadequacy of such systems can be seen in their application to the functioning of photocopy machines in busy offices – a far cry from their anticipated ability to deal with such difficult areas as natural language processing, speech recognition, story understanding, or language in general.

The key underlying assumption is that the human mind is a giant information-processing machine, the only way we are able to conceive and programme computers to reproduce the workings of that mind – a non-productive tautology. It assumes that the mind operates on the principle of learning and applying rules to solve problems using stored knowledge and other aspects of knowledge. It follows that the way to reproduce such human thinking is to programme computers to absorb large amounts of knowledge and apply the necessary rules to solve problems. Such knowledge of necessity suffers from being isolated and artificial. The search for the characteristics of knowledge as held by humans has been frustrating, but no more so than the search for the rules which humans use to apply that knowledge in smooth, fluid and effortless ways to solve incredibly complex problems.

It is interesting that such rules generally have *not* been found to explain human problem-solving. The assumption has been tenaciously clung to, that such rules do in fact exist, and if people and human experts are unable to explicate them, it is because they have forgotten them since they are longer needed on a conscious level after years of experience. Such thinking goes back to Plato's accounting of Socrates' experience in probing Euthyphro on the essential and definable elements of piety. It seems that Socrates, believing as he did in the logical, calculative, rational essence of man, held that such concepts as piety would be best defined in terms of the rules that experts used in evaluating piety by its acts. He consequently sought to induce such rules by probing the prophet Euthyphro. Unfortunately, all of his quizzing led to great frustration since Euthyphro claimed that he knew piety when he saw it, but he was unable to provide replicable rules. We can leap from that experience all the way to the most fearful hypothesis to artificial intelligence researchers: there are no rules! That is, humans form judgements and make decisions on the basis of thousands of 'special cases' – a thoroughly horrifying outlook for the future of expert systems.

One can trace back the roots of Western thinking to the philosophy of the Greeks, inventors of logic and geometry, with their willingness to reduce human thinking and expertise to calculative reasoning. At one point, *logos*, the essence of human faculties connotated the ability to grasp whole situations. When the word was translated from Greek into Latin, the emphasis was placed on *ratio*, the ability to calculate or reckon – leading to man as the reckoning or rational being. While the skirmish between the mystical and the rational has been raging for centuries, the hegemony of the rational has been clear from Plato to Leibnitz in Western civilization. My purpose here is to show that we need to guard against an imbalanced emphasis upon rationality and, most certainly, not to over-credit it with our overall progress in technology.

One conception of the controversy contrasts intuition and rule-based, calculative reasoning. Artificial intelligence researchers are forced to focus upon making rules in constructing a model to reproduce human mental activity. There is no doubt that much of human thinking and reasoning can be accounted for on this basis. The point is that an extremely large amount of human behaviour of all kinds, including school-level activities, are more parsimoniously explained by intuition-like phenomena. There is virtually no evidence to assume, for example, that the rule-based approach explains such simple things as riding a bicycle, recognizing a face in a crowd or demonstrating that most complex and irreproducible phenomenon called 'common sense'. It is assumed that the whole process of pattern recognition is carried out by humans as it might be done by machines, that is by identifying salient features of a pattern or situation and then comparing those key elements with stored images of key elements from past perceptions. It is hard to believe that the process of an owner recognizing the bark of his dog, for instance, is not a holistic act.

We all have our rational sides and our intuitive sides; the trick is to cultivate both and when faced with a given task, let the brain itself decide which type of solution mechanism is most appropriate. The research on chess playing has demonstrated not only the heavy role of knowledge, but more significantly that the process of using that knowledge is more intuitive than analytic. In fact it has been suggested that one reason there are so few master-level women chess players is that the only women who are attracted to the game are those who are analytically orientated. Tim Gallwey proposes allowing for the proper role of both brains in playing tennis, as explained in *Inner Tennis*. He emphasizes the necessity of learning when to let each type of mechanism take control.

As Socrates believed we must be using rules to make decisions about piety, so current researchers believe that even though we are unable to extract and cite the rule, we are still operating upon those rules. Socrates explained this problem by posing the thought that our difficulty in retrieving the rules was based on the fact that we had learned them so long ago that we had forgotten them. Current researchers have gone slightly beyond this explanation but are still searching for a satisfactory alternative. They have learned, however, that it is extremely difficult for experts, that is any of us, in solving thousands of every-day problems to cite the rules. When forced to produce the rules, we probably revert to a very early form of expertise, which may match our behaviour at an early learning stage, but is totally inappropriate in explaining the facile, fluid, smooth mental and physical performance we all possess as real-life 'experts'. In fact the whole process of asking people what they are doing and thinking as they're performing is questionable. It reminds one of the centipede who was unable to walk when asked by the toad which leg came after which. Unfortunately, researchers are still limited to protocol analysis as a main source of information about the process.

The evidence is clear that the mind can recognize whole scenes without decomposing them into features. Chess players do not refer to elements, nor even to large chunks and patterns, but rather to patterns of patterns. We know that people suffering from brain damage, especially a particular condition called agnosia, must decompose objects into component parts in order to recognize them. The process of recognizing a triangle for them is a cumbersome one, limiting their functioning considerably. Even Donald Broadbent (n.d.) had to revise his theory of perception and learning to account for the two types of behaviour: those that provide for verbalization of the knowledge vs those that seem almost miraculously to account for the matching of similarities between two situations. Apparently humans rely on this experience-based, holistic recognition process rather than operating as logic machines or inference-making machines. They seem to have some kind of built-in holistic imaging devices still not reproducible by our sophisticated technology. Several years ago, Professor Pribram, a neuropsychiatrist at Stanford University, posited that the brain may well function as a holograph, since it clearly does so, to the extent that extirpation of key brain tissue merely reduces the intensity and clarify of the associated function.

However it works, this ability is profound. In most cases, it is so obvious that we do not recognize it. The sheer ability to speak, the ability to begin sentences not knowing how they are going to come out, should be considered one of the wonders of the world, but we take it totally for granted. While driving an automobile, we make thousands of split-second judgements without realizing the complexity and efficiency of those judgements. We do not think of what might be coming up around the corner, but automatically adjust for surprise events Chess players who are able to use rapid-fire techniques of playing chess at the rate of one move every five to ten seconds obviously are relying upon some special combination of knowledge, skill and intuition.

The power of intuition is implicitly granted in many other aspects of life. We do not expect our judges to explain their decisions because we know that they know, as we do, much more than they are able to verbalize. The bases for our decisions are in fact so complex that the Western emphasis upon reasoning often forces us to create reasons to publicly defend our intuitive judgements. We know that that is the case, yet in our official business and judicial capacities we require such reasons so they can be publicly examined. This has led to a situation where the emphasis on verbalizing and rationalizing sometimes becomes more highly valued than that of being right!

The efficiency of apparently non-ruled based behaviour is impressive, and can be found to take varied and unexpected forms. The US poultry industry looked to the Japanese for the solution to an age-old problem – discriminating baby hen chicks from cockerels. One Hikosoboro Yogo was able to detect the sex of baby chicks at the rate of approx. 1,400 an hour, with 95 per cent accuracy, and was unable to explain how he did it. Mr Ben Salewski could do a 1,000 chicks an hour, with 99.5 per cent accuracy. He claimed to do it merely by touch, but he was unable to explain what that meant. The proof of the power of these examples is that the process of training chick sexers at the present is one of having novices work with experts, going through the process and forming their own intuitive impressions until they reach a high state of proficiency – which they do – yet not knowing how it is done. Perhaps this is a homely example of what Pascal might have meant when he said that 'The heart has reasons that reason does not know'.

New approaches and models are being developed to overcome the inadequacies of earlier, more linear sequential approaches. The two new approaches, both of which draw upon the work in distributed associative processing, are: (1) those using holographic approaches with their own new concepts, such as convolutions, and (2) those working from a neuronal net standpoint. Both approaches are being studied by the community of researchers often called the New Connectionists. The fundamental problem, however, is how to represent knowledge such that it matches the real world and bears appropriately upon the tasks in question. Researchers still have great difficulty representing the common-sense knowledge possessed by a four-year-old. In fact it is this very 'common-sense' aspect of the knowledge that proves to be such a conundrum. Human knowledge representation and manipulation is so profound and complex: for example, people instantly know whether they know something. We know those things that we definitely know; we know those things that we could think of and we know which things we have no knowledge of. Computers, on the other hand, are unable to know without scanning the data base. With the speed of scanning, this in and of itself is not a serious problem, but it represents the nature of the qualitative difference between human and computer representations. Another example is the ability of humans to recognize problems, as well as solve problems. This may be the epitome of our knowledge – i.e. our ability not just to solve problems, but to recognize or 'feel' when a situation is not right.

What can we learn from this excursion into the world of rules vs intuition? It seems the first principle is that of balance. While throughout this paper we have engaged in exaggeration to make a point, we are aware that balance and moderation are necessary, that some truth lies in all arguments and points of view. We can only agree with Pascal who said that 'There are two equally dangerous extremes – to shut reason out and to let nothing else in'. We know that the tendency of rationalists is to disparage anything that cannot be quantified; we know that romantics rebel against this rationality, as did Goethe, and return to his old adage 'feeling is everything'. Our responsibility is to encourage children to cultivate their intuitive capacities not instead of, but in addition to, their facilities for logic and calculative reasoning. We need to be open-minded and prudent about our introduction and use of rules and procedures in teaching children. We need to allow for other modes of learning as well – especially those types that would allow the student to capture *en masse* the complex of sub-skills and routines in a given learning exercise. For some areas, it seems wisest to allow students to learn by imitation, observation and a general absorption process in taking on a fully formed proficiency. For assessment, it means that while we may want to assess the application of rules, or evidence of the student's familiarity with the rules, we must not let this become the sole focus. We need to emphasize the student's actual production and communication of knowledge in holistic ways, in addition to its application to specific circumstances. It means we need to respect the diverse and seemingly irrational methods students will use to solve problems, in addition to how well they follow prescribed sequences.

Implications for assessment

Given our new curriculum and new conception of learning, it is obvious that assessment must change. The traditional purpose of assessment – providing information about the effectiveness of the system to inform changes – must now become secondary, if not tertiary. The two chief purposes of an external assessment programme in a school reform environment are proposed as follows:

- to illustrate and portray the outcomes of an instructional programme centred on meaning, understanding and thinking and, by inference, on the instructional practices leading to those outcomes;

- to provide non-monetary, publicity-oriented incentives for local personnel to adopt those practices with all possible speed.

An instructional programme based upon (a) the goals of a worthwhile and demanding curriculum, and (b) an enlightened view of the nature of knowledge and learning, ought to be distinctly different from what we see in most US schools. We leave the description of that instructional programme to others, moving on to the implications it carries for an assessment programme expressly designed to illuminate and clarify the goals of the curriculum and support efforts to improve the instructional programme. The following are 11 overlapping characteristics of the type of assessment programme we believe is needed.

1. *Emphasis on production rather than discrimination:* Norman Frederiksen, a distinguished psychologist at Educational Testing Service (ETS), has described the real bias in mental testing as that inevitably associated with a reliance on the multiple-choice test format (Frederiksen, 1985). Although it is true that persistence and cleverness can yield multiple-choice items that draw upon the highest mental processes, it is also true that those response formats limit a student to marking a bubble. If the goal of instruction is to teach students the expressive side of communication and problem-solving, tests must be patterned after instruction; they must emphasize production, creation and performance – doing

rather than discriminating. Beyond school we demonstrate knowledge through production of original conversation and writing; through repairing and building; and through artistic, musical and athletic performance. It is obvious that such tasks focus on the end-product rather than the skills and knowledge propositions that may be called upon to solve the problem or make the product. Assessment is most meaningful when it carries benefits beyond the evaluation of students, that is when achievement on an assessment task has aesthetic or utilitarian value apart from determining the competence of the learner. This aspect of authenticity stands out as we imagine children or adults trying to succeed in a variety of activities they consider important such as writing letters, news articles or insurance claims; when they speak a foreign language; or when they develop blueprints or build a stereo cabinet. Achievement of this sort has special value that tasks contrived only for the purpose of assessing knowledge do not have.

2. *Modelling good instruction:* the assessment exercises must, by their very nature, reflect ideal instructional settings and strategies. They should be mirrors of instructions. Furthermore, assessment should provide a learning opportunity in and of itself. By and large, this has not been the case in the USA because multiple-choice items are less likely than constructed response test formats to ask students to think about relationships or form new understandings.

3. *Focus on integration:* the assessment tasks themselves must be intentionally complex, moving away from the clean, unidimensional factorial purity of the past. Only tasks that call for integrating and applying learning can reinforce the highest goals of instruction. The tasks will be multi-dimensional in skills assessed, multi-sensory in stimuli presented and multi-modal in response formats.

4. *Fewer tasks of greater depth and breadth:* complex integrated outcomes cannot be assessed with a multitude of unidimensional items that call for quick answers, but only by items that require thought and provide the opportunity to do it. The right kind of exercises will take approx. five to ten times as long as normal multiple-choice questions and the test will therefore consist of a relatively small number of tasks.

5. *Interdisciplinary learning and assessment:* the complex multidimensional tasks will cut across disciplinary lines, providing opportunities for students to write about science, tell how they would solve a social problem, and so forth. Instruction focused on large, real-life problems, such as deforestation of the earth or world hunger, will promote multidisciplinary opportunities for learning and then, quite naturally, for assessment.

6. *Writing to learn and to communicate learning:* Students will be asked to write, not as a mode of expressing pre-packaged, pre-digested truth so much as a way of promoting learning through writing and reinforcing the importance of writing in the curriculum.

7. *Valuing face validity:* measurement textbooks have long listed face validity as a poor cousin in the validity family. In assessment focused on improving instruction, however, tasks that look like good measures go to the head of the class. The test must have credibility to teachers, parents and students, as well as provide meaningful results.

8. *Learning and assessment in groups:* educators are increasingly aware of the significance of group learning and assessment. They recognize that productive participation in group problem-solving is essential to success in life beyond the

classroom. To promote the necessary skills, instruction must move towards the group mode and assessment must follow suit. The ability to interact, negotiate and cope with different opinions to achieve common ends is too important to be left out of the assessment picture.

9. *Renewed emphasis on speaking and listening:* Since the advent of mechanical means for recording answers, we have downplayed the importance of spoken communication in instruction and assessment. Speech training has been limited to circumscribed educational courses and to large-group presentations rather than focusing on its most common occurrence in one-to-one interactions. Perhaps because children speak early and few require formal instruction to do so, we have treated speaking as a primitive form of literacy not deserving of the attention given to writing. We now realize that this view of oral language is too limited. Oral examinations can take several forms, for example: student debates, peer problem-solving sessions, teacher examinations of small groups that have done research together or teacher examinations of individual students.

10. *Intentional lack of definition:* Assessment exercises must no longer provide neat, tidily structured problem situations, but call upon students to structure problems before they can be solved. This is especially obvious in mathematics, but not necessarily any less true of other fields.

11. *Flexible use of time:* It is unrealistic to expect assessments of authentic learning to take place within rigidly, and frequently short, pre-specified time periods. In the real world adults are not always asked to work within rigid time constraints to solve problems, to write effective pieces or to produce designs for products. If the curriculum does not purport to develop these types of skills, this doesn't matter; if the curriculum does, then it is a travesty to require responses on short time periods that match the mentality of short, right answers.

A call for new assessment designs

Creative designs are required to match the purposes of assessment with ways of collecting, analysing and reporting assessment results. We have been pleased with the success of the matrix-sampling approach for programme evaluation, but we are also certain that the move towards more open-ended, holistic assessment will place even greater demands on existing designs. Because our assessment programme must be concerned with the reliability and validity of scores for school units, we have not varied the sampling base. As we move towards a new programme to reflect our new curriculum, one interim design may be to assess groups of students within a school on various open-ended tasks drawn randomly from a pool of tasks, and randomly test all other students on other types of instruments. Such a design would provide broad coverage and still incorporate open-ended tasks in the overall assessment. It is crucial that some number of open-ended exercises 'count' for the school score in order for the assessment to be taken seriously and have its full impact on instruction. We look forward to this and the many other challenges facing us in implementing an assessment programme worthy of the students we serve.

References

ANDERSON, R.C., SPIRO, R.J. and MONTAGUE, W.E. (Eds.) (1977). *Schooling and the Acquisition of Knowledge*. Hillsdale, NJ: Lawrence Erlbaum.

BOCK, R.D. and MISLEVY, R.J. (1981). 'An item response curve model for matrix-sampling data: the California grade-three assessment'. In: CARLSON, D. (Ed) *Testing in the States: Beyond Accountability*. New Directions for Testing and Measurement No. 11. San Francisco, Calif.: Jossey-Bass.

BOCK, R.D. and MISLEVY, R.J. (1987). 'Comprehensive educational assessment for the states: the duplex design', *Evaluation Comment*, November, 1–20.

BROADBENT, D.E., FITZGERALD, P. and BROADBENT, M.H.P. (1986). 'Conscious and unconscious judgement in the control of complex systems', Department of Experimental Psychology, University of Oxford (preprint), p. 21; cited in DREYFUS, H.L. and DREYFUS, S.E. *Mind over Machine*. New York: The Free Press.

BRUNER, J.S. (1962) *On Knowing: Essays for the Left Hand*. Cambridge, Mass.: Harvard University Press.

CALIFORNIA STATE DEPARTMENT OF EDUCATION (1978). *Science Framework for California Public Schools, Kindergarten and Grades One through Twelve*. Sacramento, Calif.: California State Department of Education.

CALIFORNIA STATE DEPARTMENT OF EDUCATION (1984). *Science Framework Addendum for California Public Schools, Kindergarten and Grades One through Twelve*. Sacramento, Calif.: California State Department of Education.

CALIFORNIA STATE DEPARTMENT OF EDUCATION (1985a). *History – Social Science: Rationale and Content*. Sacramento, Calif.: State Department of Education (draft).

CALIFORNIA STATE DEPARTMENT OF EDUCATION (1985b). *Mathematics Framework for California Public Schools, Kindergarten through Grade Twelve*. Sacramento, Calif.: California State Department of Education.

CALIFORNIA STATE DEPARTMENT OF EDUCATION (1987a). *English-Language Arts Framework for California Public Schools: Kindergarten through Grade Twelve*. Sacramento, Calif.: California State Department of Education.

CALIFORNIA STATE DEPARTMENT OF EDUCATION (1987b). *History–Social Science Framework for California Public Schools, Kindergarten through Grade Twelve*. Sacramento, Calif.: California State Department of Education.

CHOMSKY, N. (1959). Review of *Verbal Behavior*, by B.F. Skinner. *Language, 26–58*.

DREYFUS, H.L. and DREYFUS, S.E. (1986). *Mind over Machine*. New York: The Free Press.

FREDERIKSON, N. (1985). 'The real test bias: influences of testing on teaching and learning', *American Psychologist*, 39, 193–202.

HIRSCH, E.D., Jr (1987). *Cultural Literacy: What Every American Needs to Know*. Boston, Mass.: Houghton Mifflin.

KNOBLAUCH, C.H. and BRANNON, L. (1984). *Rhetorical Traditions and the Teaching of Writing*. Upper Montclair, NJ: Boynton/Cook.

LUNSFORD, A.A. (1986) 'The past and future of writing assessment'. In: GREENBERG, K.L., WIENER, H.S. and DONOVAN, R.A. (Eds.) *Writing Assessment: Issues and Strategies*. New York: Longman, p. 5.

MESSICK, S. (1984). 'The psychology of educational measurement'. *Journal of Educational Measurement*, 21, 215–37.

MOFFETT, J. (1968). *Teaching the Universe of Discourse*. Boston, Mass.: Houghton Mifflin.

NATIONAL COMMISSION ON EXCELLENCE IN EDUCATION. (1983). *A Nation at Risk: The Imperative for Educational Reform*. Washington, DC: US Government Printing Office.

RESTLE, F. *et al*, (Eds.) (1975). *Cognitive Theory*. Hillsdale, NJ: Lawrence Erlbaum, Vol. 1.

SHARKEY, N.E. (Ed.) (1986). *Advances in Cognitive Science*. New York: Halsted Press.
SMITH, F. (1986). *Insult to Intelligence: The Bureaucratic Invasion of Our Classrooms*. New York: Arbor House.
TRAVERS, R.M.W. (1983). *How Research Has Changed American Schools*. Kalamazoo, Mich.: Mythos Press.

7 Feedback of Assessment Results to Teachers, Students and Parents: The Role of Indicators

Ingemar Wedman, Staffan Karp, Tommy Lyxell, Eva Andersson and Tomas Åström

What does Johnny learn in school? is an eternal question. The history of education is rich with questions of this and related content: their significance stems from an interest in making things happen while in school. However, what happens while in school may be explained in many different terms, depending on who is answering the question.

Many things go on in school. Generally speaking, however, most schools have at least one thing in common, namely the fostering of competencies in different subjects, competencies that are supposed to be important both for the individual student and society in general. Much money and time are devoted to strengthening each individual's competencies while in school.

Therefore, it seems quite natural to ask how schools manage in developing proficiency and skills. In order to obtain an answer to such a question, some sort of evaluation has to take place. A large-scale assessment might be one such evaluation activity.

In light of what has been said above, the Swedish National Board of Education formed an informal evaluation group about ten years ago. On the agenda was the question of what Johnny learns in school. No answer was given, mostly because there was no information available that could answer that question. At that time, groups and persons outside the National Board began to show a growing interest in what happened in school and what Johnny learned. Even the mass media began to ask questions about education and the students' competencies. For instance, one of the biggest evening papers in Sweden published an article in which it was asserted that the National Board of Education each year educates 20,000 students who are illiterate.

Based on discussions within the informal group at the National Board of Education, and also the external interest in what school did with the individual student, a minor research project was initiated with the purpose of examining the prerequisites and the possibilities for what might be called a Swedish National Assessment Programme. The contract was given to the senior author.

Our first task was to find out more about the two existing National Assessment Programmes then available in the USA and UK respectively, namely National Assessment of Educational Progress (NAEP) and the Assessment of Performance Unit (APU). Later on we added experiences from the Australian programme (ASSP). Briefly, we soon came to the conclusion that a common difficulty for all three mentioned programmes had to do with the use of the information obtained from the different programmes or rather the non-use of the information obtained.

One common experience from all the programmes, as it seems from an external point of view, is the limited use the information has resulted in. Gipps and Goldstein (1983), in the evaluation of the APU programme, presented the following answer to a question asked of local education authorities (LEAs) about the influence that they had found the APU to have:

> The biggest group, however, almost a third (30 per cent), made no response to this question or gave an answer which was irrelevant. This, together with the high proportion which said the APU had no effect, suggests that perhaps half the LEAs in the sample had not really taken much note of the APU, as though it was going on elsewhere which did not affect them.

Power and Wood (1984) gave a similar picture from the Australian programme:

> Less than 2 percent of schools made changes in lesson-time allocation curriculum, remedial activities, teaching, or testing practice as a consequence of the testing program. In most schools, staff did not even discuss the results. Half of the parent organizations contacted knew nothing of the project and only 11 percent said they were clear about what was being tested and what interpretations were justified. Teachers' unions, professional organizations, and other groups with a potential interest were aware of the results from media reports, but only 12 percent had discussed them, and even fewer took action.

Based on such experiences, we successively come to the conclusion of stressing the pedagogical component in developing a national assessment programme in Sweden. The logic behind such a conclusion is that without a strong pedagogical component, the information obtained will not appeal to those responsible for the teaching process (i.e. teachers, students and parents), and consequently not used and, furthermore, that such a component has to contain information of direct relevance for the teaching process going on in the different classrooms. In short, the pedagogical component seen in our eyes contains two separate parts, namely an interpretation tool based on indicator information, and feedback information to persons responsible for the teaching process (teachers, students and parents). Below, we will elaborate a little on the idea of the pedagogical component seen in terms of feedback of information and indicator information for use in the interpretation work.

The consumers of the programme and problems of reaching them

At first, it may seem obvious that a national assessment programme is addressed to those who really are responsible for education – i.e. politicians and decision-makers at different levels. Such an ambition corresponds rather well to the administrative system most countries have for education, but no more. If, however, the ambition is that the programme should have pedagogical effects (e.g. leading to concrete discussions about competencies and what goes on in school), teachers, students and parents are as important consumers, perhaps even more important consumers. Why are these groups so important? Their importance stems from the fact that it is between these groups that the actual enterprise of education is constructed and it is also between these groups that the curriculum is concretized in active teaching. Under such circumstances, an exclusion of these extraordinarily important groups is to reject the possibilities of creating a school for all, in a democratic sense.

Of course, decision-makers at different levels are also important consumers of the programme. However, it is not, in the first place, as decision-makers that they operate, but as creators of synthesis, of reviews, and as interpreters of the results. Those reviews and interpretations are then to be used to stimulate thought about the pedagogy in schools, and by so doing, strengthen the role of the school in bringing competencies to the students.

The significance of teachers, students and parents as consumers of the programme can also be expressed as follows: without active contribution from these groups, the pedagogical discussion may be discussion for its own sake, or one that only partly exploits the potential to strengthen competencies.

In order for a national assessment programme to be effective, horizontally as well as vertically, information flows and discussion are presupposed. In order to take into account and use fully the results of the programme in a constructive way, the results need to be known and debated within *all* groups of consumers of the programme – by teachers, students and parents – and, in addition, within boards of education at different levels and by politicians and those responsible within the National Board of Education. In order for the programme to have a real supporting capacity, dialogue between the different consumers and between different levels within the education organization needs to be improved.

Something that is probably true for many large organizations is that internal problems are so many and complex that they take up more resources than are allocated to the work of realizing and providing the primary goals of that organization. Often this is mirrored in the daily work of the schools. A national programme must ensure that the important factors really are related to the internal problems, that today in many ways work as a hindrance to development. In this connection, let us digress a little.

What opinions do teachers have on the pedagogical debate, on pedagogical materials and the discourse relating to the curriculum? During our work with the Swedish National Assessment Programme we have tried to answer that question. Our study has involved talks with teachers and headteachers working at the primary level within the Swedish school systems. The discussion dealt mainly with questions concerning the pedagogical discussion and materials and contacts between teachers and heads, as well as between teachers and parents.

The teachers and the heads in the study were also asked to give their opinions as to the forthcoming National Assessment Programme as it has been described by the National Board of Education in their proposal to the government for the fiscal year 1986/87.

All teachers in the study were critical of the pedagogical materials addressed to them. They emphasized that mostly the materials correspond poorly to the reality of their work, that is problems that teachers find most difficult to handle are not often those dealt with in the official reports and materials. Also that criticism holds for the materials connected with the curriculum for the support in local development work.

In answer to one direct question, however, it turned out that not one of the persons asked had taken any part in the production of the materials that they were so critical of. In this connection, it is necessary to point out further that not one of the teachers had contributed in any part to the materials dealing with their own subject.

Will that mean that the criticism mentioned is to be neglected? Of course not. Instead we have to ask ourselves why teachers don't take an active part in producing the materials that are addressed to them. The question isn't easy to answer, and the reasons for the criticisms have a number of different points of departure – e.g. the layout of material; the teacher as central to the criticism of the materials; increased workload for teachers arising from the materials; etc. However, we are still left with the question as to why teachers are critical of the materials that they de facto have not used. Perhaps it may at least partly be explained by the fact that they haven't had the opportunity to gain the knowledge that is necessary to be able to handle the additional materials (associated with the curriculum) in their daily work.

What consequences will the above factors have for development of the National Assessment Programme? It seems to us that if we in the future are going to use those information channels that up until now have been used for presenting result, then the programme will be received in the same way as the other materials of pedagogical interest. Few of the teachers will consider the results while most will be critical of or even neglect the materials. The complexity of the problem involved has been illuminated by some of the paradoxes, myths and opinions that often characterize the large organizations (Stevrin, 1984). Of that phenomenon presented by Stevrin, the following may be of special interest in connection with the development of a National Assessment Programme:

1. *More of the same sort.* This phenomenon is marked by the attempt to solve problems in exactly the same way as before, but more so.

2. *Negative problem-solving.* In this, one emphasizes the problems at hand, in order to point to how one would like things to be done.

3. *The utopia syndrome.* The objectives of the operations are assumed to be good, but the individuals involved in attaining those objectives are judged to be bad as the objectives are not realized.

4. *Over-subscription for the future.* By this is meant an unwillingness to make any sacrifices to future advantage. Resources are locked up at the present time, and they will not be sufficient solution for the coming problems.

5. *Reduced self-regulation.* Here, when external control is strengthened, it is implied that the internal control is weakened; this, in turn, is taken as a reason to increase the external control.

National assessment: an indicator perspective

In discussing the problem of making use of the huge quantities of information collected in any large-scale assessment programme, several critical factors should be identified. The first has to do with *meaning* – i.e. that of the information obtained; and that meaning can be articulated in a number of different ways. In a national assessment programme of great importance, in our view, is to have those persons responsible for the teaching process able to play an important role in defining the meaning; and the basic argument is simply that those persons actually form the teaching process itself. In order for them to influence and change ongoing activities, then they must understand the reasons for change. However, this does not mean of course that teachers alone supply that definition of meaning, but rather that their meaning must be taken into account; other meanings may very well, and should be, articulated.

What do we mean by saying that we have to identify the **meaning of interest**? Usually, assessment programmes will present the information obtained in terms of different types of averages; much work and money are devoted to finding good estimation techniques of such averages. Much less work and money, it seems to us, are devoted to find a meaningful frame of reference for interpreting and understanding the information obtained. In other words, we usually spend much effort on estimating important parameters and almost none on what use these parameters have for the purpose the whole programme is supposed to fulfil. That wouldn't be a problem if there was a prime way of interpreting the information, known to everybody; however, this is seldom the case. In fact, in an educational context, every parameter can be interpreted in many different ways. Such is the case too with different types of average. Here the problem is that we can know only of few in education. A grand theory is surely not at hand and probably never will be. We are therefore left with a complex of influences that affects the teaching process and what Johnny learns. But to know that learning and teaching are complex processes, and that what Johnny learns may be the result of many factors in combination, must not leave us overly passive in trying to understand better what interrelates and to develop rationales for relating seemingly critical factors in the teaching process. In that work, teachers, students and parents are important contributors.

Such rationales might take different forms. We are, in this context, arguing for an **indicator perspective** as an interpretative frame of reference. In the light of our lacking a theory for answering what Johnny learns and why he learns it, it is important to try to mirror the results obtained in, say, mathematics on what we know about educational variables, or in short educational indicator information. Such variables form the frame of reference against which the achievement is to be interpreted and understood. Here what we are talking about is a number of background variables, each one included so as to help us better understand a certain result. It is through such 'understandings' that the results will serve to influence our forthcoming pedagogical activities, with the aim of helping Johnny to learn more. Further, indicator information of the type we are talking about will be of use when trying to interpret the information obtained. Without such indicator information, we are left with results of limited pedagogical value, especially for those responsible for the teaching process.

It is, however, to be understood that (lacking a grand theory of education and learning) our indicator information will not give us the answer as to why certain results have been obtained. Rather, it will help to strengthen our thinking about critical factors in the learning process, thereby stimulating further activity in the realm of schooling and the competencies it produces.

An empirical example of interpretating national assessment data

To illustrate the use of what we here have called **indicator information** we will present some data from a try-out evaluation study in connection with the Swedish National Assessment Programme. The main purpose of the pilot evaluation study was to test the pedagogical component within the National Assessment Programme.

One hundred and sixty students from a school in the northern part of Sweden participated in the study, divided into two classes in each of grade 2, grade 5 and grade 8 respectively. Our instrument measured drawing, mathematics, music, science, social science and Swedish language. Besides this, we collected a great deal of background information (indicator information) from students, teachers and parents through questionnaires, to tap our indicator information.

To present the idea of different ways of using information from large-scale assessment programmes, we will take here as our point of departure the results obtained in mathematics.

Generally speaking, we found in grade 5, that the two classes involved differed as to their average results; however, that difference was fairly small. Such information does not provide much help in understanding results, or in stimulating pedagogical activities. In most cases, the general standard of a class is fairly well known by the individual teacher.

Proceeding with the analysis one step further, we found (as almost always, of course) that average values hide tremendous individual differences. For the individual teacher, it is often of greater interest to know the spread of the scores in his/her class than to know the general mean. Individual differences have direct consequences for an individual teacher and his/her way of preparing teaching.

Let us, then, make use of the sex variable. As to the total score, we found a small difference between the averages for boys and girls, to the advantage of the boys. However, looking at the results on the individual items and controlling for sex gives a more interesting picture. The p-values for boys and girls respectively on the following addition problem:

Calculate 428 + 966

was about the same for the sexes (p = 0.60). However, a similar problem, phrased verbally, gave a rather larger difference between the sexes, again to the advantage of the boys (p = 0.61 vs p = 0.21).

Pursuing this a bit further, we looked at the results in Swedish language. Those students who scored on the verbally phrased maths item all scored highly in Swedish language. Therefore, a low result in maths may be affected by, in this case, other competencies than those of mathematics. Such information is naturally of great interest for the mathematics teacher when preparing his/her teaching.

In terms of mathematics, we also found that seven out of ten students rated their own achievements in maths as 'good' or 'very good', although only half of them scored above the average result in their class. Furthermore, their parents did the same and often overestimated the achievements of their children. It seems to us that such information is of some pedagogical value to the individual teacher; one consequence, then, might be enabling these students, together with their parents, to obtain better ability to evaluate their own competencies in maths.

Furthermore, six out of 54 students had a strong positive attitude towards maths and, perhaps more interestingly, as many as 16 students (out of 54) rated maths lowest among the subjects in school; in this group, there are more girls than boys. Furthermore, we know from other results that maths loses its popularity steadily from grade 2 to grade 8, and especially so for girls; such information is naturally of real importance to a mathematics teacher. It also tells us that factors other than those directly related to the teaching of maths might well be of crucial importance for increasing skills in that subject.

Aside from the above attitudes, we also found in our study, through use of background information, that parents often regard themselves as rather active persons concerning school-related questions. And, at the same time, they regard many teachers as rather passive participants. The picture, it should be noted, is inverted when asking teachers the same questions about parents. Knowing that the students are fostered in such an environment, then, might instigate further investigation of that environment and what it means to the different achievements measured.

Of course, much more could be present about interpretations based on background information from large-scale assessment programmes. Here our purpose has only been to try to go beyond the 'average achievement' presentation, in order to better understand a certain achievement, and also to put forward pedagogical questions of interest for further examination, to clarify the situation, so that learning will be strengthened.

Discussion

A national assessment programme, of whatever sort, is marked by many problems. Some of them concern technical matters – e.g. how best to estimate statistical parameters of different types of competencies. Others deal with rationales for measuring contents of different kinds. Here an often overlooked problem area has to do with the use of the information collected within a national assessment programme. This paper has dealt exclusively with the last group of problems, especially with the arguments concerning use of **indicator information** in combination with **traditional achievement measures** and with the problems of having the collected information used by those responsible for the leading process – i.e. teachers, students and parents.

Our paper certainly advances no solutions to the somewhat tricky problems it raises. Rather, we have looked at some of the possible sources of inspiration in order to attack seriously the problem of making some real use of the data collected within a national assessment programme. Primarily, we have argued for observing background information as an important tool for making sense out of achievement data, and of having those responsible for the teaching process to participate in interpreting the results obtained.

Behind such a rationale our conviction is supported by the empirical evidence that a national assessment programme can only work successfully if the primary target, better educated students, is supported by those responsible for the targets. In that group of persons we include teachers, students and parents as the obvious candidates.

References

GIPPS, C. and GOLDSTEIN, H. (1983). *Monitoring Children: An Evaluation of the Assessment of Performance Unit.* London: Heineman.

POWER, C. and WOOD, R. (1984). *National Assessment in Australia. An evaluation of the Australian Studies in Student Performance Project*, EDRC Report No. 35.

STEVRIN, P. (1984). *Professionell problemlösning [Professional problem solving]* (in Swedish). Lund: Student-litteratur.

8 Use of Assessment Results for Managing Instruction

Paul D. Sandifer

To **manage**, according to *Webster's New Collegiate Dictionary*, is 'to handle or *direct* [emphasis added] with a degree of skill'. Directing anything requires a clear understanding of the desired outcome or destination. Directing, or managing, instruction requires a clear understanding of the goals of instruction, as well as precise information about the extent to which those goals have been achieved.

What is there that has more potential than assessment for evaluating student achievement, identifying student and curricula strengths and weaknesses, focusing instruction, and informing educators and the public about the extent to which the goals of instruction have been achieved? Nothing of which this writer is aware. The rewards to be reaped from using assessment results as a tool in directing instruction are, at first glance, so obvious that the notion hardly seems to require discussion. Sadly, however, that which should be obvious is frequently overlooked, maligned or, worse yet, ignored. This may be due, in part, to the fact that assessment systems, *per se*, are not inherently useful for directing instruction.

Assessment which occurs as an afterthought, rather than as an integral part of a total instructional programme may have little, if any, utility in managing instruction. Ill-conceived and/or poorly implemented assessment programmes may actually have the potential for doing more harm than good. Popham (1987) points out that 'educators must reconceive the relationship between measurement and instruction, so that tests are employed as vehicles of instructional clarification'. When tests are conceived as an integral part of the instructional programme, assessment results are useful in managing, directing or driving instruction.

Measurement-driven instruction (MDI), a concept which has been the focus of considerable debate in recent years, has been defined as occurring 'when a high-stakes test of educational achievement, because of the important contingencies associated with the students' performance, influences the instructional programme that prepares students for the test' (*ibid.*). MDI has obvious potential for improving educational achievement, but as indicated earlier, that which has obvious potential benefit is often maligned – MDI is no exception. Among the criticisms which have been levelled at MDI are fragmentation, narrowing and trivialization of the curriculum (Bracey, 1987). Others might express their fears or concerns as curriculum reductionism, and valuing what we test rather than testing what we value. Another concern is that test results can be used as a basis for making unfair comparisons and drawing unwarranted conclusions.

The criticisms levelled against MDI are not necessarily without substance. On the other hand, the criticisms gain substance only when assessment programmes are poorly conceived and implemented. The critics of MDI, if they maintain a fair degree of open-mindedness towards the results of effective MDI programmes, provide a service in identifying *potential* pitfalls and shortcomings. Likewise, the critics do students a disservice if they would automatically deny them MDI's potential benefits on the basis of their fears or experiences with less than useful programmes.

In the remainder of the paper, I will set forth some of the requirements for an assessment system that can be used in effectively managing instruction; describe South Carolina's* experience in developing such a system; present evidence that the South Carolina system is working; and close with a summary of some of the issues which must be addressed in the initial development and subsequent revisions of an assessment system.

Requirements for an effective assessment system

As stated earlier, large-scale assessment programmes, or small-scale ones, are not inherently useful for managing instruction. Utility for purposes of instruction is achieved only if the assessment is designed as an integral part of the total instructional programme. Unfortunately, too many educators still view instruction and assessment as essentially unrelated activities. Teachers who use test results only as a means of assigning grades, and not as a means of improving instruction, ignore most of the potential of teacher-made tests. The policy-makers who view large-scale assessment only as a means of 'checking the pulse' of education, rather than as a means for improving instruction, ignore some potent medicine that can be used to strengthen that pulse.

What, then, are the requirements for an effective assessment system? It seems that they can be classified in two general categories: those related to the system itself – *system requirements*; and those related to the process of system development – *process requirements*. The following characteristics which, on the basis of the writer's experience seem essential, will be discussed more fully in the remainder of this section.

System requirements
- Assessment must be viewed as an integral part of a total instructional system.
- The instructional goals and objectives to be assessed must be important, manageable in number, defensible, clearly defined, and communicated to those responsible for instruction – i.e. teachers, principals and curriculum coordinators.
- Tests should be criterion-referenced, rather than norm-referenced.
- There should be a pool of tests items to permit the construction of alternate forms for the purposes of maintaining security and credibility.

---

* South Carolina, one of the 13 original states, is located in the Southeastern region of the United States of America. The state is 30,138 square miles in area and has a population of approximately 3,300,000. The public school system includes 91 school districts, 1112 schools, approximately 612,000 students, and 40,000 professional personnel.

- Reports of tests results must be timely and useful to teachers, principals and curriculum coordinators.

Process requirements
- Those most likely to feel threatened by the system must be provided the opportunity to develop 'ownership' through meaningful participation in its development.
- Development of the system should be a collaborative effort of specialists in the areas of curriculum and measurement.

System requirements

INTEGRATED SYSTEM

Assessment must be conceived as an integral part of the instructional programme. To be useful in managing instruction, assessment must be more than a checkpoint or mileage marker on the highway of education. True, assessment results can tell us whether we are progressing towards our goal or destination; however, their real potential is realized when they are used for remediating weaknesses at the pupil level *and* for adjusting instruction for entire groups. Teachers responsible for remediation are well served by knowing the specific strengths and weaknesses of individual students. Additionally, information on common strengths and weaknesses for entire groups (classes and schools) should be used as feedback for adjusting the instructional programme at the class or school level.

Assessment results obtained at, or near, the end of the school year should be useful to two groups of teachers: those who taught the students who were assessed, and those who will be teaching them in the next grade. Teachers who were responsible for the instruction prior to testing should use the results to monitor the effectiveness of their instruction and, if necessary, to make adjustments in instructional emphases and strategies. Teachers at the next-highest grade should use the results as an aid in identifying students' strengths and weaknesses, so that instruction can be effectively focused.

GOALS AND OBJECTIVES

The critical considerations in identifying goals and objectives are that they be important, defensible and manageable in number. Although it is also important that they be clearly defined and communicated to those responsible for instruction, there is little benefit in clearly defining and communicating a multiplicity of trivial objectives.

The targets of instruction (and assessment) should deal with a manageable number of important and desirable student outcomes. Good teachers will attend to that which is important if a manageable number of priorities is clearly established. Faced with large numbers of competing priorities, all of which appear equally important (or trivial), teachers will quite logically establish their own.

Should an assessment system measure only that which is currently included in the curriculum, or should it be used as a means of facilitating curriculum change? This issue is almost certain to be raised during deliberations about the focus of the assessment. If there exists a standard curriculum that has been uniformly implemented in all schools that are to be included in the assessment, the question then is simply: 'Is the existing curriculum adequate?' If there is no standard curriculum, or if the standard curriculum has not been uniformly implemented, the issue becomes more crucial. What should be used as the focus of assessment? In other words, what is it that we want students to know or be able to do?

Restricting assessment to those portions of the curriculum that have been implemented in all schools will surely yield tests that possess instructional validity for which content-related evidence of validity can be provided. It will just as surely lead to curricula reductionism in some schools and the perpetuation of the status quo in the others.

Developers of assessment programmes should resist the pressure to reduce the assessment to the lowest common denominator. Specialists in curriculum and measurement must work closely and co-operatively in resolving this tension between competing desires to develop tests with initial content-related evidence of validity, or tests which are anticipated to be supported by content-related evidence when the objectives on which the tests are based are incorporated into the curriculum and instruction i.e. **anticipatory validity**.

Once the goals and objectives are agreed upon and clearly defined, they must be communicated to teachers. Logically this communication should be illuminated by suggested instructional strategies related to each goal or objective and, if necessary, be accompanied by appropriate instructional materials. If new instructional materials are not necessary, existing materials should be cross-referenced to the objectives. Whether new materials are developed or existing materials are utilized, it is imperative that the relationship between instructional targets and instructional materials be clearly defined.

CRITERION-REFERENCES TESTS

This requirement flows logically from the requirement that the objectives be clearly defined. The measurement of clearly defined, rather than fuzzily focused, objectives requires a predictable and well-defined match between the tests and the goals of instruction.

Loosely defined instructional targets lead to loosely defined tests that may be only tangentially related to the intended targets of instruction. However, it is not sufficient that the tests and the targets of instruction be closely aligned. The content of the tests must also be current and relevant to good instruction. Otherwise, the tests may drive instruction in undesirable directions.

For example, one objective of instruction might be to ensure that students can locate and utilize desired information in reference sources (reference usage). A traditional way of assessing student mastery of one aspect of this skill has been to use test items based on facsimiles of entries in the library card catalogue. This approach to assessing reference skills is becoming obsolete as more library/media centres computerize their card catalogue files. Although such items may not be relevant to good instruction, teachers may continue to instruct students on the use of the card catalogue simply to ensure good test results. Ensuring that test content remains current and instructionally appropriate requires constant monitoring both of instructional strategies and the content of the tests.

SECURITY AND CREDIBILITY

Maintaining security of the tests is necessary to ensure the validity of results and credibility with the public and policy-makers. Few, if any, teachers or other educators are likely to deliberately breach the security of the tests. Nevertheless, we must be able to assure users that the test results are valid indicators of student achievement – results that have not been artificially inflated by impropriety on the part of anyone involved in the processes of instruction and assessment.

In assessment systems that must rely on school personnel to administer the tests, the only feasible way to maintain security appears to be through the use of alternate forms of the tests. Creation of sufficient numbers of items to provide alternate forms on an annual basis is not inexpensive. In the long term, however, it is more cost-effective and feasible than employing and training special test administrators.

TIMELY AND USEFUL REPORTING

Typically, teachers and school administrators want their test results returned immediately and in formats that are useful for managing instruction. While it is not possible to return the results immediately, it is essential that they be returned in a timely manner and that reports meet the various needs of teachers, principals, curriculum coordinators, policy-makers and parents. Data which are out of date may have some utility for monitoring trends in achievement, but they are not useful for managing instruction or providing remediation for individual students.

The need for timely reporting has implications for the nature of the assessment. Complex assessments which include performance items, such as writing tasks, require more time for scoring, analysis and reporting. The assessment should not be trivialized for the sake of fast reporting. Nor should it be so complex and sophisticated that reporting is unreasonably delayed.

In the USA the typical school year begins in mid-August to early September and ends between late May and mid-June. Ideally, preliminary results of objective assessments administered in late April should be reported before the end of the school year. Complete results, including performance items such as composition, should be available before the beginning of the next school year. Under these reporting conditions, school administrators can use the results for decisions related to staffing needs and student scheduling. Teachers can use the results for directing remediation for individual students and for detecting apparent strengths and weaknesses in the instructional programme. Returning test results within a reasonable period of time facilitates planning and the use of the data for managing instruction.

Process requirements

ESTABLISHING OWNERSHIP

The assessment of student achievement is threatening to many teachers and school administrators, particularly if the assessment is viewed as an accountability measure rather than an instructional improvement strategy. Any system which is imposed upon instructional personnel is likely to be greeted with suspicion and to meet resistance.

Teachers and other instructional leaders are much more likely to attend to the established goals and objectives if they feel 'ownership' towards them as a result of substantive involvement in the development process. In large-scale assessment programmes such 'ownership' is not easily established, but strategies for involving teachers in the development process can, and should, be established and implemented.

COLLABORATIVE DEVELOPMENT

Effectively developing an assessment system which can be used for managing or driving instruction requires a collaborative effort of specialists in the areas of curriculum and measurement. This requirement seems so obvious that it may appear trivial, but it is so essential that it warrants mention. Systems that are designed by one group to the exclusion of the other are almost certain to be seriously flawed in either the objectives to be assessed or in the assessment itself.

Neither the identification of objectives nor the development of tests should be viewed as the exclusive domain of one group. Although the identification of objectives should be primarily the responsibility of those responsible for curriculum, measurement specialists can provide valuable and needed assistance in clarifying objectives and ensuring that they are amenable to measurement. In a like manner, test development is primarily the responsibility of specialists in the field of measurement. Curriculum specialists, however, are essential to the process of developing test item specifications, determining appropriate and relevant test content and deciding the emphasis to be placed on each objective tested.

The South Carolina Experience

The preceding portion of the paper should properly be viewed as my own perception of the requirements for an assessment system that can be used effectively in managing instruction. These perceptions were developed through experience gained in assisting with the development and implementation of South Carolina's Basic Skills Assessment Program (BSAP).

The intent here is not to extol the virtues of the BSAP, but to use the programme as a means of illuminating the requirements and issues set forth in the preceding section of the paper. The BSAP is not perfect – it was designed by imperfect beings and it now needs substantial revision. It has, however, been effective as a means of managing and focusing instruction and improving student achievement.

The South Carolina Basic Skills Assessment Program

The BSAP was mandated by legislation enacted in 1978 by the South Carolina legislature. Among the provisions of the original law were the requirements that the State Board of Education establish educational objectives in the basic skill areas of reading, writing and mathematics for kindergarten through grade 12; administer a readiness test to all public school students at the beginning of grade 1; administer criterion-referenced tests (CRTs) in reading and mathematics at the end of grades 1, 2 and 3; administer CRTs in reading, writing and mathematics at the end of grades 6 and 8; administer a test of adult functional competency at the end of grade 11; and establish minimum standards of achievement for readiness and the other areas to be tested at each grade. The purposes of the testing, as stipulated in the legislation, are those of diagnosing student deficiencies and in aiding in remediation.

In 1984 the BSAP was amended by eliminating the grade 11 test and replacing it with an exit examination in grade 10. Passing the exit examination becomes an additional requirement for the receipt of a high school diploma in 1990. The legislation was also amended to require the identification of science objectives for grades 1–8 and the testing of science at the end of grades 3, 6 and 8. Because of the recent legislative changes, and in the interest of brevity, the following discussion of the programme will focus primarily on the reading and mathematics programme in grades 1–8.

IDENTIFICATION OF OBJECTIVES

The Department of Education employed the services of a contractor to assist in the identification of objectives for grades 1–12. The objectives were assembled after a careful review of objectives in reading, writing and mathematics submitted by 23 South Carolina school districts in response to an invitation to all 91 districts by the South Carolina Department of Education, existing objectives collections such as those possessed by the Instructional Objectives Exchange and the National Assessment of Educational progress, and sets of basic-skills objectives secured from approx. 30 state departments of education. Thus basic skills objectives, reflecting both the South Carolina and national perspectives, were used in the initial assembly of grades 1–12 objectives.

Prior to their adoption by the State Board of Education, the objectives were reviewed and modified by large numbers of educators and lay citizens in South Carolina. Committees of curriculum specialists and classroom teachers spent several days in reviewing and modifying the objectives. Approx. 18,000 public school teachers in South Carolina reviewed and reacted to the objectives. (The objectives were sent to all South Carolina public schools for review at the school level.) In addition, eight regional public meetings were held to allow South Carolina citizens to register their reactions to the objectives. All of these reactions were presented to the South Carolina Basic Skills Advisory Commission, a group consisting of lay citizens and educators, which reviewed and endorsed the objectives prior to their adoption by the State Board of Education.

Rather than containing almost endless sets of objectives to serve as instructional targets for South Carolina schools, the objectives were deliberately formulated to be broad in scope, yet still measurable. Each objective subsumes a series of lesser enabling skills. By limiting the focus of educators to a manageable number of broad-scope objectives, more effective instruction could be designed and more valid measures could be created. Teachers implementing the BSAP have a reasonable number of major instructional targets to which to attend. For purposes of classroom instruction, of course, the isolation of sets of sub-skills which students would need to master prior to achieving the broad-scope objectives was necessary. A series of documents entitled 'Teaching and Testing Our Basic Skills Objectives' (T&T) were developed and pilot-tested in the schools. The documents were revised to incorporate teachers' suggestions and final copies were given to every teacher in South Carolina who had a responsibility for instruction in the areas of reading, writing or mathematics. The T&Ts include the objectives, a description of essential sub-skills, suggested teaching strategies and sample test items.

Throughout the entire process of identifying objectives an effort was made to establish ownership by obtaining broad-based participation of educators and lay citizens. The process constantly focused on what students *should* know or be able to do rather than concentrating on the existing curriculum. (This was particularly true in the area of writing since evidence existed that writing instruction was not occurring in the primary and intermediate grades in most South Carolina schools.) The efforts to establish ownership of the programme were continued through all phases of system development.

TEST DEVELOPMENT

The CRTs required by the legislation were developed following generally accepted procedures for developing detailed item specifications; developing items to meet the specifications; and constructing initial test forms. The test development was a collaborative effort of the contractor, measurement specialists from the State Department of Education and the University of South Carolina; curriculum specialists from the State Department of Education, institutions of higher education and school districts; and committees of classroom teachers.

The item specifications and test items, initially developed by the contractor, were subjected to thorough review and frequent revision by the committees of teachers and specialists in the areas of curriculum and measurement. Only after a consensus was reached among the committee members was an item specification, and ultimately a test item, judged to be acceptable. The influence which teachers and curriculum specialists had in shaping the programme is best illustrated by the nature of the writing test. Initially, the measurement specialists had conceived the writing test as consisting of a combination of multiple-choice items and having students write a very short paragraph. The curriculum specialists and teachers objected to the multiple-choice items, and consequently the writing tests for grades 6, 8 and 11 (not grade 10) consist of having students write a composition in response to a specific assignment or prompt.

STANDARD-SETTING

Standard-setting for the reading and mathematics tests in grades 1, 2, 3, 6 and 8 was accomplished through application of the 'undecided group' procedure. Prior to the first test administration in 1981, representative samples of approx. 4,000 students per grade were identified. Teachers of the students included in the sample were asked to make judgements for each student concerning the level of the student's mastery of the skills reflected in the objectives for reading and mathematics. The nature of the judgements requested were whether the student had 'adequate' mastery of the skills to be successful at the next grade, 'inadequate' mastery or, in cases where the teacher was uncertain, 'undecided'. The teachers' judgements concerning students in each grade and subject area were matched with the students' actual test performance and the resulting score distributions were used to inform the standard-setting process. Ultimately, the median score for the 'undecided' group in each grade and subject was established as the prescribed minimum standard.

SECURITY

Test security and credibility of the results are maintained in two ways. First, new test forms are constructed each year by replacing approx. two-thirds of the items on all reading and mathematics tests. Additionally, writing exercises, or prompts, are not re-used. Secondly, strict accountability procedures are employed in the distribution and return of all secure materials. Each test booklet is identified with a unique number which permits tracing the booklets to school districts, schools and teachers. As stated earlier, maintaining credibility of the assessment results is crucial to public acceptance. Although there may be few, if any, teachers who would breach the security of the test by teaching specific test items, it is necessary to reduce the potential for the appearance of any impropriety.

ADMINISTRATION, SCORING, AND REPORTING

The tests are administered in late April of each year and preliminary results for reading and mathematics are reported to the school districts in late May. Scoring of the approx. 150,000 compositions is accomplished in June and complete results for all tests are reported to the school districts in late July. Preliminary reports identify students who qualify for special funding to address their deficiencies in the areas of reading and mathematics. The final reports include a report for parents, individual reports for students identifying strengths and weaknesses for each objective tested and summary reports at the class, school, district and state levels. In addition to the summary reports for all students, summary results are also provided for various sub-populations based on gender, ethnicity and other factors.

At the beginning of each school year, the test results from the prior year are available to teachers, curriculum coordinators, principals and others who have a responsibility for managing instruction.

Seven years of growth

The improvement in student achievement reflected in seven years of data is very encouraging. The increase in the percentages of students meeting prescribed standards in all grades and subjects has been substantial. Most encouraging is the fact that the increases have occurred in all segments of the population and that the disparity between the achievement of the 'advantaged' and 'disadvantaged' students, while remaining unacceptably large, has been dramatically reduced.

As indicated in Figure 8.1, the increases in the percentage of students meeting the prescribed standards in reading between 1981 and 1987 ranges from a low of 14.3 percentage points in grade 1 to a high of 24 percentage points in grade 6. Likewise, the data for mathematics in Figure 8.2 reflect increases ranging from 16.4 percentage points in grade 1 to 26.4 percentage points in grade 8. Obviously, no cause-and-effect relationship can be established between the BSAP and the improvement in student achievement. On the other hand, the history of South Carolina strongly suggests that the improvement would not have occurred without some type of intervention.

Educators in South Carolina and throughout the USA have long been concerned about the generally poor achievement of 'disadvantaged' students. Although disadvantage may take many forms, one of the most common constructions of the term relates to socio-economic status. Since no direct measure of socio-economic status of students is available for analysing the test results, the state uses 'eligibility for free lunch' as a proxy for the variable.*

Examination of Figure 8.3 clearly indicates that the discrepancy between the achievement levels of 'advantaged' (no F/R lunch) and 'disadvantaged' (free lunch) students decreased appreciably between 1981 and 1987. In 1981 there was a 28-point difference in the percentages of advantaged and disadvantaged students meeting the standard for reading in grade 1. In 1987 that difference had been reduced to 16 percentage points – a decrease of 12 points. Significantly, the reduction of the disparity in achievement levels has not been at the expense of the advantaged students. Data for the other grades, and for mathematics (not shown) reflect similar patterns of change. As noted earlier, new test forms are created each year by replacing at least two-thirds of the test items. Consequently, the gains in achievement cannot be attributed to familiarity with specific test items.

The critics of measurement-driven instruction may continue to denounce it and point to its potential shortcomings, but South Carolina has demonstrably benefited from such a system. Thousands of students have improved skills in reading, mathematics and writing which can be attributed to the implementation of the BSAP.

---

*In the USA the federal government subsidizes lunch programmes in the public schools and the cost to students is determined by the ability to pay. Under the guidelines of the federal government, students from low-income families may be eligible to receive lunch either free or at a reduced price. The data used to construct Figure 4 and the figures in Attachment B include all students – students eligible for free lunch, and students who are not eligible for either free or reduced-price lunch. Students who were eligible for reduced-price lunch are included in 'all students', but data for that group are not reported separately. In 1987, the percentages of free lunch eligible students ranged from 42 in grade 1 to 31 in grade 8. During the period 1981-87, the percentages have decreased by 3 points in grade 3, 4 points in grades 1, 2 and 6, and 7 points in grade 8.

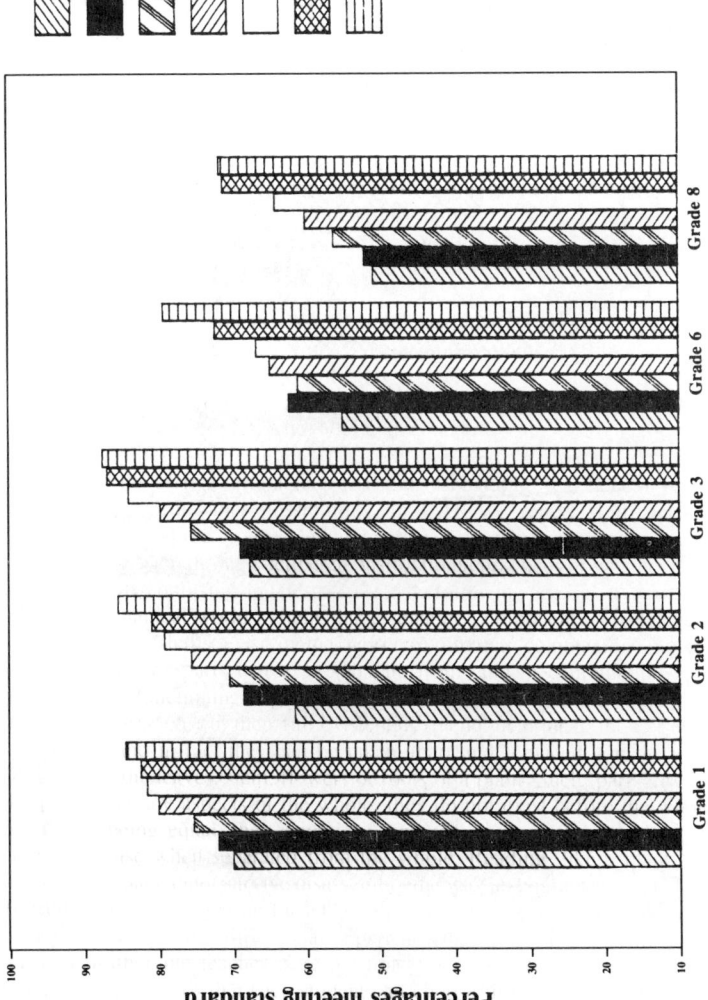

Figure 8.1: BSAP reading (percentages meeting standard)

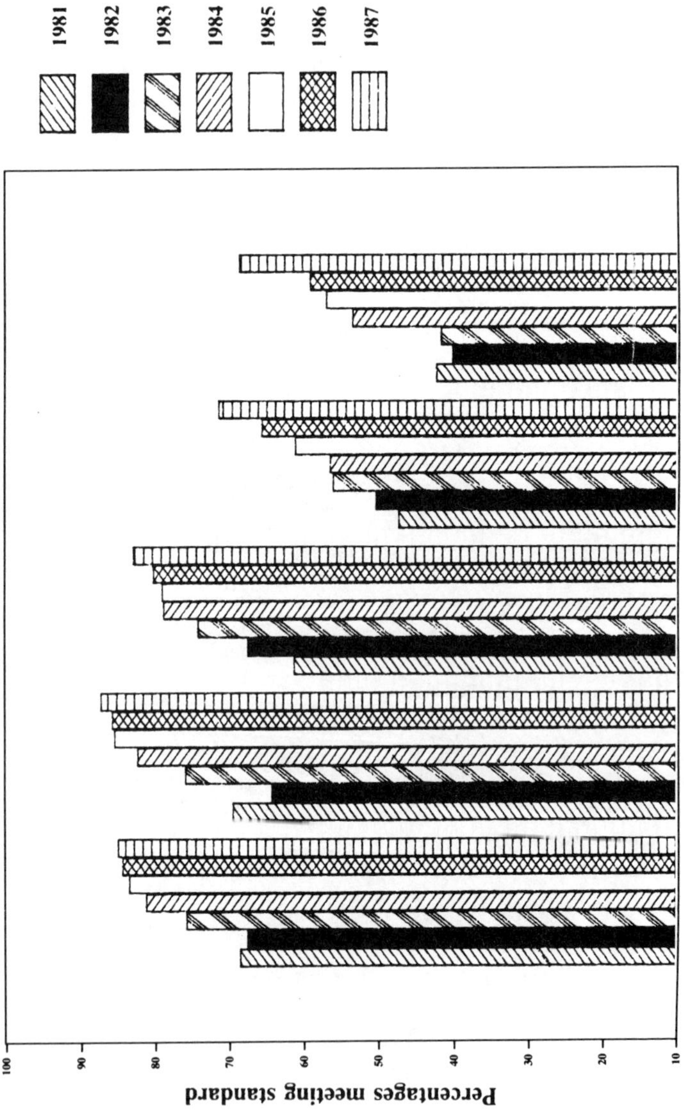

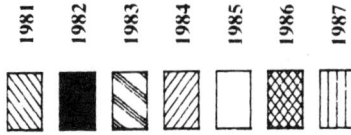

Figure 8.2: BSAP mathematics

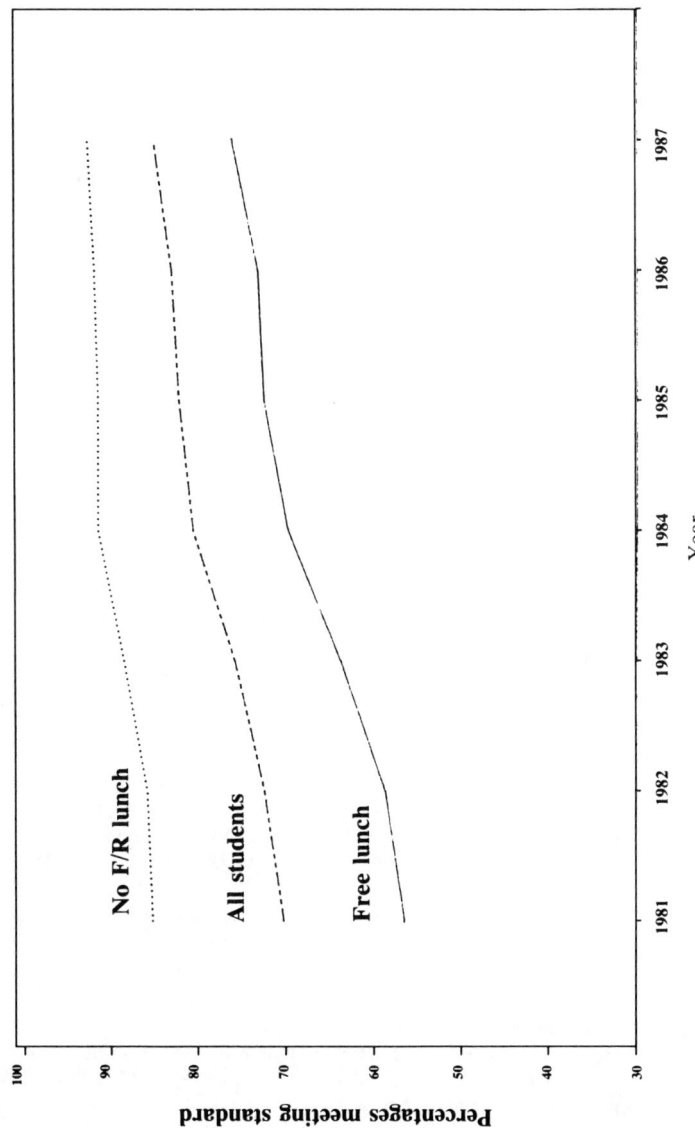

Figure 8.3: BSAP reading, grade 1 (percentages meeting standard)

Unanticipated uses of results

Opportunities for using data for purposes other than those originally intended always exist. The results obtained from large-scale assessments are no exception to the rule. In 1984 the South Carolina legislature enacted the Education Improvement Act which mandated a number of education reforms and stipulated uses of assessment results which had not been anticipated when the BSAP was developed. In addition to the original purpose of diagnosing student deficiencies and assisting in remediation, the BSAP data are now used for the following purposes: (1) school-level evaluation of remedial education programmes; (2) 25 per cent of the assessment in determining whether students are promoted or retained in grade; (3) making monetary awards to schools with outstanding achievement; (4) assisting in determining whether teachers participating in the teacher incentive programme will receive a monetary award; (5) making monetary awards in the principals' incentive programme; and (6) as one criterion in the identification of school districts in which the quality of education is 'seriously impaired'.

Certainly, many of the current uses were not envisioned when the BSAP was originally developed and many people question the appropriateness of some current practices. Although there is no way to ensure against inappropriate uses of test results, this should not deter those responsible for the improvement of instruction from pursuing appropriate uses and implementing systems that are beneficial in managing instruction. Those who would have us wait for the creation of a perfect system, or one that cannot be abused, would deprive generations of young people of the opportunities for improved achievement that are offered by clearly defined instructional programmes of which assessment is a part.

Plans for the future

Success in using measurement as a means of driving instruction brings with it a new set of issues and concerns. When improved achievement leads to large percentages of students scoring at or near the ceiling of the tests and even larger percentages meeting the prescribed standards, the usefulness of test results as a means of focusing instruction for a majority of students is greatly diminished. This is currently the situation in South Carolina and, consequently, the assessment programme needs revision.

In addition to technical issues such as maintaining comparability of data across years, revision of the system, particularly the re-defining of the targets of instruction, will likely raise concerns among teachers and other members of the education community that have expended considerable time and effort in articulating their local curricula with the objectives, skills and sub-skills of the state programme. This points to the need for a clear understanding among all concerned that assessment systems must be periodically reviewed and revised to be responsive to changing needs and conditions. All participants in the initial development should understand that useful systems must be dynamic rather than static. Advances in our understanding of the way in which students learn and of effective instructional practices may require changes in our assessment methodology. Additionally, the targets of instruction and performance standards which may be appropriate at the time a system is implemented may need to be reconsidered when effective teaching generates test results that have diminished utility for managing the instructional programme.

The fact that large percentages of students in South Carolina are now scoring at or near the ceilings of the tests is not a function of the tests' being too easy. The tests are in fact equivalent in difficulty to the first tests which were administered in 1981. The ceiling effects are due to the efforts of teachers and other educators in effectively managing instruction and focusing their efforts on a manageable number of important and clearly defined educational goals.

Summary

To **manage** is 'to handle or direct with a degree of skill'. Directing, managing or driving instruction requires a clear understanding of the goals of instruction and definitive information about the extent to which the goals have been achieved. Consequently, if the results of assessment are to be useful for managing instruction, the assessments must be based on important educational outcomes which are manageable in number and clearly stated. Effective implementation of such a system requires that those primarily responsible for its successful implementation (teachers) develop ownership in the system through involvement in its development.

To remain useful as a tool for managing instruction, assessment systems must be dynamic rather than static. Changes in pedagogy and the needs of society require constant monitoring of the goals of instruction, instructional strategies and the methods of assessment.

Through the collaborative efforts of teachers, curriculum specialists and measurement specialists, effective instructional systems can be fashioned which include assessment as an integral part. Properly conceived, developed and implemented, assessment systems can result in improved student achievement by focusing and stimulating instruction.

References

BRACEY, G.W. (1987) 'Measurement-driven instruction: catchy phrase, dangerous practice', *Phi Delta Kappa*, 68, 9, 683–6.
POPHAM, W.J. (1987). 'The merits of measurement-driven instruction', *Phi Delta Kappan*, 68, 9, 679–82.
POPHAM, W.J., CRUSE, K.L., RANKIN, S.C., SANDIFER, P.D, and WILLIAMS, P.L. (1985). 'Measurement-driven instruction: it's on the road', *Phi Delta Kappan*, 66, 9, 628–34.
Section 59-30-10, Code of Laws of South Carolina, 1976.
WILLIAMS, C.G. (1979). *Report on the Implementation of the Basic Skills Assessment Program, 1978–79*. Columbia, SC: South Carolina Department of Education, December.
WILLIAMS, C.G. (1981). *Teaching and Testing Our Basic Skills Objectives, Mathematics, Grades 7 and 8*. Columbia, SC: South Carolina Department of Education, September.
WILLIAMS, C.G. (1988). *Report on the Implementation of the Basic Skills Assessment Program, 1986–87*. Columbia, SC: South Carolina Department of Education, January.
WOOLF, H.B. (Ed.). (1973). *Webster's New Collegiate Dictionary*. Springfield, Mass.: G. and C. Merriam.

9 Educational, Political and Social Implications of the 1987 Education Reform Bill in England and Wales

Clare Burstall

(This paper was presented on 17th June 1988, before The Education Reform Act of 1988 was passed through Parliament.)

The Education Reform Bill is a major piece of legislation introduced into the House of Commons in November 1987 and to become law by the Autumn of 1988. It proposes major changes in how schools are organized and governed and provides for the introduction of a natural curriculum, with defined attainment targets for children aged from five to 16, appropriate programmes of study and the regular monitoring of pupils' progress by means of nationally prescribed tests at the ages of seven, 11, 14 and 16. At all ages except seven, the results of these tests are to be publicly reported. The Bill will have profound effects on the lives of all schoolchildren in England and Wales and on the running of the state education system: it is perhaps one of the most controversial pieces of legislation to have been put before Parliament in recent years. Certainly, since the run-up to the last general election, education has held a hitherto unprecedented salience in the public arena.

The supporters of the Bill regard it as a long-overdue move to expose education to market forces, to raise standards of achievement (widely believed to be inferior to those of our overseas trading partners), to offer greater freedom of choice of school and to increase parental and community involvement in the running of the nation's schools and colleges. Moving the Third Reading of the Education Reform Bill in the House of Commons in March 1988, the Secretary of State for Education, Mr Kenneth Baker, described the Bill as a 'landmark in our education system'. He went on:

> Future historians will see the Bill as the turning point, when the country moved forward from a long debate on education to a programme of action to improve the education system – action to improve the quality of education in our schools, colleges, polytechnics and universities; action to raise the standards achieved by pupils and students; action to extend freedom of choice and to enhance the position of parents...As a country, we have been letting too many of our children down...Legislation alone cannot put this right. What it

can do is create a framework which focuses the creativity of our professional teachers and taps into the energies and commitment of parents, employers and local communities...The Bill is a charter for better education (Hansard).

In sharp contrast to the above view, the opponents of the Bill regard it as a radical move away from the traditional local control of education towards direct control by central government: the wide powers being placed in the hands of the secretary of state are interpreted as a fundamental threat to local democracy. Speaking for the Liberals during the Third Reading of the Bill, Mr Paddy Ashdown described it as 'probably the most dangerous Bill brought forward by any government for the last 20 or 30 years'. He went on to claim·

> The damage that it will do to our education system and to the future of our children will be felt for years to come. Perhaps even more important, it is a potential threat to the nature of pluralism in our democracy...The secret aims of the Bill are to diminish the power of local government, to centralise the power over education in the hands of the Secretary of State and to reinforce privilege in our education system...We shall have schools for the chosen and schools for the trapped...We shall have freedom for the few, and state conformity for the remainder. This is a bad and dangerous Bill. (Hansard).

Speaking for the Labour Party during the same debate, Mr Jack Straw described the Bill as a 'desperate, wasted opportunity', claiming that 'the public have a great deal to fear from this Bill, especially from the free market nonsense of the Bill by which children become commodities to be left at the mercy of the market'. However, in spite of the Opposition's many attempts to introduce changes into the Bill during its passage through the House of Commons, it emerged almost unscathed from the debate and returned to the House of Lords after the Easter recess with all its main proposals intact.

At the heart of the Education Reform Bill is the notion of a national curriculum. What is proposed is that all schoolchildren aged five to 16 in the state education system should follow a national curriculum composed of a 'core' of religious education, English, mathematics and science, and seven other 'foundation' subjects, namely: history, geography, technology, art, music, physical education and, in secondary schools only, a modern foreign language. Under the current system, individual schools can determine the curriculum that they follow, and pupils are free to 'opt out' of a number of subjects at the age of 14. This means that they may choose to follow a narrow or idiosyncratic set of subjects which, later, may have the unfortunate and often unforeseen effect of closing doors to many job opportunities. It is common, for instance, for large numbers of boys to give up learning modern languages, and for equally large numbers of girls to drop mathematics and physical sciences. The aim of the introduction of a national curriculum is to ensure that all pupils will receive, as their entitlement, an education that is 'broad, balanced, relevant to their needs and set in a clear moral framework' (GB DES, 1987).

It is not intended, however, that the national curriculum will constitute the whole of what is taught in schools, nor will the amount of time to be devoted to each subject be laid down by law. The intention is that the national curriculum will establish a framework of clearly defined objectives, with attainment targets and programmes of study for each area of the curriculum devised by expert working groups, but that there will also be considerable freedom within that framework for teachers to exercise their professional skills and judgement. Schools will not be told how they should organize their timetables, for example, or what teaching methods they should employ; nor what textbooks they should use. But they will be expected to 'deliver' the national curriculum effectively, and this effectiveness will be subject to both internal and external scrutiny.

Although some reservations have been expressed about the precise nature of the proposed national curriculum, for example, the rationale underlying the choice of subjects for inclusion has been question, as has the appropriateness of applying a subject-based approach to the primary school curriculum, in general the concept that each child should be entitled to receive a similarly broad but differentiated education has commanded wide political and professional support. The main problem perceived by the critics of the Bill is that, since the national curriculum will not apply to the independent sector, its introduction could lead to an increasingly divisive, two-tier system of education. In practice, however, it seems highly unlikely that, once it was introduced into the maintained sector, the independent schools would see fit to develop in directions that were at odds with the national curriculum. It would seem to be very much to their advantage to be able to demonstrate that they were capable of delivering the national curriculum with the utmost efficiency, and more besides.

The introduction of the national curriculum will be accompanied by a national system of assessment and testing, at the ages of seven, 11, 14 and 16. These ages have been chosen because they represent key stages in a pupil's school career. Seven is the age at which children normally progress from the 'infant' to the 'junior' stage in the primary school and is seen as a crucial point at which to monitor the development of basic skills; 11 usually marks the end of the primary stage and the transfer to secondary school; 14 is the age at which decisions are usually made about the subjects to be pursued to public examination level; and 16 is the age at which pupils complete their period of compulsory schooling. At each of these ages, pupils' achievement of the national attainment targets will be assessed and, at each age except seven, the levels of achievement attained in each school will be publicly reported.

Although we have had in the UK national surveys of pupils' performance in certain subject areas for a number of years, these have always been targeted at group performance and carried out on a light-sampling basis. A totally new system of assessment had to be devised that would meet the demands of monitoring the delivery of the national curriculum to each individual pupil and provide both teacher and parent with regular and comprehensible information on the progress that the child was making, but that would, at the same time, provide schools, local education authorities and central government with aggregated data suitable for their own information needs. To this end, the secretary of state set up a Task Group on Assessment and Testing (TGAT) and charged it with the responsibility for devising an appropriate national assessment system. Working to a very tight deadline, the Task Group put forward proposals that were published by the secretary of state in January 1988 (GB DES, 1988b) followed shortly afterwards by a digest of the main proposals, (GB DES, 1988a) written with teachers in mind.

Before the Task Group's report appeared, many fears were voiced, particularly by members of the Opposition and by the representatives of the teachers' unions, that the national assessment system would be narrow, restrictive, old-fashioned, divisive, unacceptable to the teaching profession and damaging to children's self-esteem and well-being. Once the Task Group's proposals had been made clear, however, there was almost universal relief and a general acceptance of the main thrust of what was proposed. At the heart of the TGAT report is the conviction that teaching and testing should not be sharply divorced activities, rather they should go hand in hand. It recognizes that the best of the newer test materials lend themselves readily to teaching purposes and accurately reflect good teaching practice. To quote from the TGAT report:

> Promoting children's learning is a principal aim of schools. Assessment lies at the heart of this process. It can provide a framework in which educational objectives may be set, and pupils' progress charted and expressed...The assessment process itself should not determine what is to be taught and learned. It should be the servant, not the master, of the curriculum. Yet it should not simply be a bolt-on addition at the end. Rather, it should be an integral part of the educational process, continually providing both 'feedback' and 'feedforward'. It therefore needs to be incorporated systematically into teaching strategies and practices at all levels. (GB DES, 1988b).

The report recognizes that there are three essential strands woven into the process of assessment: the teachers' own informal assessments, externally provided standard tasks or tests and further diagnostic assessments of children with special needs. It places the teacher at the centre of this process, but recognizes the need for comparability, achieved through moderation.

Attention is drawn in the report to the wide range of testing techniques now available and to the desirability of employing a wide variety of approaches to assessment, avoiding a total reliance on written tests. The latter undoubtedly have their place in any scheme of assessment, but they are not always the most appropriate instrument to use. At younger ages, carefully devised integrated tasks, involving the use of language and simple scientific and mathematical activities, can provide a means of assessment which can be fitted naturally into normal classroom procedures – indeed the children themselves would not even know that they were being 'tested' – but which, nevertheless, satisfy strict psychometric criteria. There is no need whatsoever nowadays to place children under stress in order to test their capabilities. A good test is one that allows a children to produce the very best performance of which he/she is capable, that is unobtrusive to administer, that complements rather than distorts good teaching practice, yet loses nothing of its informative value, nor its psychometric precision. Recent advances in the technology of testing allow no excuse for settling for less.

The view taken by the Task Group was that any system of national assessment that would both help to inform decision-making about the educational progress of an individual child and, equally, meet the needs of those charged with decisions regarding the local and the national education system would have to satisfy four general criteria:

1. the assessment results should give direct information about pupils' achievement in relation to specified objectives – i.e. they should be criterion-referenced;

2. the results should provide a sound basis for decisions about pupils' further learning needs – i.e. they should be primarily 'formative' rather than 'summative' in their purpose;

3. the scales or grades derived from the tests should be capable of comparison across classes and schools, sharing a common language and providing common standards for the nation as a whole: this implies that the assessments should be calibrated or moderated;

4. the national assessment scheme should relate clearly to the expected educational development of children and provide a continuity of assessment at the different ages under consideration which would highlight children's progression towards the agreed attainment targets.

These criteria lie at the heart of the national assessment system proposed in the initial TGAT report and further elaborated in a series of supplementary reports submitted to the secretary of state before Easter and published by him in early June. In so doing, (GB DES, 1988c) he commented on how well the Task Group's proposals had been received and reported the government's decision to adopt, as the basis for the new national system of assessment and testing, the main principles contained in the Task Group's reports. These may be summarized briefly as follows:

(a) National attainment targets will be set to establish what children should normally be expected to know, understand and be able to do at the ages of seven, eleven, fourteen and sixteen in each of the 'core' and 'foundation' subjects. Children's progress towards these targets will be assessed and reported on at the ages concerned. Results will be presented in the form of an attainment profile.

(b) The national assessment system will involve a combination of externally-set national tasks or tests and teachers' own informal assessments. In order to safe guard national standards of comparability, teachers' own assessments will be compared with the results of the national tests and exposed to the professional judgement of other teachers.

(c) The results of the tests and other assessments will be used both formatively, to inform decisions about the next step in a pupil's programme of learning, and summatively, to convey information to parents about their children's attainment of the national targets.

(d) Pupils' different stages of achievement and their overall progress as measured by tests and assessments in the different areas of the national curriculum will be described in terms of their progression through ten levels of attainment, covering the whole span of compulsory schooling, as detailed in the initial TGAT report (GB DES, 1988b).

(e) Assessment results for individual pupils will be given in full to their parents, but no individual results will be publicly released. Aggregated data for schools and LEAs will be publicly reported at the ages of 11, 14 and 16 and, although there will be no legal requirement to do so, the government 'strongly recommends' that aggregated data for seven-year-olds should also be made publicly available.

It is the government's current intention that work on the national curriculum attainment targets and programmes of study should begin with children entering primary school in Autumn 1989, in at least the 'core' subjects. At the same time, first-year pupils in secondary schools will begin work on the new mathematics and science curriculum. The first round of national assessments will involve seven-year-olds in 1991 and 14-year-olds in 1992, although these will be seen as a trial run and it will not be until the second round of assessments, in 1992 and 1993 respectively, that the results will be made publicly available. Assessment in the other areas of the national curriculum and for further year groups of pupils will introduced progressively thereafter.

Apart from the central issue of the national curriculum and its assessment, a further major reform proposed in the Bill is that which entails the delegation of financial powers and responsibilities by local education authorities (LEAs) to the governing bodies of all secondary schools and all larger primary schools (i.e. those with more than 200 pupils), and if they wish, to smaller primary schools as well. The schools' governing bodies will thus have responsibility for most of the schools' expenditure, notably on staffing, the purchase of books, materials and equipment, and the greater part of the schools' running costs. The LEAs would remain responsible for school transport, for the provision of advisory, inspection and other general services and for the administration of pay, tax and superannuation matters. Each LEA will be required to prepare plans for the delegation of financial responsibility to its schools, which must be submitted to the secretary of state for approval. Some LEAs have already been involved in pilot schemes for what has now become known as 'local management of schools' (LMS), but the intention of the Bill is that the system should be extended on a nation-wide basis, although to be phased over several years. In the words of the secretary of state:

> The Bill pushes responsibility down the line – to the school, the headteachers and the governors. They will work to get the best value out of the resources delegated to them...They will now be able to get on with the job of managing the schools. The LEAs will be able to move out of detailed involvement into strategic management, and that must be right. (Hansard).

This view is corroborated in an independent report commissioned to evaluate the advantages and disadvantages of the proposed shift of financial responsibility from the LEAs to the individual school: 'we think that the proposals will produce considerable benefit in that they will enable LEAs to focus more attention on questions of major importance without being distracted by having to pay attention to points of detail.' (Coopers and Lybrand, 1988).

Doubts have been expressed as to whether governing bodies would be able to muster sufficient expertise to manage the school's delegated budget effectively but, on the whole, the proposals have been welcomed by the teaching profession if received with less enthusiasm by some of the LEAs themselves. The critics of the Bill regard these proposals as a blatant attack on local government. As one of them put it: 'the main objective of this measure is to distance schools from local authorities and generally deprive them of powers. The attack on local government as a whole is one of Thatcher's clearest objectives.' (Simon, 1988). Those who support the idea of local management welcome the degree of freedom and control over its own affairs that the individual school will enjoy under the new circumstances.

Allied to the idea of the local management of schools is that of the proposed ability of schools to 'opt out' of local government control and to choose instead to be directly funded by a central government grant. These schools, which would be known as 'grant-maintained' schools, are seen by the government as a means of extending parental choice:

> The Act gives parents and governors a new opportunity. They will be able to take over the running of their schools, free of the local education authority...The grant-maintained school means the introduction of competition – with no charge to the customer – into a publicly provided service. Competition for custom, for pupils, is the best self-regulating mechanism for higher standards all round. Those who foresee a divide opening up between successful and 'sink' schools ignore the dynamic nature of competition. The LEAs will have to respond to competition and to parental pressure. (Hansard).

The initiative to opt out of local authority control could be taken by the school governors or by a substantial number of parents petitioning the governors, and the application to the secretary of state would need the support of a majority of parents voting in secret ballot. In considering an application to opt out, the secretary of state would need to be satisfied that the school concerned had a viable future and that the governors and headteacher were competent to run it. The whole notion of opting out has aroused more controversy than almost any other aspect of the Education Reform Act. Those who favour it see it as:

> a spur to LEAs to raise educational standards in all their schools. Satisfied governors and parents...will not want to opt out. But those threatened by inefficient and authoritarian LEAs or by a scheme of secondary reorganisation which would close or fundamentally change the character of a successful school will be able to take advantage of the Act. (Jameson, 1988).

The view taken by the Opposition is that the proposals represent a further attack on local democracy:

> Opting out is a wild plan inspired by a sectarian hatred of the present democratic system of education built up so patiently over the years. It is a veritable leap in the dark and is bound to cause chaos. There is no precedent for it. The Government have no idea where they are going. (Hansard).

Not quite so controversial, but fairly hotly debated, have been the government's proposals for open enrolment. At the moment, it is possible for LEAs to set artificial ceilings on the number of places available at popular schools, in order to spread pupils more evenly over the schools in the area. The government takes the view that no child should be refused admission to a school unless the building is genuinely full. Under the terms of the Education Reform Act, schools will have to admit pupils at least up to their 'standard number', which will usually be the number admitted in 1979. Where admissions are higher in 1988 than in 1979, that higher figure will become the standard number. In the words of the secretary of state: 'The provision for more open enrolment will extend choice, opening the doors of good schools to more parents. The bizarre spectacle of empty desks at popular schools will become a thing of the past' (Hansard). Those who oppose this measure fear that the community use of school premises (i.e. is the use of spare classrooms for such activities as play-groups, luncheon clubs for the elderly, adult education classes, welfare clinics, community libraries, etc.) will suffer, if schools are obliged to fill their buildings to the capacity of 1979, before school enrolments began to decline. It is also argued that the proposals would increase parental choice only marginally, and only for better-off parents who could afford to transport their children to more distant schools.

The final measure proposed in the Bill to increase parental choice of school is the establishment of a new type of school: the 'city technology college'. These schools will offer free education to parents who want their children to have an education with a technological bias. The intention is that the establishment of city technology colleges (usually to be situated in inner city areas) will be made with the help of funding from industry and commerce. The first is due to open in September 1989 and others are due to follow. The curriculum in these schools will emphasize technology, science and mathematics. Pupils will be chosen 'who make a commitment to their school education and who will take advantage of a curriculum emphasising technology and science'. (GB DES. 1987). Like the grant-maintained schools, the city technology colleges will operate independently of LEAs. Those who oppose this move see it as yet another attack on local democracy and fear that the city technology schools will be better staffed and equipped than those maintained by the LEA and thus be in a position to 'cream off' the best available talent in the area. Those who support the idea of the new schools see them as enriching the variety of educational provision available and helping to counteract the acute shortage of technologically able young people.

At the time of writing (June 1988), the Education Reform Bill has emerged from the House of Lords with only minor amendments relating to religious education, the balloting arrangements for opting out of the local education system, and the safeguarding of academic freedom in the universities. It is likely that the Bill will receive Royal Assent in July. There can be little doubt that it will have a more profound effect on the education system of England and Wales than any Bill enacted in the past several decades.

References

COOPERS AND LYBRAND (1988). *Local Management of Schools: A Report to the Department of Education and Science*. London: Coopers and Lybrand.

GREAT BRITAIN. DEPARTMENT OF EDUCATION AND SCIENCE (1987). *Education Reform: The Government's Proposals for Schools*. London: HMSO.

GREAT BRITAIN. DEPARTMENT OF EDUCATION AND SCIENCE (1988a). *National Curriculum: Task Group on Assessment and Testing Report: A Digest for Schools*. London: Department of Education and Science.

GREAT BRITAIN. DEPARTMENT OF EDUCATION AND SCIENCE (1988b). *National Curriculum: Task Group on Assessment and Testing: A Report*. London: Department of Education and Science.

GREAT BRITAIN. DEPARTMENT OF EDUCATION AND SCIENCE (1988c). *National Curriculum: Task Group on Assessment and Testing: Three Supplementary Reports*. London: Department of Education and Science.

HANSARD, 130, 124. London: HMSO.

JAMESON, R. (1988). 'The Baker Bill: an outside view', *Report*, 10, 5, March.

SIMON, B. (1988). *Bending the Rules*. London: Lawrence and Wishart.

10 Design of the Dutch National Assessment Programme in Education: Enhancing the Educational Debate through Large-scale Assessment

Johan M. Wijnstra

After several years of discussion at the national policy level and the completion of a pilot study in primary education, in 1986 the Dutch National Assessment Programme in education was launched (cf. Sandbergen's paper in this volume). The Minister of Education and Science commissioned the National Institute for Educational Research in the Netherlands and the National Institute for Educational Measurement to carry out the assessment programme as a joint project. Until further notice the project is restricted to an assessment of the primary education system.

The programme's aim is to describe periodically by means of surveys the contents of the curriculum in use and the attainment of students at the end of primary education (about 11 years old) in all curriculum areas on a national basis, so as to provide a basis for a more rational discussion about the contents and the level of primary education. In a period of about five years the whole curriculum should be covered, including social studies, science, physical education, art and music. In the fields of mathematics and language additional assessments will be carried out with eight-year-olds, about midway through the Dutch primary school.

In this paper some of the guiding principles in the design of the assessment programme will be described. Data collection started in the Spring term of 1987 with the assessment of mathematics at the end of primary education, followed by the midway assessment in the Fall term; the design of these assessments is highlighted in this paper. The scale construction is described in more detail in Eggen's paper (in this volume). The report on the mathematics assessments will become available in the Fall of 1988.

The National Assessment Program is primarily intended to describe the attainment and the contents of education at the national level. In this paper, which is illustrated with examples from the mathematics assessments, special attention is paid to the way the results will be reported so as to foster the discussion about the contents and the level of education. At the local level, the assessment data are not very useful, unless local data can be related to national data. In the final section the experimental local service option for mathematics is described. In this voluntary option, which was operated for the first time in 1988, a selection of items from the national assessment is used.

Instruments

Instrument development starts with the construction of a framework, describing the structure of the curriculum area under study. The frameworks are primarily content-oriented and rather detailed, so as to provide the basis for the description of the curriculum in use and the performance of students in meaningful units for educators and curriculum specialists, more or less comparable to what Bock, Mislevy and Woodson (1982) call 'indivisible curricular elements'. The frameworks, which provide a rationale for the instrument construction, are presented for comment to several groups of relevant respondents, like teachers and curriculum specialists, of course, but also representatives of societal organizations such as political parties, unions and employers' associations. The frameworks do not imply that all the topics included are given the same degree of attention in Dutch schools. Such a restriction beforehand might curtail a discussion of the results with respect to desirable developments in the contents of education.

The frameworks provide the basis for the construction of two types of partially complementary instruments:

- questionnaires to make an inventory of the topics actually taught and the variation in the intensity of teaching;

- tests to measure the performance of students on narrowly defined content domains, in the fields of mathematics and language at two age levels (eight- and 11-year-olds).

The inventory of the contents taught constitute data in their own right. In addition, these data can be used to explore relations between performance and content of the curriculum taught.

The tests are meant to cover a wide range of skills and concepts. In the language assessment, for instance, reading and writing proficiency, as well as speaking and listening skills, will be assessed. Each individual test will cover a rather small content domain. The scope of the domains is comparable to the curricular units used in the California Assessment Program (cf. Pandey and Carlson, 1983).

The test items and exercises are developed by committees of experienced teachers under the direction of project staff members. A high degree of curricular validity is aspired to in the test construction. If the curricular validity of multiple-choice items is questionable, open-ended items and exercises will be used. In the mathematics assessment, for example, the open-ended format was used in more than 95 per cent of the items.

As item response theory has several advantages in large-scale assessment (Bock and Mislevy, 1981; Bock, Mislevy and Woodson, 1982; Messick, Beaton and Lord, 1983); these models will be applied in scale construction whenever dichotomously scored items are used. In Eggen's paper the application of a mixture of the one- and two-parameter logistic model is described. The rather detailed frameworks have several advantages in this context (e.g. changes in curriculum can easily be catered for without losing comparability over time on unaffected scales), while the probability of arriving at a reasonable model fit is greatest (Traub and Wolfe, 1981; Hambleton and Swaminathan, 1985).

Populations and sampling

Compulsory education in the Netherlands starts at age five years, but almost all children enter primary school on a voluntary basis at the age of four years. The primary school contains eight grades, the first two grades are more or less comparable to a kindergarten programme. The Dutch National Assessment Programme will collect data about the curriculum content and achievement of students at the end of primary school, while in the fields of mathematics and language, additional assessments will be carried out midway through primary school. Since grade alone is not a satisfactory basis to categorize students, the student populations are defined as the students in a given grade (5 or 8) and all students who could have been in that grade according to their age (students of eight and 11 years old respectively on 30 September of the school year in which the data are being collected). This provides the opportunity to define three relevant populations:

1. the students in a given grade, irrespective of age;
2. the students of a modal age in a given grade;
3. the students of a given age, irrespective of grade.

The population of schools consists of all primary schools in the Netherlands. Although about two-thirds of the schools have non-public governing bodies, financially almost all of thee schools are completely publicly maintained and no difference is made in sampling. However, the population is stratified beforehand according to the composition of the school population.

To determine the number of teachers a school is entitled to hire, a weighted number of students is calculated. The weight for lower-class, indigenous Dutch students is 1.25, for example, and 1.90 for ethnic minority students. The distribution of the ratio of the weighted and the nominal number of students is heavily skewed (see Figure 10.1).

Because of the policy relevancy, this variable is used to stratify the population of schools into three categories:

1.05	: 47% of the schools;
1.06–1.15	: 35% of the schools;
> 1.15	: 18% of the schools.

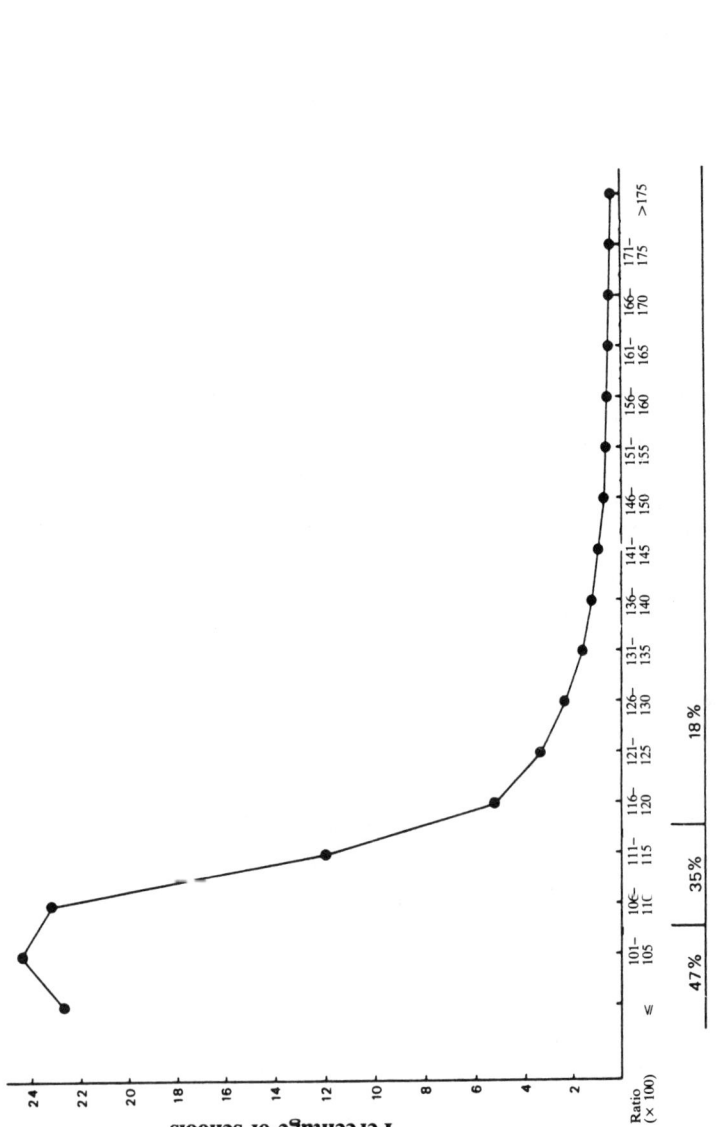

Figure 10.1: Distribution of the ratio of weighted and nominal number of students in the Dutch population of schools (1985).

In each stratum the samples will contain the same number of schools, in principle, in such a way that the mean test scores in each stratum can be estimated with a precision of 0.075. In order to retain representativity on the stratification variable, systematic random samples are planned, with two or three replacements for each sampled school (participation is completely voluntary).

All students available in the sampled schools participate in the testing sessions conducted by specially trained project assistants. To reduce the clustering effect, each student takes only a few of the tests and, at the same time, rotating the tests over students within schools. In principle, testing takes no longer than half a school day. Therefore, the sample size will also be dependent on the number of tests to be used and the time these tests take.

Mathematics assessments in primary education

As the assessment at the end of primary education as the first to be carried out, this assessment is described first. At the end of this section the analogous design of the midway assessment is described briefly.

The framework for the mathematics assessment at the end of primary school contains 27 topics of rather narrowly defined curriculum components such as:

- fractions: basic concepts;
- addition and subtraction of fractions and rational numbers;
- multiplication and division of fractions and rational numbers;
- fractions: applications.

In the curriculum inventory each topic was illustrated with three items, varying in difficulty, from the corresponding tests. Aiming at the average student in grade 8, the classroom teacher was asked the following questions about each topic:

- Have the concepts and skills necessary to solve each of the exemplar items been taught to the average student in your class?

- How much time did you spend in teaching this topic this school year?

In order to estimate the time spent per topic, first the total amount of time spent in mathematics was to be estimated. Then the relative amount of time spent on each topic was estimated with the help of 100 cardboard chips, each chip representing 1 per cent of the total time spent on mathematics. Complementary to the teacher questionnaire about the average student, the teacher was asked to indicate whether each of the students on the list with the names of the participating students had been taught the concepts and skills necessary to solve the easiest exemplar item of each topic.

For each topic a scale was to be constructed, using item response theory. With one exception, 16–20 items were constructed for each topic. The first test, on basic skills in mathematics, contained 32 items, which were administered in a structurally incomplete design. Each student took only two blocks of eight items of this topic. The blocks were systematically rotated over students. In addition to the basic mathematical skills test, each student took items on four or five topics. These topics were also administered in a structurally incomplete design, but in these cases a priori collateral information was used to assign students to tests, so as to maximize the information and to minimize the embarrassment to students. The items on each topic were divided into two test versions, a relatively easy one (A) and a relatively hard one (B), with an overlap of eight items. Basically, six A and six B booklets were needed. So as to balance order effects, each tests was produced in two item orders while, at the same time, the booklets were assembled in two different topic orders. Consequently, 48 booklets were produced: 24 A and 24 B booklets. Whether a student received a booklet containing A or B tests was decided by the classroom teacher. All students who were one or more grades behind, compared with their age mates, took the easy test versions, of course.

The tests were administered in a sample of some 320 schools during the month of May 1987. The total sample consisted of systematic random samples of about 95 schools from each of the first two strata and 130 from the third. The latter sample size was increased in order to collect data simultaneously for an evaluation programme on educational priority areas. The schools in the sample included about 8,000 students who were eligible for the assessment programme. Each item was taken by at least 500 students, while the overlapping items in the A and B tests were taken minimally by double that number. This sample size is sufficient to estimate the mean test scores in each stratum with a precision of 0.075, even when the intraclass correlation exceeds a value of 0.20.

The design of the midway assessment, which was carried out in October–November 1987, was analogous to the assessment at the end of primary education. In this assessment the mathematics domain was divided into 13 topics. Between 18 and 30 items were constructed for each topic. The tests on the first two topics, basic skills in addition/subtraction and multiplication/division, were presented orally in a complete design: every item was administered to all students available (students who were one or two grades behind only took the basic skills test on addition and subtraction). The tests on the other topics were administered in much the same way as in the assessment at the end of primary education. Because item order did not appear to be of any influence in the first assessment, this variation was deleted in the production of the test booklets. Every test was taken by about the same number of students as in the assessment at the end of primary education. Since the number of tests and items was smaller, the total sample size was reduced accordingly.

Reporting the results

Using a mixture of the one- and two-parameter logistic item response model, all topics were successfully calibrated (cf. Eggen's paper in this volume), standardizing the mean of the reference population (all students in grade 8 or 5) at an arbitrary value of 250 with a standard deviation of 50.

In addition to the technical reports, a publication will also be produced for those whose interest in the project is more general. The body of this report will contain a description of the state of mathematics education at the national level and in the three different strata. The scale constructed for each topic will be portrayed graphically (Figure 10.2), showing the percentile distribution of the reference population, while several scale points will be illustrated with items that can be answered correctly by students of that ability with a high probability (80 per cent). So, it can be seen easily how many students are able to answer a certain type of item correctly. These data will be supplemented with data on the contents taught, the time distribution, etc.

In the first cycle the assessment programme is producing baseline data, which cannot be compared with other available data. Therefore, the appraisal of the results is not easy in the educational debate. To promote this kind of interpretation, a questionnaire about the assessment at the end of primary school was sent out to three groups of relevant respondents:

1. primary school principals;

2. parent members of parents–teacher councils (every school is obliged to have such a council);

3. teachers in three types of secondary education.

These respondents were confronted with the scales without the normative information about the percentile distribution. Parents and principals were requested to indicate on each scale the appropriate level of attainment for the average student in grade 8. Principals were also requested to mark the required minimum level which should be reached by 90 per cent of the students. Correspondingly, the teachers in secondary schools were requested to indicate the minimum level of attainment for students entering their school type.

The averages of these data will be displayed alongside the actual data, so as to foster a debate about the contents and the attainment level in mathematics education, for example, the present discussion about the contents of a core curriculum. The project staff will not contribute to this debate. The project is restricted to a description of the actual situation and the promotion of a discussion of the findings. To enhance further the educational debate, two or three experts in the field of mathematics education will be invited to comment upon the results. Their comments will be integrated in the publication.

The report will be distributed among all relevant educational support and development agencies in the country. All primary schools will receive a copy of a brochure summarizing the main findings and comments. The assessment results will also be presented for discussion at a conference organized by a professional organization in mathematics education before an audience of curriculum experts, consultants, etc.

All these activities are aimed at the national level. The assessment data are not very useful for a discussion at the local level, unless local data can be related to national data, as has been shown in several state assessment programmes in the USA. The Dutch assessment programme's design is not suitable

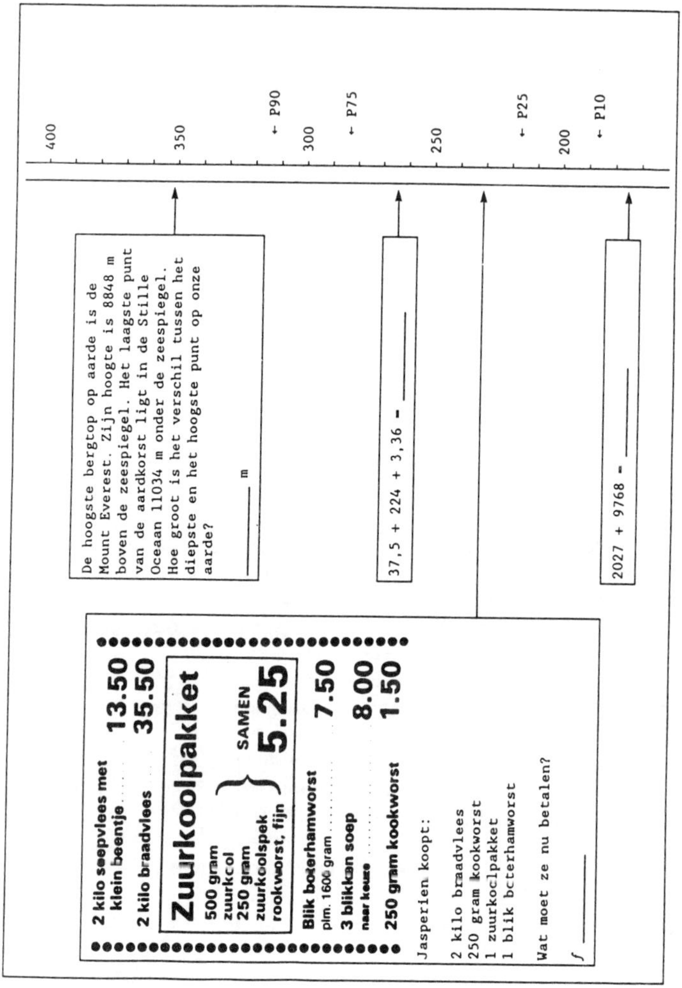

De hoogste bergtop op aarde is de Mount Everest. Zijn hoogte is 8848 m boven de zeespiegel. Het laagste punt van de aardkorst ligt in de Stille Oceaan 11034 m onder de zeespiegel. Hoe groot is het verschil tussen het diepste en het hoogste punt op onze aarde?

___ m

$37,5 + 224 + 3,36 =$ ___

$2027 + 9768 =$ ___

2 kilo soepvlees met klein beentje **13.50**
2 kilo braadvlees **35.50**

Zuurkoolpakket
500 gram zuurkool
250 gram zuurkoolspek
rookworst, fijn

SAMEN **5.25**

Blik boterhamworst **7.50**
plm. 1600 gram
3 blikken soep **8.00**
naar keuze
250 gram kookworst **1.50**

Jasperien koopt:

2 kilo braadvlees
250 gram kookworst
1 zuurkoolpakket
1 blik boterhamworst

Wat moet ze nu betalen?

ƒ ___

400
350
← P90
300
← P75
250
← P25
200
← P10

Figure 10.2: Portrait of a scale

to combine in the same operation the collection of national data and data for local assessment, as is proposed by Bock and Mislevy (1987, and their paper in this volume) in their duplex design. In order to provide data for a discussion at the local level, this year (1987) an experimental local service option has been introduced. This option will be described in the final section.

Local service option

In the national assessment at the end of primary school about 500 items were used. For the experimental local service option some 100 items were selected from this assessment, approx. four from each scale, except the basic mathematical skills tests. The schools that participated in last year's mathematics assessments were offered the opportunity to administer these items to this year's grade 8 students. To obtain the reports, the schools had to mark their students' tests and to fill out the answer sheets.

In the reporting service several of the original scales will be combined in different ways. The scales will be ordered according to content category and type of knowledge and operation. In the ordering based on content category the reporting units on whole and decimal numbers, respectively fractions, percentages and ratios, will be sub-divided on type of operation and knowledge:

- concepts and mental operations;
- calculations and applications.

The following reporting categories will be distinguished:

Content categories:

Whole and decimal numbers	–	concepts and mental operations
	–	calculations and applications
Fractions, percentages, ratios	–	concepts and mental operations
	–	calculations and applications
Measurement	–	concepts, mental operations, calculations and applications
Type of knowledge and operation concepts	–	whole and decimal numbers, fractions, percentages and ratios
Mental operations	–	whole and decimal numbers, percentages
Calculations	–	whole and decimal numbers, fractions
Applications	–	whole and decimal numbers, fractions, percentages, ratios, time and money

In addition to a listing of its students' scores and the school means on all reporting units, each school will receive a few simple summaries, in which the performance is related to the distribution of scores of some reference population –

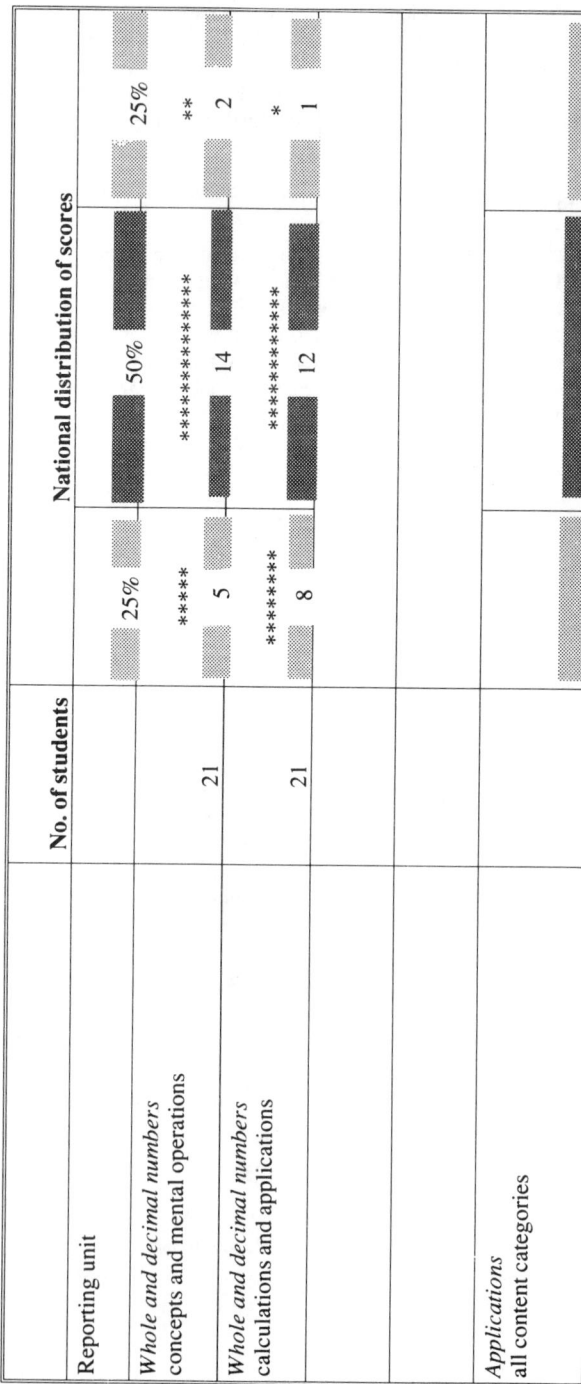

Reporting unit	No. of students	National distribution of scores		
		25%	50%	25%
Whole and decimal numbers concepts and mental operations	21	***** 5	************** 14	** 2
Whole and decimal numbers calculations and applications	21	******** 8	********** 12	* 1
Applications all content categories				

Figure 10.3: Distribution of scores in relation to national distribution

e.g. the national score distribution, the distribution in the relevant stratum or the score distribution of ethnic minority students. In Figure 10.3 an example is presented which shows the score distribution of a hypothetical school in relation to the lowest quartile in the national distribution, the middle two quartiles and the highest quartile.

If this local service option appears to be successful, the National Institute for Educational Measurement plans to offer this service to all schools and to extend it to other curriculum areas after the assessment has been carried out.

References

BOCK, R.D. and MISLEVY, R.J. (1981). 'An item response curve model for matrix-sampling data: the California grade-three assessment'. In: D. CARLSON (Ed), *Testing in the States: Beyond accountability.* New Directions for Testing and Measurement No. 10. San Francisco, Calif.: Jossey-Bass, pp. 65–90.

BOCK, R.D.and MISLEVY, R.J. (1987). *Comprehensive Educational Assessment for the States: The Duplex Design.* Chicago: University of Chicago/NORC.

BOCK, R.D., MISLEVY, R. and WOODSON, C. (1982). 'The next stage in educational assessment', *Educational Researcher,* 11, 3, 4–11, 16.

HAMBLETON, R.K. and SWAMINATHAM, H. (1985). *Item Response Theory: Principles and Applications.* Boston, Mass.: Kluwer-Nijhoff.

MESSICK, S., BEATON, A. and LORD, F. (1983). *National Assessment of Educational Progress Reconsidered: A New Design for a New Era.* Princeton, NJ: National Assessment of Educational Progress.

PANDEY, T.N. and CARLSON, D. (1983). 'Application of item response models to reporting assessment data'. In: HAMBLETON, R.K., (Ed) *Applications of Item Response Theory.* Vancouver, BC: Educational Research Institute of British Columbia, pp. 212–29.

TRAUB, R.E. and WOLFE, R.G. (1981). 'Latent trait theories and the assessment of educational achievement'. In: BERLINER, D.C. (Ed) *Review of Research in Education 9.* Washington, DC: American Educational Research Association, pp. 377–435.

11 Possible Educational Hazards and Side-effects of Assessment Programmes

Helga Thomas

Bringing up again hazards and side-effects of assessment programmes in view of decades of international experience with educational measurement and a well-known set of pros and cons is a risky enterprise.

First, new arguments against, or in favour of, educational measurement will hardly be found. Moreover, many of the debates among educationists seem to be more a battle of convictions than controversies based on solid knowledge of test theory, test analysis, assessment methods and their different ranges of interpretation. And thirdly, in many of those debates the different levels of criticism are continuously intermingled, social policy arguments are played off against methodological or educational arguments and vice versa, which considerably hampers a thorough examination of the benefit of assessment programmes.

Therefore, I will not repeat the fundamental debate on educational measurement in principle and at an abstract level, but will rather discuss some prerequisites which seem to be relevant when deciding on the usage of assessment methods, their aims and their range within the national context of the Federal Republic of Germany.

Possible educational hazards and unintended side-effects which might come along with a widespread application of tests in selection procedures or with large-scale assessments are fairly well known and have been discussed at some length in several publications (cf. Haase, 1978; Ingenkamp, 1981, 1983):

- Tests are mainly serving as a means of selection; this usage of tests will rather tend to promote hereditary concepts of ability and foster discrimination than be conducive in overcoming individual and group-specific learning disabilities.

- Objective testing is promoting competition among pupils, schools and regions; it will pave the way for broader administrative control and will reduce the scope of educational innovations within schools and within the classroom.

- Large-scale assessments might stimulate central curriculum planning processes and cross-regional or cross-national comparisons, thus provoking financial sanctions or further lowering the prestige of weaker regions.

- Achievement tests, in particular, are liable to restrict classroom instruction to imparting mere information to pupils and to repress those educational goals which are difficult to be measured on a psychometric basis; they tend to streamline the whole learning process according to specific standards and thus to discourage slow learners.

- Human beings – a complex mixture of nature and nurture – can not be 'measured' at all, unless they are 'mismeasured' (Gould, 1988), since any method of measurement is based on some hypothetical constructs, which restrict the manifold dimensions of achievement and completely neglect the varying conditions of learning.

All of the objections mentioned above are not to be denied; they are mostly even accepted, to some extent, by those who plead for educational measurement. There are two basic reasons to believe that it might be useful not to discuss any further the pros and cons, in principle, but to consider carefully the different contexts of decisions with the administration of testing programmes.

The rise of democratic societies, no longer based on privileges of birth and social class, but, in principle, on individual proficiency, combined with the modern role of schools as institutions of social selection, necessarily led to procedures of assessment and comparisons, and to the development of specific standards of achievement: marking and credit systems, more or less obligatory curricula, examination regulations, etc. But, although there is manifold evidence on the poor diagnostic and prognostic value of traditional assessment procedures, such as marks and reports, based on teachers' subjective judgement, they still remain the decisive criteria for selection and promotion within the educational system as well as the basis of comparisons between schools and school systems. On the other hand, there is also much evidence that additional testing procedures possibly played an important role in the process of educational democratization. But we have to take into account the particular factors, different in each country, which are more or less favourable to such effects.

When Eduard Spranger (1882–1963), one of the great German pedagogues of the hermeneutic school, developed the idea of a 'Law of unintended side effects in education' ('Gesetz der ungewollten Nebenwirkungen in der Erziehung': Spranger, 1962), referring to Wundt's 'heterogeneity of aims' (*Heterogonie der Zwecke*), he did not envisage that even the best intentions might be abused or thwarted by unforeseeable events. Rather he emphasized the idea of a 'law', according to which it can be generally stated that, inevitably, whenever we take action in the field of culture and education, there is always something else being produced than what had been intended (*ibid.*, p. 349). And this is due to the complexity of the cultural system and to the manifold factors with their inherent laws influencing the outcomes. Given this view, it is quite possible, at least in part, to anticipate some of those 'unintended side-effects' on the basis of experience and a systematically induced understanding of the educational process within a specific cultural context.

Comparative investigation, especially in an intercultural field, taught us to analyse carefully the context of decisions if we intend to adopt procedures and instruments which have proved a success in other countries. Let me mention some examples.

The overall application of standardized tests, and especially the use of intelligence tests, were without doubt instrumental in revealing educational discrimination, in shaking hereditary-based convictions and in promoting the democratization of school systems. Incidentally, the development of intelligence testing turned out to the particular advantage of women. Lorrain J. Daston (1988), a fellow at the Institute for Advanced Study in Berlin, convincingly described in a recent lecture on 'Female Intelligence' – a pilot study of historical patterns of thought, referring mainly to the Anglo-Saxon tradition of intelligence testing – how the transition, from concepts of qualitative polarities to the perception of a continuum, established the idea of fundamental equality of men and women, at least at the level of the construct 'intelligence'. It goes without saying, that this change of concepts did not automatically abolish unequal opportunities.

Yet a quick glance at the history of educational reforms proves that steps towards more democratization were not primarily taken because testing procedures were available, but rather were due to a political and social atmosphere, which favoured or hampered the use of objective testing.

A similar social-egalitarian impetus which, for instance, led to the development of comprehensive schools in the USA and to the spread of testing as early as after the First World War, only arose in many European countries mainly along with social repercussions after the Second World War.

In the UK, for example, unexpected results in overall intelligence testing within the army, pointing to a vast reservoir of abilities, raised an important issue in the discussion on better and more valid selection procedures for the tripartite system; on the other hand, a relatively long tradition of standardized selection methods eased the new discussion on promoting equal opportunities in the context of the 1944 Education Act. Even Cyril Burt, whose work has been vastly criticized in the meantime, and whose theories of heredity played a decisive role within the UK's educational psychology for decades, repeatedly argued against any attempt to justify scientifically the establishment of a tripartite system on the basis of research on intelligence, although he supported the political decision (Thomas, 1975a, p. 134; Zimmer, 1975).

Finally, in the Federal Republic of Germany, the application of social scientific and empirical methods of evaluation gained some reluctant acceptance, mainly during the 1960s, after a long period not only of reconstruction, but of restoration as well, when economic reasoning gave strong impulses to the idea of democratizing education. This has been thoroughly discussed, especially by Kuhlmann (1970), who analysed the long German tradition of prevailing hereditary concepts of ability and the ideologically based reforms since the 1920s.

As a result of this tradition, neither sufficient testing procedures were available, since the development of experimental research and of objective evaluation had been disrupted with the rise of the Nazi system, nor were politicians (and large parts of the public) ready to take into account empirical research when presented; neither were they keen to have it published. This has been reported for some research evidence on the amount of social stratification in the 1950s (Kuhlmann, 1970, p. 133).

It was only in the late 1950s that a new 'realistic approach' (Heinrich Roth) to education opened the field to empirical studies, which now, by means of quantitative methods, showed the extent of social and cultural barriers and contributed to the establishment of comprehensive schools at least as pilot models. But this uprising soon ran into a new radical criticism of quantitative methods and especially of educational measurement, though in the Federal Republic of Germany tests never had been used to any extent comparable to that in the USA (e.g. Haase, 1978; Ingenkamp, 1981; Ingenkamp, Horn and Jäger, 1986).

In part, the political front lines were completely reversed. In the early discussions on social democratization 'conservatives' showed little interest in scientific justification of their convictions. Parts of the 'progressive' league in education now reject the use of tests, fearing that eventually weaker results than expected of educational experiments might be used against any innovation by political opponents; their fears are not groundless.

Ingenkamp himself often stated the relationship between test criticism and a radical criticism of society (1981, 1983). But most interestingly, those who support testing and those who oppose it agree in one point, namely that radical test criticism led to the complete neglect of the development of educational diagnostics at all levels, which now hampers effective models of innovation (Begabung-Lernen-Schulqualität, 1987; Ingenkamp, 1985).

I will not repeat this feature of a broadly published debate; the historical remarks above have merely aimed to stress the indissoluble relations between measurement procedures, the purpose and use of testing and the social and political background of a society, which are not to be counterbalanced by mere information on test theory.

It is therefore necessary to try to consider very carefully the eventualities of misuse or abuse in a given society, which always consists of different interest groups and manifold and varying targets.

This is even more important in the field of achievement tests than, for instance, in administering intelligence tests since achievement results are even more subject to the influences of a whole set of variables, which are only partly represented by measured outcomes – not to speak of the inevitable limitations to specific fields of learning. Again, I do not intend to raise once more the obviously not very fruitful dispute on why those areas of learning, which cannot be exactly defined, nor observed or described, should have much more importance than achievements which can be measured, even though in a limited way.

Let me stick to the moderate purpose of large-scale assessments, namely to investigate achievement results and achievement changes more exactly than it can be done by means of less valid instruments like teachers' marks or subjective reports – in a case where formal qualifications are indeed decisive for a pupil's career and public expenditure for education is quite high.

The different crucial points of criticism of large-scale assessments in different countries like the USA or UK, which have longer experience with assessments, may teach us how to counteract undesirable use – at least, theoretically – by means of sampling methods, evaluation procedures and a proper presentation of results (cf. Forbes, Pandey, Carlson and Hadley, 1986; Schreiber, 1986). Those undesirable cross-national comparisons may be counteracted by not choosing states as sampling elements, as it is the case with the National Assessment of

Educational Progress (NAEP) – an important issue in a federal system with little central competencies. On the other hand, schools or school districts may be chosen once assessments are aimed at investigating the different achievement levels of single schools and districts within a system of regional control, as it is the case with the California Achievement Program (CAP).

Generally speaking, sampling procedures should be chosen according to the different possible purposes of large-scale assessments and the varying administration and financial structures of an educational system to allow for identifying desirable elements – be it states, school systems, single schools, classes, groups of pupils, etc. – or not to do it.

All these provisions will not automatically exclude any misuse; but, at least, wrong interpretations are not to be justified from a scientific point of view.

Only this consolation seems to be rather a weak one – at least, when speaking of the Federal Republic. We may be reminded of the school reform period, when in the discussion on comprehensive schools vs the tripartite system, each of the conflicting parties mobilized their scientific informants – and found them.

In the Federal Republic we face a legally mixed system of educational control. On one hand we have a fervently upheld cultural federalism with high centralization within the states and on the other hand national control mechanisms, like through the *Permanent Conference of the Ministers of Culture*, which negotiate for example the mutual acknowledgement of formal school qualifications. This creates a network of varying interests, additionally complicated by changing political majorities at regional, state and federal level. I suspect that in spite of all methodological scrupulousness, the best we could do is to complain of the perversion of scientifically sober results afterwards. The ill-starred discussion on a bonus-malus system for university admissions, based on numerical state averages of teachers' marks, might be taken as an awful example. We should be cautious in view of a certain mania for regulations and prescriptions, which seems to be a German tradition.

The crucial point with large-scale assessments is to be seen not only in providing descriptive information on achievements and changes of achievement, but enabling us to ascribe outcomes and changes in specific factors and thus help educators to shape better educational methods. Examples and approaches currently exist in different countries: combining the assessment results with expert reports and observation schemes at school or classroom level; fostering valid evaluation of pilot models; involvement of teachers in test construction; and generally furthering teachers' assessment competencies beyond merely using standardized tests.

But taking into account a combination of assessments and indicators to explain differences is obviously bound to prevailing features of educational policy in a specific country. It is no accident that a country like Sweden envisages this approach since its policy for decades has been to provide manifold programmes to overcome learning deficiencies and educational inequality.

The GDR might be taken as another example, where advancement programmes for gifted and highly gifted pupils and students are discussed in a less cramped way than is possible in the FRG – but on the solid basis of a common and relatively high standard for all pupils. There is no comparable consensus on educational policy in the FRG, in spite of significant changes during the past two decades.

The prerequisites for a combination of assessments and indicators are even more problematical. The FRG may be definitely taken as a developing country, in terms of measurement methods, evaluation procedures and interpretation schemes. Therefore, it is very likely that the work of teachers especially might be affected by large-scale assessments: provoking didactical reductions, restricting instructions to transmitting knowledge and releasing teachers from personal responsibility by providing seemingly objective criteria.

These possible effects are also due to considerable deficiencies in teacher training; but they certainly cannot be overcome within a short time. Teacher curricula are state-controlled, changes in examination regulations occur at the rate of up to ten years and decreasing numbers of pupils and financial cuts limit the recruitment of young teachers.

Moreover, what has been called the 'professionalization' of the teaching profession is more characterized by focusing teacher training on subject learning and shifting it to the universities, less by providing educationally and psychologically founded competence. This too may indicate the different importance attached to areas of teachers' competence in our society, since state authorities are deciding on the share of training content.

Quite obviously, the atmosphere in our schools has changed during the past 20 years; teachers are certainly more engaged and open for pupils' needs, in general. Yet we know from some studies that mere devotion without a solid diagnostic and didactical competence does not increase pupils' performance (Begabung-Lernen-Schulqualität, 1987, p. 59; Thomas, 1987); and we know as well from several studies on teachers' attitudes (summarized in Begabung-Lernen-Schulqualität, 1987, p. 78 f.) that teachers still differ in their concepts of ability. Those who work in the prevailing selective tripartite system take a more static view than those teaching in comprehensive schools; and even comprehensive school teachers are now more sceptical on the possibility of influencing pupils by means of education than during the early times of reform. Helplessness and uncertainty are spreading.

The issue is not to criticize teachers, nor to plead for leaving things unchanged and rather retain the traditional subjective assessment methods. But given the situation just described, teachers are likely to perceive objective methods as a welcome means to reduce personal responsibility, and with school work getting harder, to rely on 'easy' procedures: objective assessments, separation of pupils and teaching 'facts'.

We should also take into account the new task for our schools, to integrate a multitude of migrant workers' children of different nationalities. Assessments and comparisons on the basis of assessments might also be used as a justification to evade difficult or disliked demands.

To summarize:

- The primary intent of my contribution has been to point to the relationship between aims, purposes, modes of analysis and the specific social-political climate at the stage of planning large-scale assessments.

- Secondly, the contribution is geared to stimulate discussions no longer focused on supposedly mechanical effects of testing procedures, but on the identification of largely foreseeable side-effects. It is not so much a matter of providing technical safeguards against misuse, but of reaching acceptance and desirability; consensus-building too is not merely a technique but should also be based on careful analyses of national requirements.

- Thirdly, it needs to be asked in what ways differentiated knowledge among educators and teachers, and an informed public interest in improving the quality of schools, could be enhanced as a precondition for large-scale assessment.

The problems raised relate to the possible hazards accompanying general implementations in the FRG. Eventually further experiments and evaluations at school level, as well as regionally limited implementations, could prepare the field in a better way such as feasibility studies to prove assessments are supportive of schools and teachers.

References

BEGABUNG-LERNEN-SCHULQUALITÄT (1987). *SOESTER SYMPOSIUM 1987*, Hrsg. vom Landesinstitut für Schule und Weiterbildung, Soester Verlagskontor.

DASTON, L.J. (1988). *Weibliche Intelligenz: Eine historische Fallstudie von Denkstrukturen*, Vortrag im Rahmen der Colloquien am Wissenschaftskolleg zu Berlin (Institute for Advanced Study), 19 May.

FEND, H. (1977). *Schulklima: Soziale Einflubprozesse in der Schule*. Weinheim: Beltz.

FORBES, R.H., PANDEY, T., CARLSON, D. and HADLEY, C. (1986). 'Überregionale Testprogramme im Bildungswesen der USA'. In: INGENKAMP, K., HORN, R. and JÄGER, R.S. (Eds) *Tests and Trends 5*. Weinheim: Beltz., pp. 118–65.

GOULD, S.J. (1988). *Der falsch vermessene Mensch*. Frankfurt: Suhrkamp; *The Mismeasure of Man*. New York: W.W. Norton, 1981.

HAASE, H. (1978). *Tests im Bildungswesen. Urteile und Vorurteile*. Göttingen, Toronto and Zurich: Hogrefe.

INGENKAMP, K. (1981). 'Testkritik ohne Alternative. Eine kritische Darstellung der Argumentation radikaler Schultestkritik in der deutschen Fachliteratur'. In: JÄGER, R.S., INGENKAMP, K. and STARK, G (Eds) *Tests und Trends 1*. Weinheim: Beltz, pp. 71–101.

INGENKAMP, K. (1983). '1960–1980: Two decades of educational measurement in Germany: developments, controversies and results', *Studies in Educational Evaluation*, 9, 131–45.

INGENKAMP, K. (1985). *Lehrbuch der Pädagogischen Diagnostik*. Weinheim and Basle: Beltz.

INGENKAMP, K., HORN, K., JÄGER, R.S. (Eds) (1986). *Tests and Trends 5*. Jahrbuch der Pädagogischen Diagnostik. Weinheim and Basle: Beltz.

KUHLMANN, C. (1970). 'Schulreform und Gesellschaft in der Bundesrepublik Deutschland 1946–1966. Die Differenzierung der Bildungswege als Problem der westdeutschen Schulpolitik'. In: ROBINSOHN, S.B. *et al.* (Eds) *Schulreform im gesellschaftlichen Prozeb*. Stuttgart: Klett, Vol. 1, pp. 7–206.

LIGHTFOOT, S.L. (1985). *The Good High School*. New York: Basic Books.

ROBINSOHN, S.B. and KUHLMANN, J.C. (1967). 'Two decades in West German education', *Comparative Education Review*, Special issue: 'Ten Years of European Educational Reform 1956–1966, pp. 311–30.

RUTTER, M., MAUGHAN, B., MORTIMORE, P., OUSTON, J., with SMITH, A. (1979). *Fifteen Thousand Hours. Secondary Schools and Their Effects on Children*. London: Open Books.

SCHREIBER, W.H. (1986a). 'Methoden und Ergebnisse überregionaler Lernerfolgskontrolle', *Zeitschrift für Pädagogik*, 32, pp. 31–50.

SCHREIBER, W.H. (1986). 'Die Schule von innen erneuern! Untersuchungen und Erkundungen zur Wirksamkeit und Qualität schulischen Lernens', *Die Deutsche Schule*, 78.

SPRANGER, E. (1969). 'Das Gesetz der ungewollten Nebenwirkungen in der Erziehung'. In: BÄHR, H.W., BOLLNOW, O.F. EISERMANN, W., ENGLERT, L., FLITNER, A., MEYER, H.J., and WENKE, H. (Eds) *Gesammelte Schriften*. Heidelberg: Quelle and Meyer, Vol. 1, pp. 348–405.

THOMAS, H. (1975a) *Schulreform und Gesellschaft in England und Wales 1944–1970*. Stuttgart: Klett.

THOMAS, H. (1975b). 'Soziale Schichtung und Schulreform. Sozialpolitische Motive und Bedingungen der Reform der Sekundärschulstruktur 1945–1965'. In: *Schulreform und Gesellschaft. Vergleichende Studien über die gesellschaftlichen Bedingungen von Schulreformen in sieben europäischen Ländern*, Max-Planck-Institut für Bildungsforschung, Materialien zur Bildungs-Forschung Nr 3, Teil I, Berlin.

THOMAS, H. (1987). 'Modellversuch "*Integration ausländischer Schüler in Gesamtschulen*". Abschlußbericht der Wissenschaftlichen Begleitung. Gesamtschulinformationen', Sonderheft 1 und 2, Pädagogisches Zentrum (Ed), Berlin.

ZIMMER, J. (1975). 'Wissenschaft und Schulreform. Ein interkultureller Vergleich zur Funktion der Psychologie im Ablauf von Schulreformen'. In: *Schulreform und Gesellschaft. Vergleichende Studien über die gesellschaftlichen Bedingungen von Schulreformen in sieben europäischen Ländern*, Max-Planck-Institut für Bildungsforschung, Materialien aus der Bildungsforschung Nr 3, Teil II, Berlin.

International Roundtable: Educational and Didactic Aspects of Large-scale Assessment

Chair:
Professor Dr K Aurin, Albert-Ludwigs-Universität Freiburg (FRG)
Minutes:
Dipl.-Päd. W.H. Schreiber, M.A. Zentrum für empirische pädagogische Forschung der EWH Rheinland-Pfalz, Landau (FRG)
Participants
Dr C Burstall, Director of National Foundation for Educational Research in England and Wales (UK)
Dr P.D. Sandifer, Director of Office of Research, State Department of Education South Carolina (USA)
Professor Dr. M. Thomas, Technische Universität Berlin (FRG)
Dr J. Wijnstra, Director of the Dutch National Assessment Program (PPON) (NL)

The chairman picked up the question that was raised by Larry Cuban in the *Harvard Educational Review* (1984): 'How is it possible to transform the frog into a Prince, a bad school into a good school, the teacher into a master teacher, and the curriculum into a task curriculum?' Is the large-scale assessment researcher such a magician?

Dr Sandifer expressed the opinion that a bad school may become a good school through changes in the curriculum if, at first, one forgets about assessment and just looks at what one wants students to know and do and one defines that and communicates it to teachers. Then assessment can be used as part of the total process. But we focus on assessments instead of desired outcomes. In South Carolina, when mandated writing assessment started and the measurement specialists, trapped into initial specifications for writing assessment, primarily with multiple-choice items and a short paragraph in writing, the teachers said: 'There is just no way. If you want to test writing, let students write'. The problem was that they did not teach writing in grades 6 and 8; they do now. You can change the curriculum; but you have to change the curriculum and then do assessment.

Dr Burstall added that if one waits for a perfect system, one doesn't get anything. Assessment is only one component in a very complex process of change. Setting targets by themselves will not change anything; the framework needs to be set up to achieve those targets.

Professor Thomas requested that the difference between a good school and a bad school be defined. The most important thing about a good school is consensus about goals among teachers – consensus about what students should learn at every stage of their schooling, before one tries to shape the curriculum according to one's own ideas.

The chairman, Professor Aurin, phrased the following statement: 'A good school has a lot of problems, but a good school will be able to reflect on its own problems better, it will have a better strategy to solve its own problems. We can understand the developments in large-scale assessments: the underlying philosophy has changed from a more ability- and scale-oriented approach, to a more holistic cognitive-structure approach, as Carlson pointed out. This change has consequences for test construction and test development. Can someone express more of these changes in theoretical positions and paradigmata? Which elements of these changes would be welcomed in the eyes of school administrators or teachers?'

Dr Burstall gave the first answer: 'The most important set of changes is on the assessment side. Namely, the swing towards performance assessment, not what a child can write about, but what a child can actually do, what he or she knows and can do. We actually expect them to write and talk, and manipulate materials and carry out experiments. Ten years ago we were happy to fill out blanks in sentences or tick boxes. We made a change in emphasis, which is very welcome.'

Dr Sandifer gave his opinion from the point of view of a US state: 'I agree with what Dr Burstall said, one of the major changes is the movement towards performance assessment. Another thing that is observed is that the scope of assessments is broadening. In South Carolina we just have Reading, Writing, Maths and Science in grades 6 and 8. I expect other areas to be added. This would offset some of the concern about narrowing the total curriculum. If assessment is only focused on a few subjects, there is always a danger that time is taken away from Music, Art, etc.'

Dr Wijnstra addressed the question of exercises: 'Which type of exercises are welcomed by teachers? There are those which resemble classroom work, and especially those types of exercises which can act as eye-openers. I don't know if there is a shift from the ability- or skill-approach to a more holistic approach. The level of detail necessary for one's assessment instruments should be relevant to the kind of discussion one wants to stimulate and the decisions one wants to make.'

Dr Sandifer explained: 'Concerning the move from skills to a more holistic approach, there are a few states in the USA which are moving in that direction with reading assessment. They are trying to take a more holistic approach to reading, as opposed to assessing discrete skills, such as decoding word meaning, etc. They are still in the early stages with it, and when they are a little further on, we can all benefit from their experience.'

Professor Aurin asked what the participants thought about this development in West Germany.

Professor Thomas answered, based on her research experience in Germany: 'I think that Germany is still behind in the international discussion. In my paper I alluded to a long-lasting dispute among the ministers of education on the subject of a core curriculum and I used the term "negotiation" and not "consensus". Because what evolved did so on the basis of a political negotiation and not a consensus on a modern core curriculum, and I think that might give you the right picture about the sort of discussion in West Germany. Education in the Federal Republic has not been a political issue in the 1980s. It had been one in the 1960s and 1970s, but since then no one has really been willing to speak about education, to foster education, to spend money on education or to try to improve education.

On the other hand, there are a lot of new requirements in schools – the impact of new technology, of higher cognitive standards, to name a few. These are again overloading curricula, different subject-matter is required, more content is packed into an already full curriculum; and with this overloading of the curriculum there is, at the same time, overburdening of teachers. Thus, I think, if the idea of assessment at whatever level gained ground, it might move the whole discussion of the curriculum on to a more moderate, feasible level.'

Dr Forbes addressed another topic raised by the audience: 'I guess the caution on the measurement of art and music is that if it is going to be done right, it is extremely important and it is extremely costly, too. Measuring writing is difficult and expensive. Carlson mentioned in his remarks the shift in the State of California, that we have to think of ways to measure groups of students, not group administration of the test, which include what students do. We must start moving towards formulating items, exercises that can measure group activities. But how do you translate that into individual scores or measures, so that the teacher can deal with individual students. And then, how do we ever explain it to our parents and our public that we are measuring group activities, and how do we assign some type of measurement to them?'

Dr Burstall, addressing some experiences from the UK, answered: 'We measure group performance in our assessment of talking. We have children, who as a group, discuss a problem and then reach a solution orally, or they may write something down. But we have become very interested indeed in group performance and also, as part of that development, we, became very interested in the measurement of integrated tasks when we started out, about 15 years ago, with our language tests of speaking and writing. The view was reached that such a separation was quite false, in real life that is not how language is used at all: and so, in our Language Department, we have moved very much towards the idea of having tests which integrate all communication skills. In our forthcoming national assessment programme we intend to test children at the primary level by means of integrated tasks, which will draw on the children's linguistic, mathematical and scientific abilities.'

Another question from the audience: 'How are weaknesses and strengths of language performance reported to the teacher, including specific aspects, in order to allow for remedial teaching?' was then addressed.

Dr Burstall replied, 'One form of assessment does not do all things for all men. Tests are created for a given purpose, one cannot validly use them for a completely different purpose. Detailed information is obtained by means of diagnostic testing, not by large-scale assessment, although there is a place for both.

The chairman, Professor Aurin, posed another question: 'In large-scale assessments the researcher can learn from teachers, curriculum experts and others, as well as from feedback from indicators and on the basis of pedagogical didactic or instructional information frames, as Wedman has pointed out. But have the participants from other countries examples like the one reported from Sweden – are there special indicators for teachers, which are helpful at the classroom level, that tell us about the individual development process? If large-scale assessment is involved in the pedagogical transfer of these results, if the researcher is not only an informant, but a worker in in-service training, is this the intention?'

Dr Burstall answered first: 'I don't know if this is the intention; it certainly becomes the spin-off of APU work. A lot of work over the past years has been going into transferring the data into practical advice for teachers in the classroom. We have done a lot of very detailed analyses of the data, and we have been particularly concerned with spelling out for teachers, in an accessible way, what we consider to be the practical classroom implications of the findings. We started off with mathematics, for example, where we found that there were some persistent errors that children were making in mathematical calculations. These errors were present at age 11, and were still there at age 15; they therefore need particular attention. We have done this with language and with science and we are now doing it with foreign languages. We are really going through the data very carefully to see where there is some practical pay-off for teachers in the classroom. That has been quite a successful endeavour.'

Dr Sandifer answered next: 'We have done some of the same type of analysis with South Carolina data from the criterion-referenced tests in reading and maths, in particular, and taking data from several years across different test forms and looking at persistent patterns. Error patterns of students are given to teachers as video tapes and are related to specific aspects of the problem and how particular skills might be addressed.'

Dr Wijnstra, for the Netherlands, added: 'We have only just started with the assessment project, and from that project we have not planned any in-service training. That is because of a kind of departmentalization of educational agencies in Holland. But we have very good contacts with other agencies in the educational support structure, like teacher training and consulting facilities at the school level, and these agencies are very interested in the findings that come out of the assessments and they are very happy to have the possibility of directing their attention to a real problem situation. Concerning helping schools to interpret the findings, we provide some in the local school reporting service, as I have described in my paper. Schools can compare their situation with several reference groups; I think we are not as optimistic as the Swedes, who direct the attention of the schools to very specific aspects. We leave that up to the schools.'

Mr Sandbergen added some further examples from the audience: 'In our research we have been trying to link the characteristics and indicators of a school and achievement. This was a spin-off of the feasibility study in mother tongue that was conducted by people other than Wijnstra. It was really interesting because what we thought is one important indicator is the number of hours of teaching in mother tongue. But this was not the case after refined and detailed analysis. This confirmed some of the conclusions of Coleman, in his last report, which were that there are large influences of social class and all the well-known and notorious variables which influence the achievement of schools, and that there is a considerable proportion of variance left unaccounted for. Perhaps this has to do with something holistic, as Coleman finds, and gives some sort of perspective to encouraging such kinds of analyses. Perhaps too it is not very easy to translate to individual schools?'

Professor Wedman was asked by the chairman if he was content with the contributions concerning the pedagogical problem and answered: 'I am totally in favour of indicator information for the teachers, and aid in explaining variance in achievement tests. The crucial thing is to come up with information for the teachers that looks interesting because it stimulates teachers to act. They might come up with interesting ideas to be pursued, or come back to you to investigate or apply for a new research project.'

Professor Thomas referred to her own research: 'During the past eight years, I have evaluated two pilot model schools which were geared to integrate Turkish children into the German education system. There we used some semi-standardized tests, to test the language competency of pupils. The schools had different philosophies: one school aimed to provide lots of opportunities for communication to pupils which, they believed, would generally foster language competence; the other school provided some special remedial courses, to improve language competency. We finally find out, for it took us nearly two years to have the teachers willing to co-operate in testing, that the first philosophy of stimulating communication did not improve language competency; there was a halt at the age of about 13 or 14, and pupils, especially Turkish pupils, actually declined after that point. Whereas, whatever the structure of the remedial courses was (it could be good or bad), some significant improvement in language competency was achieved. Obviously, it was not the content of the course, but rather the more structured approach to teaching, which made the difference. So I think that feedback, if structured specifically for teachers, might well improve the management of instruction. And it is not so much a problem of having integrated testing: one can have integrated testing and then a systematic report of results, which can assist teachers to structure their own teaching.'

Mr Forbes from the audience added: 'Dr Burstall mentioned that assessment is just a small part of the total system, and I think feeding information back to teachers – based on analysis – on results of large-scale assessments is another part of the system. Several times people have said "you are not going to get there, unless you know where you are going". So I question the effectiveness of just doing the analyses and generating reports and putting them out for consumption. We did some of that for teachers of mathematics in the USA. We might have affected one-tenth of 1 per cent in all of the country. I don't think anything will happen until someone does something very creative with this information. At state level, one would take the information and impress it upon the staff-development people and then make it the basis of a programme that they provide statewide in the USA. That may work. At present, the state is just putting the reports out, assuming that people are going to take the information and use it. That is not the correct way to get a feedback back into the system. I am a born optimist and the only aspect of education I am cynical about is teacher education in the USA. The problem is to get the published results of large-scale assessments into the teacher education system. There are ways to build a programme to make sure that this does take place, and I assume that is what the Swedes are going to do.'

Dr Silvester responded: 'We have to be realistic about what large-scale assessment can and cannot do. It can measure attainment, it can feed some of that information out to people who want to know about this. It can analyse results, in the way that has been described. So we can feed information to teachers about what children are doing at different stages. In other words, we could say what performance should be on a number of tasks. But I think one has to look at other methods to examine the totality of the schools as an organization or a system and must not expect national monitoring to answer those questions, because one is talking about things like quality of teaching, resources, accommodation and the curricular structure. And there is no way that national monitoring can pick up those very tenuous things. I am asking for more people, who could pick up those things, to go into schools and get a total picture of what goes on in those schools. We have to be realistic about the strengths and weaknesses of different systems.'

Dr Sandifer made some comments about some other uses of data in relation to identifying non-effective schools: this is done using certain variables as a means of classifying schools or grouping them into categories, where they have similar characteristics as far as student population, resources availability, and other factors related to student achievement, are concerned. Data can provide a means of stimulating discussion within a school or of doing some internal examination of what is going on. Schools can be grouped into broad categories, so that a school can look at its performance in relation to other schools similarly situated — school X, that has a 90 per cent minority, is outperforming school Y, with the same essential population and resources available. There we try to have them look at themselves and find out why that difference exists. We can encourage them to ask "what is being done in the other school that stimulates achievement that is not happening in our own school?" It is not a question of this being an indicator of a good school, but of looking at themselves and avoiding negative reactions. Looking at the results, one does not say: 'We have a 90 per cent minority population, we do not have the resources', but there is another group of schools just like ours and they are doing more for the students than we are.'

The chairman, Professor Aurin formulated the next question: 'What are the desirable pedagogical effects of large-scale assessments at the state or national level? What are the directions of those effects, which are connected to risks, problems or possibly misunderstandings?'

Dr Burstall doubted that large-scale assessments were planned in this way: 'The desirable effects I would not describe as 'pedagogical'. The desirable effects are on the children. The name of the game is to improve children's standards of performance. The pedagogical effects might be a secondary by-product, not something the assessment has set out to do. Obviously, one hopes that with a good assessment and a good curriculum in place, these will result an improvement in the quality of instruction.'

Professor Aurin asked if there were large-scale assessments corresponding to reform activities, like environmental education, ecological education, civic education or computer education.

Dr Wijnstra answered: 'One must ask, what the primary goal of education in school is. Is it to develop skills or to give students the opportunity to get acquainted with certain activities which are going on and they should know of? These types of goals, expressive objectives, students are not supposed to learn completely. It is supposed to mean that every student gets acquainted with some of these activities, and some of the topics you addressed lie in this direction. For us, the focus of assessment should be on the skill level of the student or on the teacher, who develops the lesson, as well as the quality of the lesson.'

Dr Sandifer reported from the US side: 'I do not think there is any trend in the USA to move beyond Mathematics and Reading, Science and Social Studies. There is a little bit of interest in Civics. But some of the other topics are probably not addressed at all.'

Professor Thomas addressed some concerns: 'I am not a methodologist, but the experience of the last two days has pointed to the fact that we should be a little less ambitious about what can really be measured by assessment programmes. So I am not sure if we should include Civics, Arts and Music, the whole set of important, but not skill-oriented tasks of the school, in such an assessment programme. This could be done by means of other techniques, and other diagnostic measures, but not by means of large-scale assessment.'

Dr Silvester added for the UK: 'There will be guidelines only, and there will be no national monitoring.' The decision in the UK not to attempt the latter was probably due to lack of resources, lack of the ability to measure, Mr Forbes added.

Methodological Aspects

12 Using Item Response Models in Educational Assessments

Ronald K. Hambleton and H. Jane Rogers

The educational accountability movement, which has been important in the USA for the past 20 years, had led to profound changes in the scope and direction of educational testing. Included in these changes have been: (1) criterion-referenced testing (Hambleton, in press; Popham, 1978), (2) matrix-sampling (Shoemaker, 1973; Shoemaker and Shoemaker, 1981) and (3) item response theory (Hambleton and Swaminathan, 1985; Lord, 1980; Wright and Stone, 1979). Most educational assessment programmes, whether focused on providing group or individual information, or both, have used criterion-referenced testing methods – goals and objectives are developed and items are written to measure them. Score information is reported in relation to the goals and objectives. The concept of matrix-sampling, which was introduced by Lord (1962), has also been popular in large-scale assessments such as the National Assessments of Educational Progress (NAEP) and the California Assessment Program (CAP) (Pandey and Carlson, 1983). This technique has contributed to large-scale assessment programmes by permitting broad coverage of content without burdening examinees with overly long tests.

The potential of item response theory (IRT) for solving a number of technical problems associated with educational assessment programmes would appear to be substantial too in view of the many other promising applications of the theory (see e.g. Hambleton, 1983; Hambleton and Swaminathan, 1985; Lord, 1980; Messick, Beaton and Lord, 1983). But this third major psychometric advance in the past 20 years has been far more controversial than the other two advances (see e.g. Nuttall, 1983). Part of the problem is that the advantages derived from an IRT model, which will be described in the next section, cannot be achieved when the fit between an item response model and the test data of interest is less than adequate. And unfortunately, the IRT models are based upon strong assumptions. In view of the comprehensive content coverage, the diversity of item formats, and variability of item statistics found in many assessment programmes, concerns about model data are justified.

The principal purpose of the research reported in this chapter was to investigate the fit of the one-, two- and three-parameter logistic models to the test results obtained from the administration of several forms of the mathematics tests used in the NAEP. Details on this national assessment programme were described in the section by Dr Archie Lapointe (p. 7). The intent of the research was to demonstrate several practical approaches to addressing IRT model fit. One of the approaches has not been previously reported elsewhere. Other recent papers that share the same general orientation include Dorans and Kingston (1985), Hambleton and Murray (1983), Hambleton, Murray and Simon (1982) and Kingston and Dorans (1985). Other purposes of the work described here included the investigation of bias or differential functioning of test items and a discussion of test-score reporting based upon item response theory concepts and features. In the next section, a brief introduction to item response theory is provided.

Item response theory

In a few words, item response theory (IRT) postulates that (1) examinee test performance can be predicted (or explained) by a set of factors called traits, latent traits or abilities; and (2) the relationship between examinee item performance and the set of traits assumed to be influencing item performance can be described by a monotonically increasing function called an **item characteristic function**. This function specifies that examinees with higher scores on the traits have higher expected probabilities for answering the item correctly than with lower scores on the traits. In practice, it is common for users of item response theory to assume that there is one dominant factor or ability that explains performance. For example, the ability might be called 'mathematics competence' if the test measures mathematics skills. However, what a test actually measures needs to be substantiated with a construct validity investigation.

In the one-trait, one-dimensional model the item characteristic function is called an **item characteristic curve** (ICC), and it provides the probability of examinees answering an item correctly for examinees at different points on the ability scale. In addition, it is common to assume that item characteristic curves are described by one, two or three parameters. In a three-parameter model item characteristics refer (generally) to difficulty, discriminating power and the likelihood that low-performing examinees will guess the correct answers to questions (for an expanded discussion, see Hambleton and Swaminathan, 1985).

In any successful application of item response theory, parameter estimates are obtained to describe the test items, ability estimates are obtained to describe the performance of examinees and evidence is collected to show that the chosen item response model – at least to an adequate degree – fits the test data-set. In large-scale assessments, such as NAEP, there is usually no interest in the individual scores for reporting purposes, though examinee scores can often be produced as part of the overall data analysis (see, for example, Bock and Mislevy, 1987). When the fit between the chosen IRT model and the data is poor, item and person–parameter estimates have limited usefulness (Hambleton and Swaminathan, 1985).

Item response theory (or 'latent trait theory', or 'item characteristic curve theory', as it is sometimes called) has become a popular topic for research in the testing and measurement field. There have been numerous published research studies, conference presentations and diverse applications of the theory in the past several years (see e.g. Hambleton, 1983; Hambleton, 1989; Lord, 1980). Interest in item response models from testing agencies stems from two desirable features that are obtained when an item response model fits a test data-set: descriptors of items (item statistics) are not dependent upon the choice of examinees from the population of examinees for whom the items are intended, and the expected examinee ability scores do not depend upon the particular choice of items from the total pool of items to which the item response model has been applied. Invariant item and examinee ability parameters, as they are called, are of immense value to measurement specialists for (at least) two reasons: (1) invariant item parameters are valued because they make it possible to build tests using item statistics without regard to the particular sample of examinees used in obtaining the item statistics, and (2) invariant ability estimates permit examinees to be placed on a common ability scale, although they may not have taken the same set of items.

Today item response theory is being used by many of the large test publishers, credentialing agencies, state departments of education and industrial and professional organizations. It is used to construct both norm-referenced and criterion-referenced tests, to investigate item bias, to equate tests and to report test-score information. In fact the various applications have been so successful that discussions of item response theory have shifted from a consideration of its advantages and disadvantages in relation to classical test models to consideration of such matters as model selection, parameter estimation and the determination of model data fit.

Nevertheless, it would be misleading to convey the impression that issues and technology associated with item response theory are fully developed and without controversy. But, it appears safe to say that item response theory technology is more than adequate at this time to serve a variety of uses (see e.g. Lord, 1980), and there are several computer programs available to carry out item response theory analyses (see Hambleton and Swaminathan, 1985).

Assessing model data fit

With respect to the selection of an IRT model, our preference at this time is to recommend the use of the more general IRT models (two- and three-parameter), whenever sample sizes are large enough to provide proper item and person parameter estimates. With smaller samples, and when the fit is adequate, the one-parameter model may suffice. In large-scale assessments, however, sample sizes are normally very substantial. Also there are serious questions about the fit of the one-parameter model to assessment data (Messick, Beaton and Lord, 1983). For example, NAEP does very little fieldtesting of its items, and items are included in the tests because of their perceived importance, not because of their desirable statistical properties. Thus it is common to find test items which vary substantially in their discriminating power. Also items with widely different difficulty levels are often used – recall that some of the same test items are given to students at ages nine, 13 and 17. Hard test items lead to more guessing. A psychometric model, such as the one-parameter model, that fails to account for item variability in discriminability and examinee propensity to guess is unlikely to fit examinee item performance data.

Regardless of the model or sample size, goodness-of-fit between any model of interest and the test data to which it is applied must be established prior to using any of the model parameter estimates. It seems especially appropriate to recommend that a *wide array* of investigations be carried out prior to judgementally determining the usefulness of a particular IRT model in a given situation. Certainly, ETS in the USA has invested large amounts of time in pursuing the applicability of logistic models to the NAEP data (see e.g. Beaton, 1988; Mislevy, 1988; Zwick, 1987). Assessing model fit is analogous to assessing test-score validity, though the research questions and analyses are quite different. A researcher does *not* prove a test is valid. Rather, evidence is collected to determine if the scores obtained from the test are consistent with the intended uses or interpretations. Likewise, IRT researchers attempt to determine the extent to which a model fits the test data, and the consequences of the misfit, which will always be present to some extent.

Statistical significance tests themselves have limitations that restrict their usefulness in model selection: the results of these significance tests are directly tied to sample size. Use small samples, and any model can probably fit the data; use very large samples and probably no model will appear to fit!

Some of the current thinking with respect to suggestions for assessing IRT model test data fit is as follows:

1. Investigate the adequacy of model assumptions with the test data.

2. Assume the IRT model of interest is valid, and check the invariance properties of item and examinee statistics (e.g. check that the values of the item parameters do not depend upon the particular sample of examinees).

3. Conduct several prediction studies (e.g. residual analyses that consider the match between the estimated parameters and the actual data) and try to determine the consequences in practice of less than perfect model data fit.

IRT is *not* a magic wand to wave over a test data-set to correct all of the shortcomings. However, when it can be shown that the chosen model fits the type of test data available, the model can help to solve a variety of measurement problems. In the remainder of this section a number of goodness-of-fit analyses will be described. The analyses were carried out on several mathematics tests for nine- and 13-year-olds in the 1977–78 NAEP. Readers are referred to Hambleton (1989) for a longer discussion of goodness-of-fit studies with IRT models.

Description of the tests

Four NAEP test booklets from the 1977–78 assessment were selected for analysis:

9-year-olds
Booklet No. 1, 65 items, 2,495 examinees
Booklet No. 2, 75 items, 2,463 examinees

13-year-olds
Booklet No. 1, 58 items, 2,422 examinees
Booklet No. 2, 62 items, 2,433 examinees

Each booklet contained test items measuring various mathematical skills in the areas of definitions, story problems, geometry, measurement, and graphs and figures. The test items in the NAEP assessment were either multiple-choice or open-ended. Finally, these data sets were unusual (compared to the popular standardized achievement and aptitude tests used in the USA, in that the test items varied substantially both in their range of difficulty (0.02 to 0.98) and their range of item discrimination levels (-0.01 to 0.99). These ranges far exceed those normally found in achievement and aptitude tests. Because of the wide range of classical item discrimination indices and the high level of guessing due to the substantial number of difficult items, we expected that the three-parameter model would fit the test data substantially better than the other two more restrictive models. In our experience, we have found the review of classical item analysis results to be highly worth while as a first step in becoming familiar with the test data and making some initial predictions about the suitability of possible IRT models to fit the test data.

Assessment of dimensionality

This type of analysis is especially helpful in determining the viability of the unidimensionality assumption. Clearly, there was a dominant first factor, accounting for 17.4 per cent of the total test score variance. Also there appeared to be a weak second factor, though the second factor did not look very much different than the remaining factors. Certainly, there needs to be a more careful look at the possibility of a second factor; however assuming a single factor is not implausible or unreasonable with this test data. Similar results were obtained with the other three tests we analysed.

In NAEP Math Booklet No. 1 (13-year-olds) all but 11 of the 58 items had loadings of at least 0.30 on the first factor. Of the remaining 11 items, five items had values between 0.10 and 0.29. These results also lent support to the unidimensional assumption.

Other more advanced approaches to assessing unidimensionality are described by Hambleton (1989), along with analyses for addressing violations in the test data of other model assumptions.

Residual analyses

Each analysis in this part of the research began with the calculation of 'residuals'. Raw residuals are comparisons of predicted performance results with actual performance results. To calculate residuals, an item response model is first chosen. For this study, the one-, two- and three-parameter logistic test models were used in separate but identical analyses. Next, item and ability parameter estimates were obtained using the LOGIST computer program (Wood, Wingersky and Lord, 1976). To find the actual performance results, an examinee is placed in an ability category based on his/her estimated ability level. For this investigation, ability categories were chosen that divided the ability scale between -3.0 and 3.0 into 12 equal intervals. Ability estimates that fell beyond these maximum and minimum ability levels were deleted from the analysis. In every investigation, this was usually less than 10 cases. For each of the 12 ability categories, the average observed performance (P_{ij}) for an item i in ability category j was found. For example, if 10 of 50 examinees in ability category j answered item i correctly, then P_{ij} would be 0.2. The process was repeated for each ability category ($j = 1, 1, ..., 12$) and for each item ($i = 1, 2, ..., n$) in a test booklet.

Using the midpoint of each ability category (i.e. -2.75, -2.25, . . ., -0.25, +0.25, . . ., +2.75) as the average ability level for that group of examinees, the expected performance (P_{ij}) for item i in ability category j was found in the usual way:

$$\hat{P}_{ij}^{(3)} = c_i + (1 - c_i) \frac{\exp\left\{1.7a_i\,(\theta_j - b)\right\}}{1 + \exp\left\{1.7a_i\,(\theta_j - b_i)\right\}}$$

for the three-parameter logistic model:

$$\hat{P}_{ij}^{(2)} = \frac{\exp\left\{1.7a_i\,(\theta_j - b_i)\right\}}{1 + \exp\left\{1.7a_i\,(\theta_j - b_i)\right\}}$$

for the two-parameter logistic model, and:

$$\hat{P}_{ij}^{(1)} = \frac{\exp\left\{(\theta_j - b_i)\right\}}{1 + \exp\left\{(\theta_j - b_i)\right\}}$$

for the one-parameter logistic model. In these equations a_i, b_i and c_i are the item parameter estimates for item discrimination, item difficulty and pseudo-chance level respectively, obtained from LOGIST (Lord, 1980) and θ_j is the midpoint of the jth ability category.

The raw residual (R_{ij}) for item i in ability category j is:

$$R_{ij} = P_{ij} - \hat{P}_{ij}$$

This difference is an index of the degree of misfit between the test data and the expected item performance, based on the chosen model. Large positive raw residuals indicate that examinees are performing considerably better on an item than is predicted by the item response model. Large negative raw residuals reveal that the model is predicting a much higher performance level by the examinees on the item than is actually observed. Finally, evidence of sufficient model data fit occurs when the residuals are small and there are no obvious paterns in the residuals across ability levels.

These raw residuals are transformed to standardized residuals (SR_{ij}) by dividing R_{ij} by the sampling error associated with the average expected performance level in an ability category; that is:

$$SR_{ij} = \frac{P_{ij} - \hat{P}_{ij}}{\sqrt{\dfrac{\{P_{ij}(1 - P_{ij})\}}{N_j}}}$$

where N_j is the number of examinees in ability category j.

Raw and standardized residuals differ in several ways. Raw residuals are simpler to calculate and easier to interpret than standardized residuals. On the other hand, standardized residuals take into account the sampling errors associated with each P_{ij}. When N_j is small, other things being equal, big differences between actual and expected differences should be obtained for the differences to be taken as an indication of model test data misfit because the residuals are very unstable. For example, suppose two different ability categories for an item i have the same computed raw residual (0.3 – 0.2), but differ in their examinee sample sizes (10 vs 100). Using the raw residuals, it appears that model data fit is the same in both examinee samples. But the greater number of examinees (N_j) produces a smaller standard error of expected performance level because a more accurate estimate is possible. Then the corresponding standardized residuals are 0.79 and 2.5. Clearly, the two statistics seem to give a very different picture of model data fit and the standardized residuals are more useful. Therefore, standardized residuals are usually emphasized in our goodness-of-fit work.

Table 12.1 highlights the distributions of standardized residuals obtained after fitting the one-, two- and three-parameter logistic models and the distributions of standardized residuals obtained with simulated test data to fit the models. These results were obtained with Maths Booklet No. 1 for the 13 year-old

Table 12.1: Summary of absolute-valued standardized residuals with three logistic test models applied to NAEP maths test data and simulated data*

Logistic model	Descriptive Statistics mean	SD	Percentage absolute-valued standardized residuals** 0 to 1	1 to 2	2 to 3	over 3
		NAEP				
1	1.90	2.54	40.2	25.4	14.5	19.8
2	0.96	1.20	60.1	30.3	7.0	2.6
3	0.87	1.08	69.3	24.3	4.7	1.7
		Simulated				
1	0.76	0.92	72.6	24.3	2.9	0.3
2	0.75	0.91	72.8	23.1	3.7	0.3
3	0.72	0.90	73.6	23.4	2.3	0.7

* Booklet No. 1, 13-year-olds, 1977–78.
** Total number of residuals is 696.

sample. A comparison of distributions shows clearly that the distribution of standardized residuals obtained from fitting the three-parameter model looks very much like the distribution obtained with simulated data that fits the three-parameter model. In contrast, the one-parameter model appears to provide a very poor fit to the test data. The two-parameter model provided a substantially better fit to the test data than the one-parameter model, but not as good as the three-parameter model. In Figures 12.1–12.3, a comparison is made between the actual distribution of standardized residuals and the distribution that would be expected if the model fit the test data. The closer the two distributions, the better.

Table 12.2 provides a comparison of the residuals and standardized residuals for the one-, two- and three-parameter models obtained at six ability levels. Again, the results are clear: the three-parameter model provided a substantially better fit to the test data than the other two models.

Figure 12.4 provides a comparison of some typical standardized residual plots obtained from applying the one- and three-parameter models. Figure 12.4 (a) highlights the problem of fitting a one-parameter ICC to a low-discriminating test item. The fitted curve is too steep to account for the test data at the bottom and top of the ability scale. With a three-parameter ICC, the item discrimination parameter can be set low, to produce a flatter ICC to fit the available test data. Figure 12.4 (b) highlights the reverse problem of attempting to fit a one-parameter ICC to a (relatively) high-discriminating test item. The three-parameter ICC can do the job, one-parameter ICCs cannot. Figure 12.4 (c) highlights the case where both models can do the job of accounting for the test data. In the data analysed in this investigation many of the standardized residual plots looked like Figure 12.4 (a) and (b). Clearly, the three-parameter model was needed to account accurately for the test data.

Research hypotheses

The residual analysis results in the last section are valuable for evaluating model data fit, but additional insights can be gained from supplemental analyses of the residuals. Our preliminary studies showed a relationship between the one-parameter model absolute-valued standardized residuals and classical item difficulties (see Figure 12.5). The outstanding features were the large size of the residuals and the tendency for the most difficult items to have the highest residuals. Possibly this latter problem was due to the guessing behaviour of examinees on the more difficult test items. In a plot of three-parameter model residuals and classical item difficulty estimates (see Figure 12.6) the standardized residuals were substantially smaller, *and* it appeared that by estimating item pseudo-chance level parameters, the tendency for the highest residuals to be obtained with the most difficult items was removed.

Figure 12.7 provides the results of a second analysis: a plot of one-parameter model, absolute-valued standardized residuals and classical item biserial correlations for four of the Math Booklets combined. A strong curvilinear relationship is evident. Items with relatively high- or low-biserial correlations had the highest standardized residuals. Figure 12.8 provides the same plot as

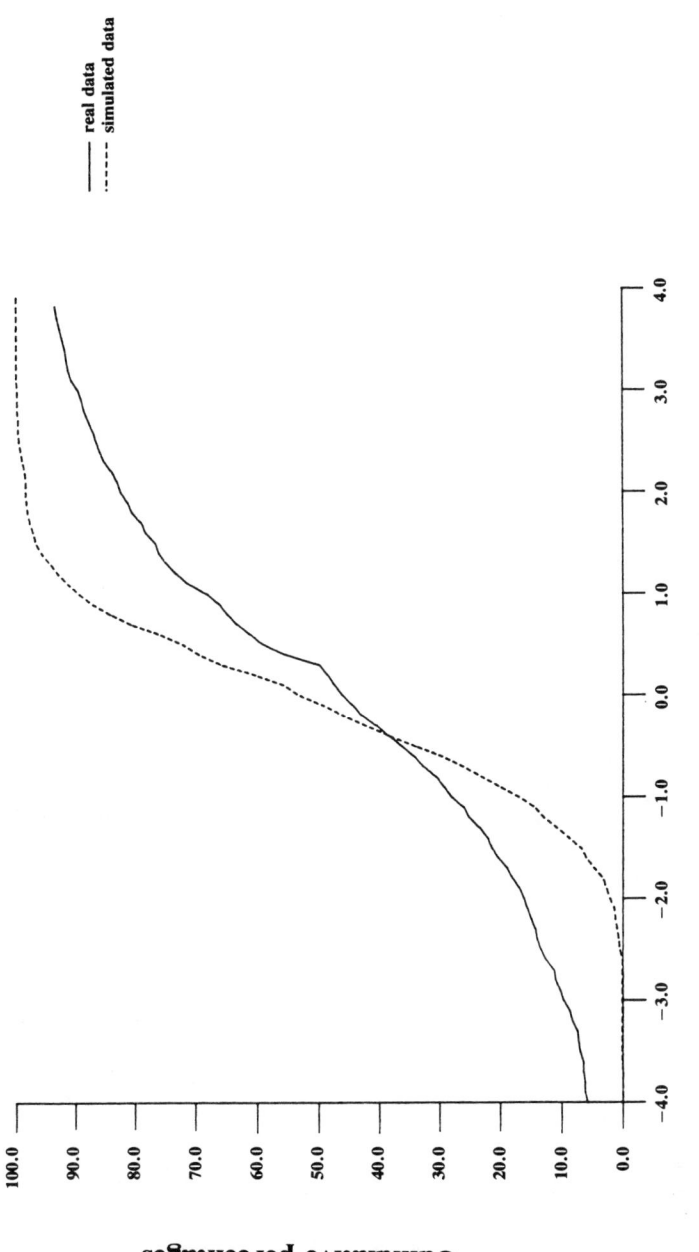

Figure 12.1: Comparison of the distributions of standardized residuals for the one-parameter model fitted to the NAEP Mathematics test items (Booklet No. 1, 13 Year Olds, 1977–78) and to simulated test data.

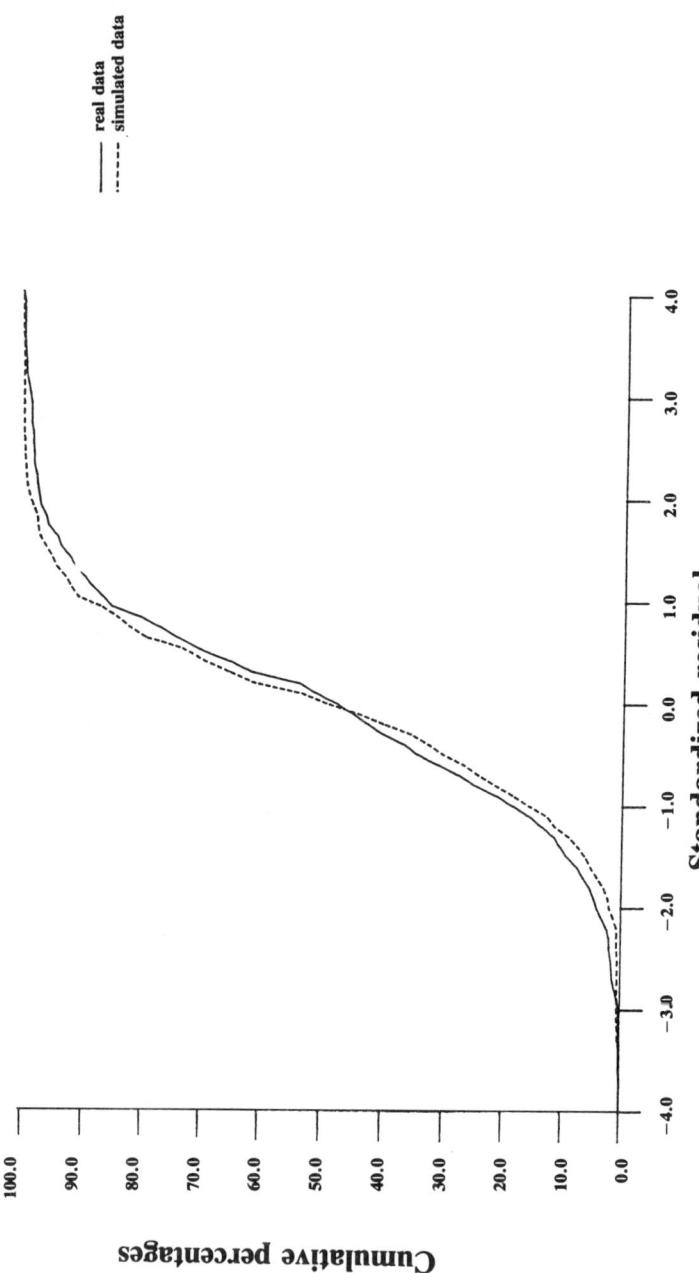

Figure 12.2: Comparisons of the distributions of standardized residuals for the two-parameter model fitted to the NAEP Mathematics test items (Booklet No. 1, 13 Year Olds, 1977–78) and to simulated test data.

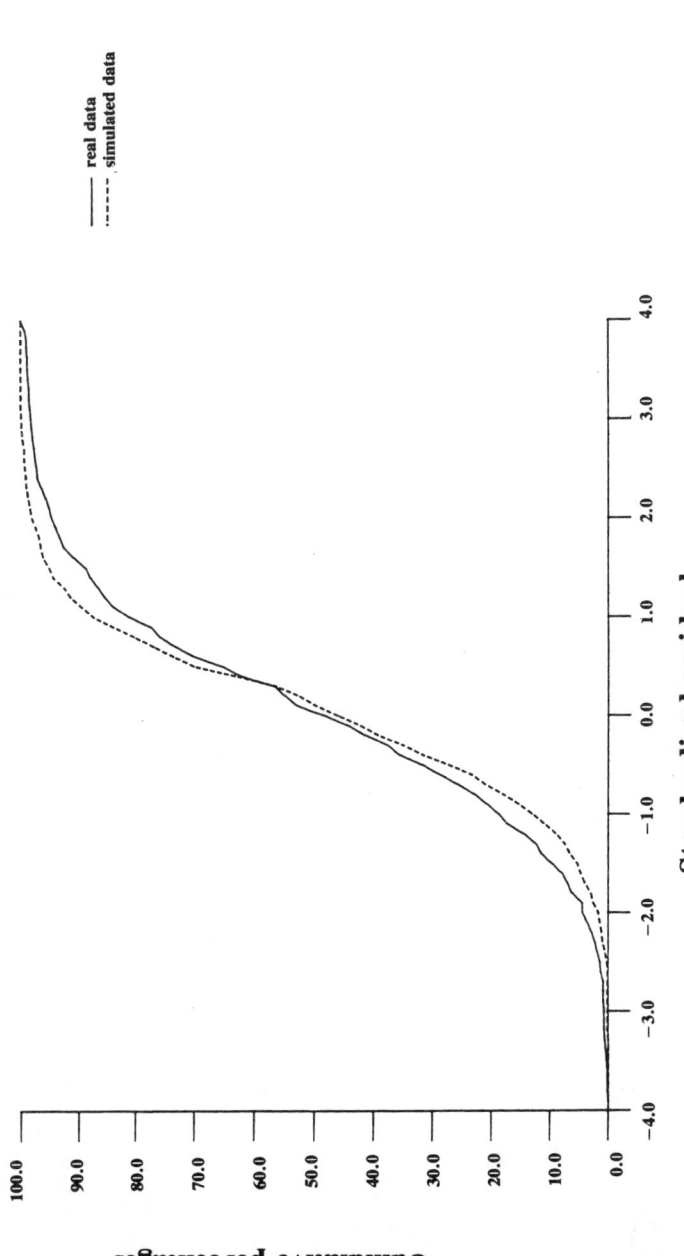

real data
simulated data

Figure 12.3: Comparisons of the distributions of standardized residuals for the three-parameter model fitted to the NAEP Mathematics test items (Booklet No. 1, 13 Year Olds, 1977–78) and to simulated test data.

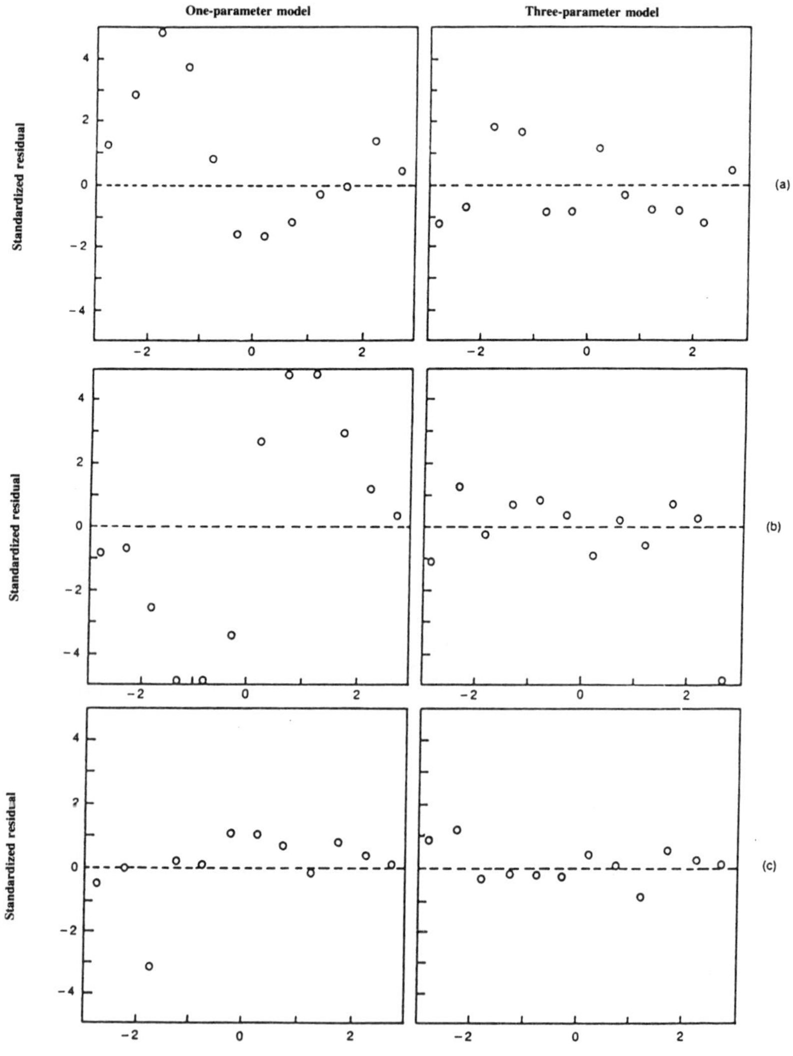

Figure 12.4: Comparison of one- and three-parameter model standardized residual plots for three test items: (a) low, (b) high, and (c) moderate point-biserial correlations (NAEP Mathematics test items, 13 Year Olds, 1977–78).

Figure 12.7, except that three-parameter model, standardized residuals were used. The curvilinear relationship disappeared. Substantially better fits were obtained when variations in discriminating powers of test items were accounted for by the three-parameter logistic model.

These analyses were encouraging because they provided several insights into possible reasons for item misfit. It appeared that the one-parameter model did not fit the data well because the model was unable to account for variation in the discriminating power of test items and/or the guessing behaviour of examinees on the more difficult test items. Two hypotheses were investigated:

1. Is there a relationship between the size of the standardized residuals and the content of the items in the test? (If there is, the assumption of unidimensionality is possibly violated in the test items.)

2. Is there a relationship between the size of the standardized residuals and items classified by difficulty and format? (If there is, the results would suggest that the model could be revised to provide a better fit to the test data.)

Results relating to hypothesis one and two are shown in Tables 12.3 and 12.4 respectively. A graphical display of the results for hypothesis two is given in Figure 12.9.

For hypothesis 1, the pattern of standardized residuals was the same across content categories. Misfit statistics for both the one- and three-parameter models were clearly unrelated to the content of the test items. Of course, the standardized residuals are substantially smaller for the three-parameter model because the fit was considerably better. For hypothesis 2, the hard multiple-choice items had substantially larger absolute-valued standardized residuals when fit by the one-parameter model than easy items in either format, or hard items in an open-ended format. This result suggests that the problem with the one-parameter model was due to a failure to account for guessing behaviour (NB: the fit was better for hard open-ended items where guessing behaviour was not operative). The differences between the average one-parameter and three-parameter model, absolute-valued standardized residuals, except for the hard multiple-choice test items, were probably due to the difference in the way item-discriminating power was handled. With the hard multiple-choice test items, the difference was due to a failure to account for both item-discriminating power and examinee guessing behaviour in the one-parameter model. There were no relationships among item difficulty level, item format and absolute-valued standardized residuals obtained from fitting the three-parameter model.

In summary, the results of our hypothesis testing showed clearly that the test items in the content categories we worked with were not in any way being fit better or worse by the item response models, and failure to consider examinee guessing behaviour and variation in item discriminating power resulted in the one-parameter model providing substantially poorer fits to the various data-sets than the three-parameter model.

Table 12.2: Summary of standardized residuals with the one-, two- and three-parameter logistic models fitted to NAEP mathematics test items*

Statistic	Logistic model	Ability level						
		−2.75	−1.75	−0.75	0.75	1.75	2.75	Total
Number of examinees	1	14	120	353	312	123	16	938
	2	9	101	364	334	103	17	928
	3	22	118	326	369	94	10	939
Average standardized residual	1	0.58	0.74	0.49	−0.14	0.09	0.03	0.25
	2	0.22	0.49	0.13	−0.14	0.34	0.24	0.16
	3	0.15	0.10	0.10	−0.11	0.21	0.12	0.05
Average (absolute-valued) standardized residual	1	1.62	3.07	2.18	1.98	1.75	0.97	1.90
	2	0.82	1.24	0.78	0.90	1.01	0.83	0.96
	3	1.11	0.88	0.82	0.90	0.97	0.57	0.87

* Test Booklet No. 1, 13-year-olds, 1977–78.

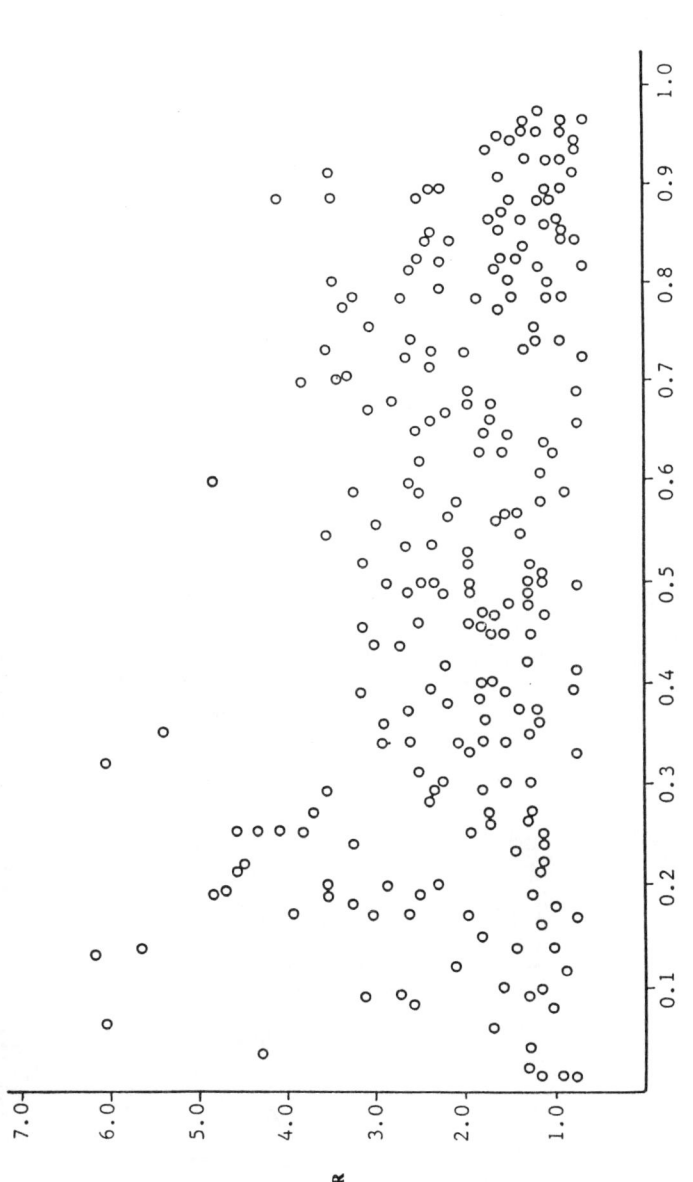

Figure 12.5: Scatterplot of one-parameter absolute-valued standardized residuals and classical item difficulties (p-values) for NAEP Mathematics test items (Math Booklets No. 1 and 2, 9 and 13 Year Olds, 1977–78).

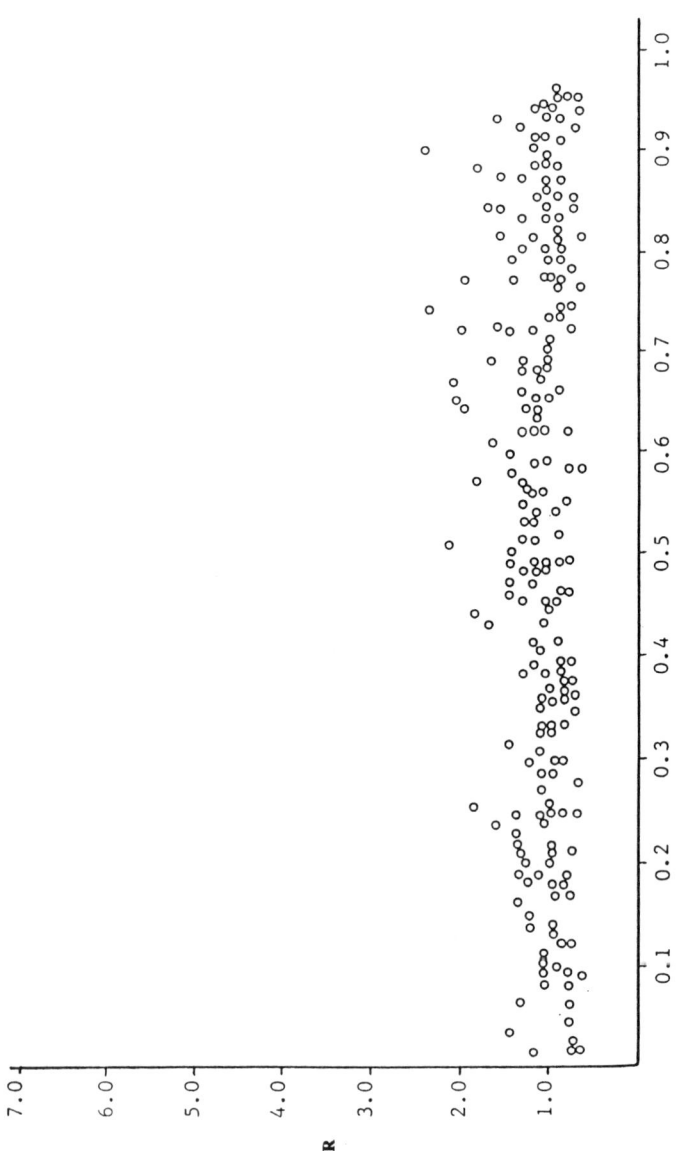

Figure 12.6: Scatterplot of three-parameter absolute-valued standardized residuals and classical item difficulties (p-values) for NAEP Mathematics test items (Math Booklets No. 1 and 2, 9 and 13 Year Olds, 1977–78).

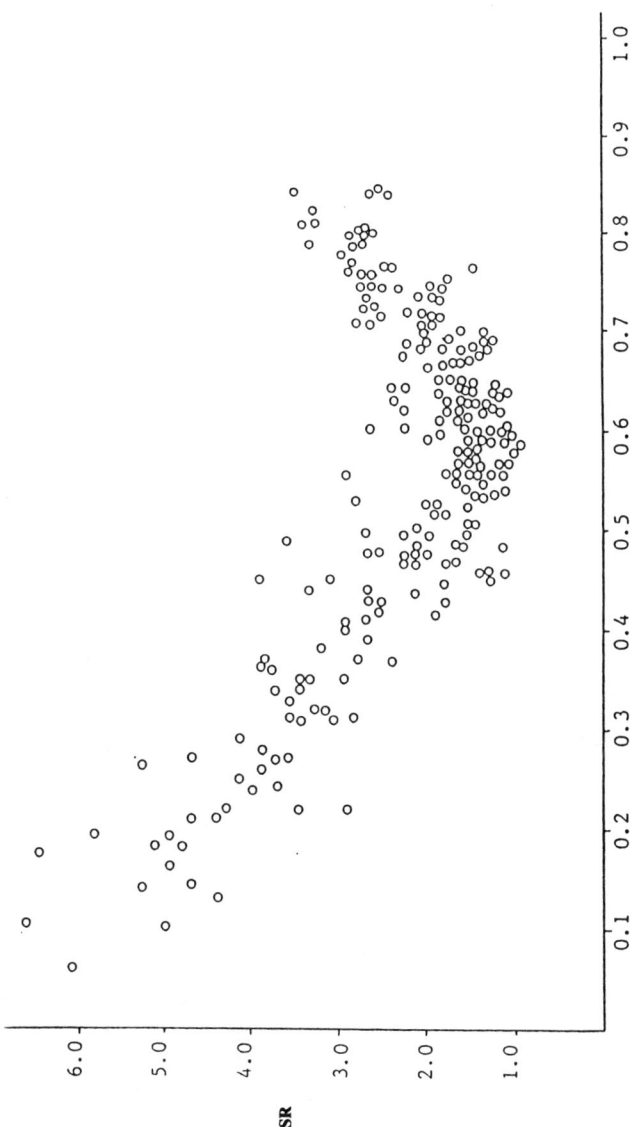

Figure 12.7: Scatterplot of one-parameter absolute-valued standardized residuals and item biserial correlations for NAEP Mathematics test items (Math Booklets No. 1 and 2, 9 and 13 Year Olds, 1977–78).

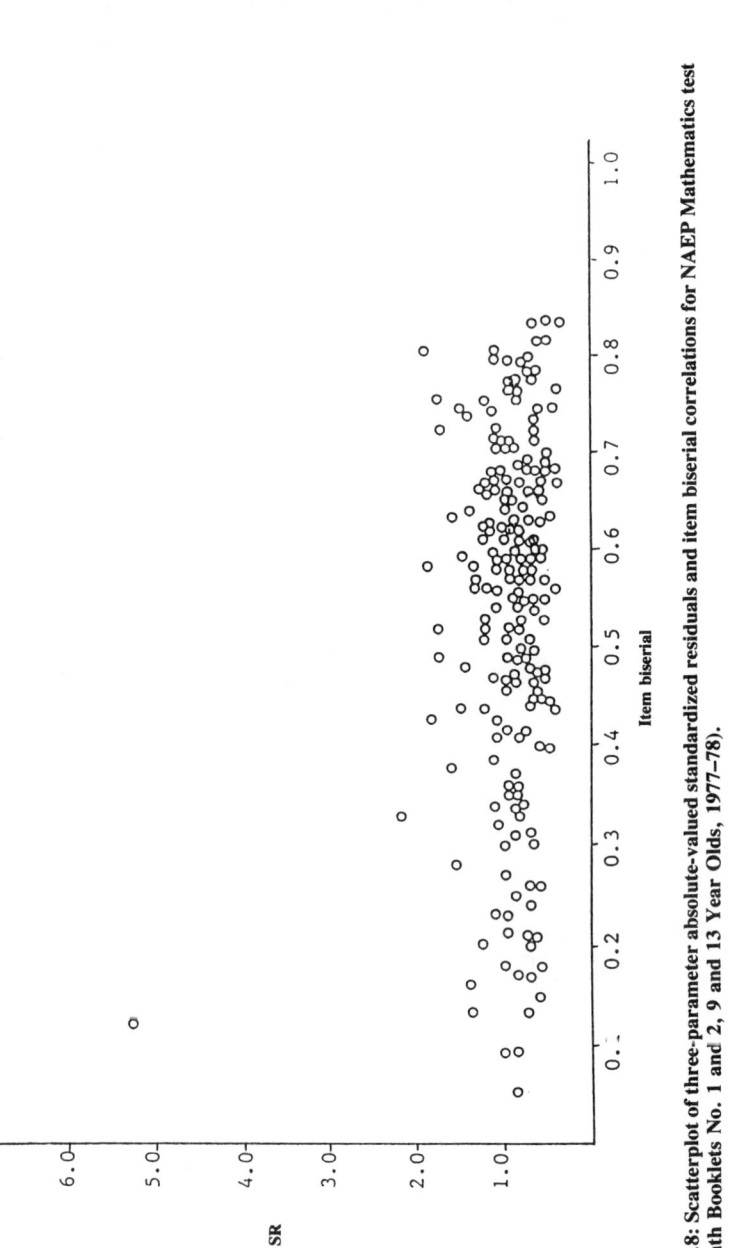

Figure 12.8: Scatterplot of three-parameter absolute-valued standardized residuals and item biserial correlations for NAEP Mathematics test items (Math Booklets No. 1 and 2, 9 and 13 Year Olds, 1977–78).

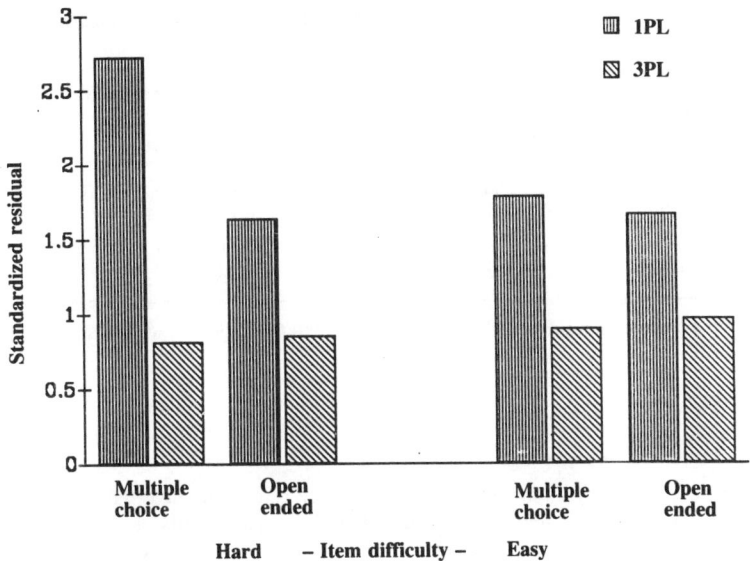

Figure 12.9: Absolute-valued standardized residuals with the one- and three-parameter models for NAEP Mathematics test items organized by format and difficulty (Math Booklets No. 1 and 2, 9 and 13 Year Olds, 1977–78).

Table 12.3: Association between absolute-valued standardized residuals and NAEP item content classification*

Content category	No. of items	One-parameter model SR (≤1.0) (n = 48)	One-parameter model SR (>1.0) (n = 212)	Three-parameter model SR (≤1.0) (n = 197)	Three-parameter model SR (>1.0) (n = 63)
Story problems	52	21.2	78.8	82.7	17.3
Geometry	48	22.9	77.1	75.0	25.0
Definitions	42	16.7	83.3	78.6	21.4
Calculations	83	15.7	84.3	69.9	30.1
Measurement	17	11.8	88.8	82.4	17.6
Graphs and figures	18	22.2	77.8	72.2	27.8
		$\chi^2 = 2.08$		$\chi^2 = 3.65$	
		d.f. = 5 p = 0.838		d.f. = 5 p = 0.602	

* Test booklets Nos 1 and 2, 260 items, nine- and 13-year-olds, 1977–78.

Table 12.4: Descriptive statistical analysis of the absolute-valued standardized residuals*

Difficulty level	Format	No. of items	One-parameter results X̄	One-parameter results SD	Three-parameter results X̄	Three-parameter results SD
Hard	Multiple choice	70	2.73	1.55	0.82	0.23
(p < 0.5)	Open ended	54	1.64	0.81	0.86	0.28
Easy	Multiple choice	70	1.79	1.10	0.90	0.64
(p ≥ 0.5)	Open ended	66	1.67	0.72	0.97	0.38

* Test mathematics booklets Nos 1 and 2, 260 items, nine- and 13-year-olds, 1977–78.

Bias analysis

One of the most important applications of IRT is in the investigation of item bias or differential item functioning (DIF). IRT is particularly useful in studying bias and, indeed, is considered the theoretically preferred approach (Shepard, Camilli and Averill, 1981; Ironson, 1983; Shepard, Camilli and Williams, 1984) because of its close connection to the accepted definition of bias. This definition states that an item is biased if examinees of the same ability but from different sub-groups do not have the same probability of getting the item right. Thus the study of item bias within an IRT framework is a matter of comparing the item characteristic curves (ICCs) for the two groups. Since the ICCs represent the probability of success on an item at each level of ability, any difference between the ICCS for the two groups indicates a difference in the probability of a correct answer for examinees at the same ability.

Because of its natural connection to the definition of bias, IRT has a major advantage over classical methods for detecting differential item functioning. IRT DIF methods explicitly control for ability before the groups are compared. Classical methods, such as the transformed item difficulty method and the analysis of variance method, do not take into account group differences in ability, which can become confounded with item difficulty or discrimination to produce the appearance of DIF when none is present (Rudner, Getson and Knight, 1980). Chi-square approaches control for ability to some extent by comparing groups at different score levels, but this approach is generally considered an approximation to the IRT approach (Shepard, Camilli and Williams, 1984).

Another advantage of IRT methods is that they are sensitive to both uniform and non-uniform DIF. Uniform DIF occurs when the difference in the probabilities of a correct response for the two groups is more or less constant across the ability range. Non-uniform DIF occurs when the difference in the probabilities is not the same at different levels of ability. In simple terms, uniform DIF occurs when an item is differentially difficult for the two groups; non-uniform DIF occurs when an item is differentially discriminating for the two groups. Classical DIF methods and methods such as the Mantel-Haenszel method are not sensitive to non-uniform DIF.

A number of statistics have been proposed for quantifying the difference between ICCs. Most often, the area between the curves is calculated and used as an index of DIF. Variations on the area statistic include the signed area, the sum of squared differences between ICCs and the signed sum of squared differences. Signed statistics are obtained by attaching a positive or negative sign to each of the component areas or differences before summing, according to which group has the higher probability of success in that interval.

The purpose of this part of our investigation was to highlight the application of IRT methods in the investigation of item bias through an analysis of test data for blacks and whites taking the NAEP tests. The methods more than the results seem pertinent here and therefore the methods will be emphasized.

Method

The test data used for this part of the investigation were the responses of the 2,422 13-year-olds to NAEP Math Booklet 1. This data-set contained the responses of 1,906 white students and 339 black students. A sample of 336 whites was randomly drawn, so that the sample sizes for the two groups were approximately equal. In this way, the standard errors associated with item statistics obtained in the two groups would be approximately equal, a feature which facilitates interpretations of the item statistics.

The IRT DIF method used was the area method described previously. In implementing the area method, the first step is to choose an IRT model. In this study the three-parameter model was used because it had been shown earlier to fit the data well; however, if model data fit had been shown earlier for the one- or two-parameter model, the more parsimonious model would have been chosen.

The three-parameter model was fitted separately for blacks and whites. Parameter estimation was carried out using the LOGIST program (Wood, Wingersky and Lord, 1976). Because of the smallness of the samples, it was expected that problems would arise in estimating parameters. To circumvent this problem, an IRT model was fitted to the data for all 2,422 students, and the theta values and c-parameters obtained from this analysis were used as known values for the separate group analyses.

After parameter estimates were obtained for the two groups, each set was rescaled. This step is necessary because the scale for item and ability parameters is not unique, hence parameter estimates obtained for the one group are not necessarily on the same scale as those for the other group. Re-scaling was done by calculating the mean and standard deviation of the b-parameters in each group, then scaling each set of b-parameter estimates, so that its mean was zero and its standard deviation was 1. In calculating the mean and standard deviation, items with extreme parameter estimates should not be included since these values are usually the result of estimation problems. In this study, items with b-values exceeding ± 3.5 or a-values less than 0.01 were excluded from the calculations. Items excluded from one set of parameters for this step should also be excluded from the other set, so that the means and standard deviations of the b-parameters for the two groups are based on a common set of items. All b-parameters in each set were then scaled by subtracting the mean and dividing by the standard deviation. Once the b-values were scaled, the a-values and theta values were scaled correspondingly: a-values were scaled by multiplying by the standard deviation of the b-values; theta values were scaled in the same way that the b-values were scaled (see e.g. Hambleton and Swaminathan, 1985).

After parameter estimates were placed on the same scale, the area between the ICCs was obtained. In calculating the area, a decision must be made regarding the ability range of interest. In our work, the area was calculated first over the interval (lower group mean - 3 standard deviations, upper group mean + 3 standard deviations) and then over the narrower interval (lower group mean ± 2 standard deviations). This was done primarily to demonstrate the effect of the choice of ability interval. In calculating the area over the wider interval, it can be expected that some items will show differences in ICCs that do not reflect differential performance between groups in the region where most examinees fall. It may be of greater interest to focus on the region of the ability scale where the effect of DIF is most serious – i.e. the region containing most of the minority examinees. For this reason, the area was calculated over the narrower interval centred at the mean of the minority group.

To calculate the area a numerical method was used: the ability scale between the specified limits was divided into narrow intervals (0.01 units), the p-value difference at the mid-point of each interval was calculated and multiplied by the width of the interval, then these small rectangular areas were summed over all intervals.

After the area statistics were calculated, a criterion was needed to determine which values were large enough to warrant flagging of the item. One disadvantage of IRT DIF statistics, such as the area statistic, is that they do not have a known sampling distribution under the null-hypothesis that bias or differential item functioning is not present. A way of overcoming this problem is to obtain a 'baseline' distribution of the statistic by carrying out an analysis for two groups for which it is known that there is no DIF (Rogers and Hambleton, in press). Given that there is no DIF, the values obtained for the DIF statistic are due to sampling fluctuations. From this comparison, then, the sampling distribution for the DIF statistic can be estimated. The largest value of this distribution or the 95th percentile can then be used as the 'cut-off' value for the statistic in determining which items need closer review.

One means of obtaining groups for which there is no DIF is to randomly select two samples from one of the groups of interest. This approach is feasible only if the sample sizes are sufficiently large. Another problem is that the samples obtained do not reflect differences in the ability distributions of the two groups of interest. Since these differences may affect the estimation of IRT parameters, they should be preserved. A way of overcoming this problem is to simulate data with the same ability distributions as the real data, and with the same item parameters for each group, so that there is no DIF. In this study data were simulated for two groups using the ability and item parameter estimates obtained in the total group analysis. Hence the two groups simulated reflected as closely as possible the ability distributions and the item characteristics of the real data. Area statistics were then obtained for each item, with the area calculated over both the full ability scale (lower group mean - 3 s.d., upper group mean + 3 s.d.) and the narrower region (lower group mean ± 2 s.d.). The distribution of area statistics for each of the two ability regions was constructed, and the largest value obtained in each case was used in the corresponding analysis of the real data (for more details see Rogers and Hambleton, in press).

Results

When the area was calculated over the wider ability interval (- 2.14, 2.50), ten items were flagged. When the area was calculated over the narrower interval (-1.5, 1.0), seven items were flagged. ICCs for the first four test items flagged in the narrow interval are presented in Figures 12.10–12.13. One of the seven, item 36, was flagged because of parameter estimation problems rather than DIF, hence it was not considered in this analysis.

Three items (items 11, 12 and 35) were flagged in both intervals. Items 11 and 35 (not shown) appeared to be exhibiting uniform DIF; item 12 appeared to be exhibiting non-uniform DIF.

Six of the ten items flagged over the full range were not flagged in the narrower interval. When the ICCs for these items were examined, it was seen that these items either had ICCs which diverged only in the upper region of the ability scale, or ICCs which crossed in the narrower interval. Thus, for these items, the area between ICCs was small within the ability region of interest (see, for example, Figure 12.10).

Of the three items flagged in the narrower interval, but not in the wider interval, all had area statistics fairly close to the cut-off value; these items simply did not have a sufficiently large area relative to the other items to be flagged in this analysis.

The purpose of this part of our investigation was to demonstrate the use of IRT procedures for investigating differential item functioning. Test data for black and white 13-year-olds taking Booklet 1 of the NAEP tests were examined. Such analyses are important, to determine whether one set of item statistics is appropriate for describing the item performance of sub-groups within the population of interest. Also differentially functioning test items are especially important in the analysis and interpretation of results.

Six items were flagged by the area statistic calculated over the ability region of interest. These six items are considered to be only potentially biased; review of the items would be needed to determine if a substantive reason could be found for the differential item performance. These results also highlight the influence of the choice of ability interval on the area statistic, particularly when there is a difference in the ability levels of the two groups.

Reporting of assessment results

The ultimate aim of any educational testing programme is to produce scores which are indices of achievement or performance for individuals, or groups of

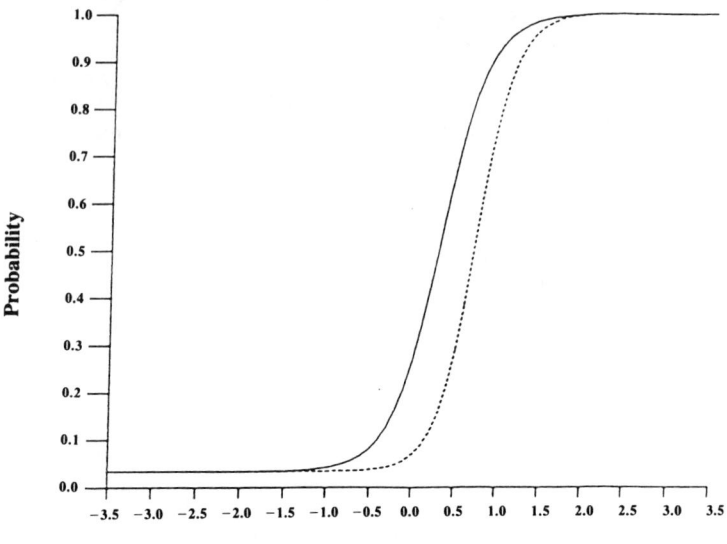

Figure 12.10: Item 4 ICCs for blacks and whites

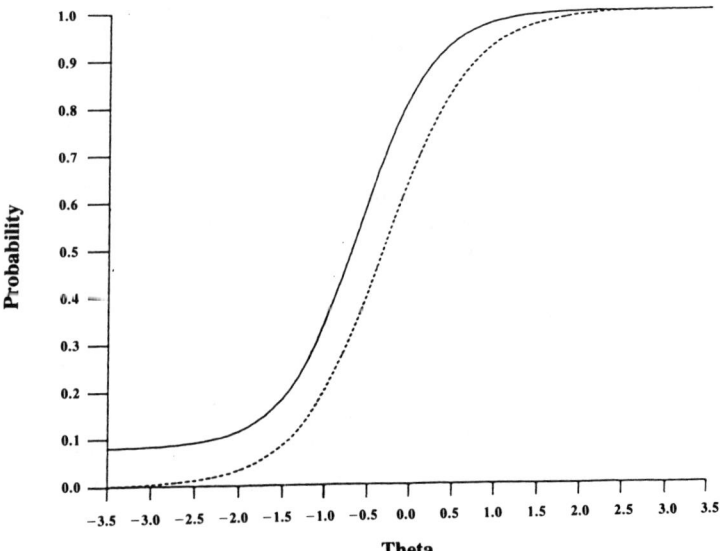

Figure 12.11: Item 10 ICCs for blacks and whites

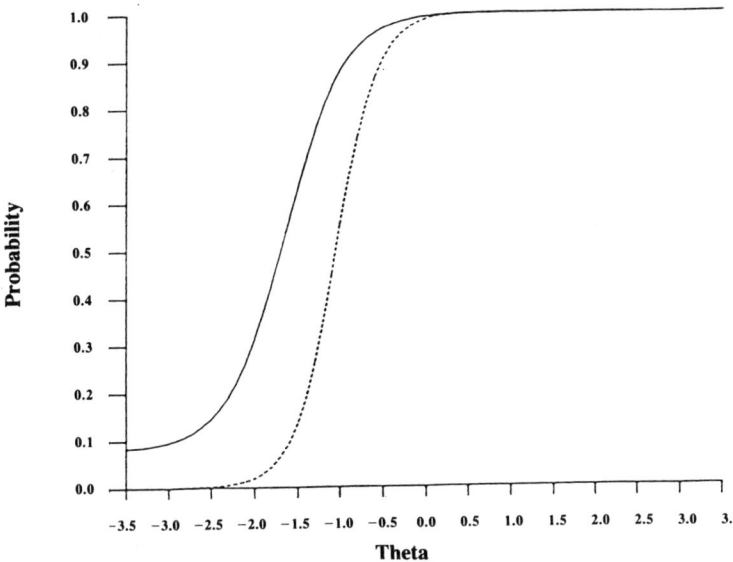

Figure 12.12: Item 11 ICCs for blacks and whites

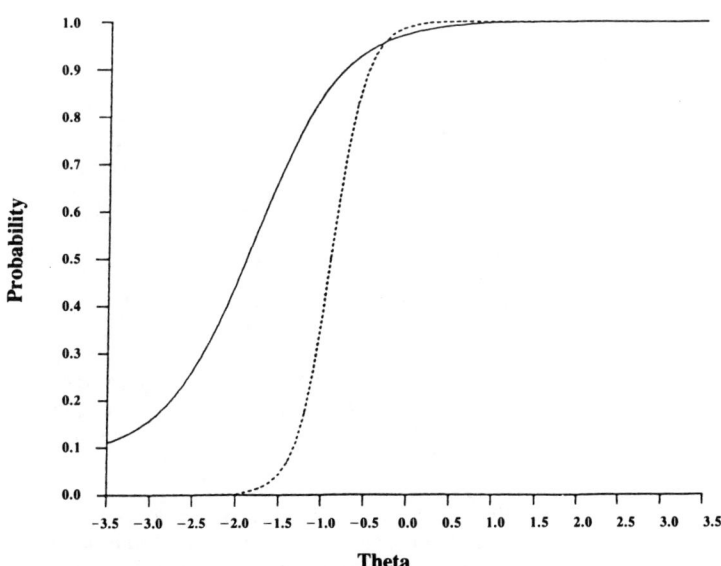

Figure 12.13: Item 12 ICCs for blacks and whites

individuals, on relevant educational dimensions. For a testing programme to be of value, these scores must be reported in a manner that is informative and readily understood by students, parents, teachers and administrators. Surprisingly, there is very little literature on the topic of test score reporting and, specifically, principles of reporting to maximize the utility of the test score information. Effective reporting is particularly important in statewide and national assessment programmes, where an enormous amount of data is gathered for the purpose of analysing educational growth and developing achievement profiles at various levels of aggregation, and where the results of the assessment are used to guide educational policy.

In the past, large-scale assessment programmes, such as NAEP, have typically used indices such as average percent correct on items or groups of items to characterize the performance of schools or school districts, or the percentile ranks of schools based on average percentages correct. While these indices are easy to understand, they have shortcomings which may jeopardize valid comparisons of performance over time or across groups of students. Two problems deserve special mention. First, percentage correct is dependent on the particular set of items administered; if the items change from one year to the next (and they must change because test security cannot be guaranteed), or different groups are administered different items, then the percentages correct are no longer comparable. Secondly, the problem with percentile ranks in score reporting is that the rank of a school will change as the performance of other schools changes, even if its own level of attainment has not changed (Bock and Mislevy, 1981). Needed is a way to measure growth or accomplishment that is tied to a body of content, not to the performance of other groups of test-takers.

A more promising approach to the reporting of assessment results is to use scores derived from item response theory. One of the main purposes of IRT is to provide a common scale on which performance can be compared across groups and sub-groups and where the test results may be collected several years apart. Other purposes for IRT include the availability of invariant item parameters and unique reporting options. The second and third purposes will be addressed next.

Because of the invariance property of the parameters of item response models, scores obtained in an IRT framework are independent of the particular items administered. Hence students taking different sets of items can be meaningfully compared, and performance over time can be examined, even if the set of items changes. This property also means that the amount of testing time can be greatly reduced since it is only necessary for students to take a representative sample of items. For a detailed discussion of design issues in large-scale assessment programmes and procedures for estimation of parameters, the reader is referred to the chapter by Bock and Mislevy, in this volume, and to the recent article by Mislevy (1988).

With scores obtained using item response theory, a number of reporting options become available. First, the scores can be scaled to a metric which is easily interpreted. For instance, both NAEP and the California Assessment Program (CAP) report scores on a scale from 0 to 500, with the mean set at 250 and a standard deviation of 50 (Bock and Mislevy, 1987). Each school or district (or for any sub-groups of students of interest) will have a scaled score on each curricular objective assessed. Along with these scores, an associated standard error can be computed, another advantage of scores derived using IRT. The standard error can be used to establish a confidence interval around the estimate of attainment or proficiency. The report for a given school (or sub-groups of interest), the, might graphically display the school's score and confidence band for each objective, along with comparison bands based on state or national scores (*ibid.*). The relative strengths and weaknesses of the school could be determined by identifying those objectives for which the schools' scores were significantly above and below its overall mean. This kind of reporting combines both norm-referenced and criterion-referenced information.

Another method of reporting and interpreting scores is to reference them to test content. One of the most useful features of item response theory is that the ability or attainment estimates and the difficulty of test items are reported on the same scale. That is, estimates of attainment can be interpreted in terms of the level of difficulty of items that can be answered correctly with a specified probability. Thus a report of the relative performance of schools within a district, for instance, could display a continuum on which each school's scaled score was marked along with the locations of various typical items (Bock and Mislevy, 1981). Bock and Mislevy suggest defining a 'mastery threshold' for items, representing the level of attainment required in order to have a specified probability of answering the item correctly. 'Benchmark' items would be those which have mastery thresholds at certain levels of attainment. For example, benchmarks such as 'basic', 'intermediate' and 'advanced' could be used as reference points (*ibid.*). From this report, it could be seen what level of attainment each school had reached in terms of specific content. These reports could then be used to guide future curriculum development. Figure 12.14, from a report by Messick, Beaton and Lord (1983) highlights some of these points. The figure shows the distributions of abilities for the three groups of interest and the location of the 25th, 50th and 75th percentile in each distribution. Shown over the same ability scale are the item characteristic curves for four exercises (or test items). These items are usually chosen to serve as 'benchmarks'. They are items with some special characteristics, such as covering content, that should be mastered by all examinees. It is then possible to determine the percentage of examinees at each quartile point in each distribution who could answer the test items correctly. The same information (and other variations) could also be reported in easy-to-read tables, along with standard errors, sample sizes, detailed content specifications for the test items, etc.

Alternatively, points along the scale could be selected (e.g. 150, 200, 250, 300, 350) and given meaning through the descriptions of the types of items which candidates can 'handle' (i.e. answer correctly with a specified probability, say, 80 per cent). Candidates in various sub-groups performing above the point (i.e. candidates who have 'mastered' the content at that point) can easily be calculated and reported.

Clearly, the use of item response theory opens up numerous possibilities with regard to the reporting of scores. Schools, or school districts, can be described by comparison with themselves over time, and with other schools and districts, and in terms of their level of mastery of curricular objectives.

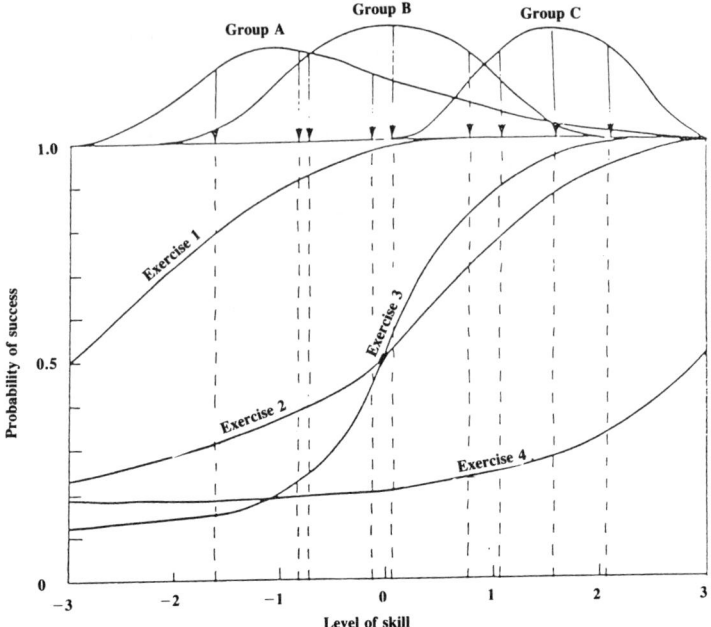

Figure 12.14: Distributions of skill in three subgroups together with expected performance levels on various benchmark exercises (From Messick, Beaton, & Lord, 1983; reproduced by permission).

Concluding remarks

Here we have highlighted several of the important analyses that are essential for assessing the usefulness of particular IRT models in large-scale assessments. The importance of a proper-fitting model cannot be overemphasized. Without it, the highly valuable invariance properties of items and examinees are not obtained. In addition, IRT item bias analyses were highlighted. These analyses can provide valuable information to guide both test development and test score interpretations. Finally, important new reporting options were highlighted which are available within an IRT measurement framework. The future of IRT models in large-scale assessments seems now to be well established in the US though, of course, there is still considerable research and development work to be done.

References

BEATON, A.E. (1988). *The NAEP 1986 Technical Report*. Princeton, NJ: Educational Testing Service.

BOCK, R.D. and MISLEVY, R.J. (1981). 'An item response curve model for matrix-sampling data: the California grade three assessment'. In: CARLSON, D, (Ed) *New Directions for Testing and Measurement: Testing in the States – Beyond Accountability No. 10*. San Francisco, Calif.: Jossey-Bass, pp. 65–90.

BOCK, R.D. and MISLEVY, R.J. (1987). 'Comprehensive educational assessment for the states: the duplex design', *Evaluation Comment*, 1–16.

DORANS, N.J. and KINGSTON, N.M. (1985). 'The effects of violations of unidimensionality on the estimation of item and ability parameters and on item response theory equating of the GRE verbal scale', *Journal of Educational Measurement*, 22, 9–262.

HAMBLETON, R.K. (Ed) (1983). *Applications of Item Response Theory*. Vancouver, BC: Educational Research Institute of British Columbia.

HAMBLETON, R.K. (1989). 'Principles and selected applications of item response theory'. In: LINN, R.L. (Ed) *Educational Measurement* (3rd edition). New York: Macmillan.

HAMBLETON, R.K. (in press). *Criterion-referenced Testing Methods*. Boston, Mass.: Kluwer.

HAMBLETON, R.K. and MURRAY, L. (1983). 'Some goodness of fit investigations for item response models'. In: HAMBLETON, R.K. (Ed) *Applications of Item Response Theory*. Vancouver, BC: Educational Research Institute of British Columbia, pp. 71–94.

HAMBLETON, R.K., MURRAY, L.N. and SIMON, R. (1982). *Utilization of Item Response Models with NAEP Mathematics Exercise Results*. Final Report – ECS Contract No. 02-81-20319. Washington, DC: National Institute of Education.

HAMBLETON, R.K. and SWAMINATHAN, H. (1985). *Item Response Theory: Principles and Applications*. Boston, Mass.: Kluwer.

IRONSON, G. (1983). 'Using item response theory to measure item bias'. In: HAMBLETON, R.K. (Ed) *Applications of Item Response Theory*. Vancouver, BC: Educational Research Institute of British Columbia, pp. 155–174.

KINGSTON, N.M. and DORANS, N.J. (1985). 'The analysis of item-ability regressions: an exploratory IRT model fit tool', *Applied Psychological Measurement*, 9, 281–8.

LORD, F.M. (1962). 'Estimating norms by item-sampling', *Educational and Psychological Measurement*, 22, 259–67.

LORD, F.M. (1980). *Applications of Item Response Theory to Practical Testing Problems*. Hillsdale, NJ: Erlbaum.

MESSICK, S., BEATON, A. and LORD, F.M. (1983). *National Assessment of Educational Progress Reconsidered: A New Design for a New Era*. NAEP Report No. 83–1. Princeton, NJ: Educational Testing Service.

MISLEVY, R.J. (1988). Item response theory in educational assessment. Paper presented at the Meeting of the National Council on Measurement in Education, New Orleans, Louisiana, April.

NUTTALL, D.L. (1983). 'Monitoring in North America', *Westminster Studies in Education*, 6, 63–90.

PANDEY, T.N. and CARLSON, D. (1983). 'Application of item response models to reporting assessment data'. In: HAMBLETON, R.K. (Ed) *Applications of Item Response Theory*. Vancouver, BC: Educational Research Institute of British Columbia, pp. 212–229.

POPHAM, W.J. (1978). *Criterion-referenced Measurement*. Englewood Cliffs, NJ: Prentice-Hall.

ROGERS, H.J. and HAMBLETON, R.K. (in press). 'Evaluation of computer simulated baseline statistics for use in item bias studies', *Educational and Psychological Measurement*.

RUDNER, L.M., GETSON, P.P. and KNIGHT, D.L. (1980). 'A Monte Carlo comparison of seven biased item detection techniques', *Journal of Educational Measurement*, 17, 1–10.

SHEPARD, L.A., CAMILLI, G. and AVERILL, M. (1981). 'Comparison of procedures for detecting test-item bias with both internal and external ability criteria', *Journal of Educational Statistics*, 6, 317–75.

SHEPARD, L.A., CAMILLI, G. and WILLIAMS, D.M. (1984). 'Accounting for statistical artifacts in item bias research', *Journal of Educational Statistics*, 9, 93–138.

SHOEMAKER, D.M. (1973). *Principles and Procedures of Multiple Matrix Sampling.* Cambridge, Mass.: Ballinger.

SHOEMAKER, D.M. and SHOEMAKER, J.S. (1981). 'Applicability of multiple matrix sampling to estimating effectiveness of educational programs', *Evaluation and Program Planning*, 4, 151–61.

WOOD, R.L., WINGERSKY, M.S. and LORD, F.M. (1976). *LOGIST: A computer program for estimating examinee ability and item characteristic curve parameters.* RM-76-6. Princeton, NJ: Educational Testing Service.

WRIGHT, B.D. and STONE, M.H. (1979). *Best Test Design.* Chicago: MESA.

ZWICK, R. (1987). 'Assessing the dimensionality of NAEP reading data', *Journal of Educational Measurement*, 24, 293–308.

13 Application of Multiple Matrix Sampling in Large-scale Assessment Programmes

Tej Pandey

Introduction

Large-scale assessments can be classified into two main types: one where the interest primarily lies at the level of *individuals*, and the second where the interest primarily lies at the level of *groups*. Individual-level assessments typically use test information to rank a student on an established norm, find an individual student's strengths and weaknesses and determine whether a student has mastered specific course content; the decision is made about individual students. Group-level assessments typically use the information to determine the achievement level of students in a system such as a school, school district or region for purposes of programme effectiveness; the decision pertains to the system. Group-level assessments generally are concerned with trends in achievement from one cycle of assessment to the next and may even incorporate provisions in assessment designs to relate trends with other factors.

It is noteworthy that group-level assessment has relied on and used for quite some time the methodology used for individual-level assessment. This fact can easily be traced through the historical development of large-scale testing programmes in the USA. As Womer (1980) has observed, testing prior to the early 1970s was used primarily for guidance and admission to colleges, using standardized or college admissions tests. However, with the intervention of federal and state programmes, such as the Title III and V of the National Defense Education Act (NDEA), testing activity began to be operated centrally, mostly through university-based testing programmes or state departments of education. For the most part, the assessment involved gathering test scores from one of the standardized tests and aggregating data for the schools, districts and the state as a whole. In carrying out assessments, there was little concern for distinguishing between assessments for individual vs programmatic purposes.

In the past two decades the character of assessment for accountability has gradually changed. Although in many programmes the interest still lies in group-level information, assessment programmes are being used more and more to improve teaching and learning practices in addition to finding out the effectiveness of existing practices. This shift in the nature of assessment is taking place to promote 'excellence' movements in many state-level programmes. The excellence movement draws upon the synthesis of research in effective school practices in the past 20 years. The new role of large-scale assessments is to use test instruments as motivators and 'drivers' of curriculum practices through well-designed accountability–incentive strategies. Most states are engaged in strategies that call for organizing *clear and visible* educational goals, providing textbooks and in-service training for teachers that support the goals, and using assessments that continually provide direction and targets for improving student learning.

The purpose of this paper is to describe the methodology of **multiple matrix sampling** (also called **item sampling**) for large-scale assessment. The paper focuses on the approach of multiple matrix sampling, its advantages and considerations in the choice of matrix sampling designs. A sample report from the California Assessment Program (CAP) is described to illustrate the application in a state-wide testing programme.

Purposes of large-scale assessments

Although the purposes of large-scale assessment vary from programme to programme they are usually designed to evaluate curriculum programmes, gather curricular and related information for policy development and stimulate educational programmes. For example, the purpose of assessment programmes to determine the effectiveness of Elementary and Secondary Education Act (ESEA)-related funds was primarily to evaluate curricular programmes. The state assessment programmes use the information for policy development and curricular improvement at the local and state levels, and the assessment programmes to support the excellence movement are designed to stimulate curricular practices. As Cronbach (1964) states:

> Outcomes of instruction are multidimensional, and a satisfactory investigation will map out the effects of the course along these dimensions separately... To agglomerate many types of post-course performance into a single score is a mistake, since failure to achieve one objective is masked by success in another direction... Moreover, since a composite score embodies (and usually conceals) judgments about the importance of the various outcomes, only a report that treats the outcomes separately can be useful to educators who have different value hierarchy (p. 236).

In other words, assessment for broader educational and societal uses calls for tests that are comprehensive in terms of breadth as well as depth. Breadth can be covered by including a large number of questions, and depth can be covered by including a variety of modes of assessments, such as open-ended questions and direct assessment of performance, besides the multiple-choice type of questions.

A typical assessment process starts with the delineation of the objectives to be assessed by the programme and writing test questions to measure those objectives. In California, for example, such documents as the Mathematics Framework for California Public Schools: Kindergarten Through Grade Twelve, Model Curriculum Standards, and the Mathematics Model Curriculum Guide serve as the key resources to develop the objectives and specifications for writing test questions. Committees composed of classroom teachers, curriculum experts, cognitive psychologists and psychometricians develop test questions that best measure those objectives. Following several field trials and review of items for usefulness, statistical criteria and bias due to linguistic or other factors, the pool of items is ready for assessment. Since the number of objectives in a year's curriculum can be large and the number of questions representing those objectives is even larger, it is obvious that contrary to a typical standardized test that uses approx. 60 questions to measure the achievement in mathematics at the sixth-grade level, the pool of questions for programme assessment may number 300–500 in order to cover the entire breadth of the curriculum.

Multiple matrix sampling

Since the interest in programme assessment is not in scores for individual students, but in how well a body of subject-matter has been learned by a cohort of students, multiple matrix sampling or item sampling can be effectively used. Under a matrix sampling or item sampling plan, a universe of test items is subdivided into more than one test form, with each form administered to a certain number of examinees selected randomly from the population of examinees. Although each examinee is administered only a portion of the test items in the total pool, the results from each sub-test may be used to estimate the parameters of the universe scores, such as the mean, variance and associated standard errors.

Item sampling procedures have several advantages over the conventional testing procedure. First, since in item sampling no student takes more than a small portion of the total item pool, the test takes less valuable classroom instructional time, is less fatiguing to the student and results in greater co-operation from students and school authorities. Secondly, since it allows for testing of a large number of questions, it results in a comprehensive assessment leading to more content-related information. Thirdly, it results in more reliable group scores. Lord (1962) showed that for a fixed number of student–item confrontations, the group mean of the item domain is estimated most reliably when the size of the item sub-set is one – i.e. when each item is taken by a different sample of students. Greater reliability is achieved because item responses tend to be positively correlated over the population: two items presented to one student will not generally supply as much information about the mean of the item domain as two items presented to different students.

Item sampling designs

Although one can think of many item sampling designs, two types of design are particularly mentioned here because of their popularity of applications. First, the non-overlapping item sampling design involves the sampling of items to forms without replacement. This means that the items in each form are unique. The non-overlapping sampling design is currently being used by the California Assessment Program. The second design, the overlapping sampling design, involves the sampling of items to forms with replacement – i.e. a particular item can appear on more than one form. The most popular design with replacement is the Balanced Incomplete Block (BIB) design currently in use by the National Assessment of Educational Progress (NAEP).

Non-overlapping designs

The theoretical developments for estimating the standard error of the pooled estimate of the mean were first given by Lord and Novick (1968) for dichotomous item scores. Pandey and Shoemaker (1975) extended these equations for polychotomous item scores. More general equations have been given by Madow (1972), Pandey (1975) and Sirotnik and Wellington (1976). The following equations for the non-overlapping designs are based upon the variance component approach shown in Pandey (1975). We define a population matrix $X = \|x_{IJ}\|$ for $I = 1, 2, \ldots, N$ examinees and $J = 1, 2, \ldots, K$ items where x_{IJ} denotes the score obtained by examinee I in item J. Assume a matrix sample taken from the population matrix is denoted as $X = \|x_{IJ}\|$ for $i = 1, 2, \ldots, nf$ examinees and $j = 1, 2, \ldots, kf$ items. Assume that there are t forms such that the number of items in the fth form is $n_f, f = 1, 2, \ldots, t$. The pooled, unbiased estimate of the mean is given by:

$$\sum_{f=1}^{t}\sum_{j=1}^{kf}\sum_{i=1}^{nf} x_{ij} \Big/ \sum_{f=1}^{t} n_f m_f$$

And an estimate of the standard error of the mean is given by:

$$(SE)^2 = \left\{\frac{1}{t^2}\sum_{f=1}^{t}\frac{1}{n_f} - \frac{1}{N}\right\} S^2{}_{x_i} + \left\{\frac{1}{t^2}\sum_{f=1}^{t}\frac{1}{k_f} - \frac{1}{K}\right\} S^2{}_{x_j}$$

$$+ \left\{\frac{1}{t^2}\sum_{f=1}^{t}\frac{1}{n_f k_f} - \frac{1}{Kt^2}\sum_{f=1}^{t}\frac{1}{n_f} - \frac{1}{Nt^2}\sum_{f=1}^{t}\frac{1}{k_f} + \frac{1}{NK}\right\} S^2{}_{x_{..}}$$

In the above equation the terms $S^2{}_{x_i.}$, $S^2{}_{x.j}$ and $S^2{}_{x..}$ are the variances corresponding to the variance components associated with examinees, items and examinee-by-items in a two-way analysis of variance random effects design. The pooled variances are computed using the following formulas:

$$S^2_{Xi.} = \frac{N-1}{N}\left\{\frac{1}{k}\overline{MSE} - \left(\frac{1}{k} - \frac{1}{K}\right)\overline{MSEI}\right\}$$

$$S^2_{Xj.} = \frac{K-1}{K}\left\{\frac{1}{n}\overline{MSE} - \left(\frac{1}{n} - \frac{1}{N}\right)\overline{MSEI}\right\}$$

$$S^2{}_{X_{..}} = \frac{(N-1)(K-1)}{NK} \overline{MSEI}$$

In the above formulas, $\overline{MSE}$, $\overline{MSI}$ and $\overline{MSEI}$ are the pooled mean squares for the pupils, items and pupils-by-items components obtained from a two-way analysis of variance procedure.

COST AND EFFICIENCY OF NON-OVERLAPPING DESIGNS

As mentioned earlier, for a fixed number of student–item confrontations, the group mean of an item domain is estimated more reliably as the number of forms increases such that in the extreme case, where each item is taken by a different sample of students, the precision of measurement is maximum. The extent of this effect was demonstrated empirically by Pandey and Carlson (1976), by sampling responses from the California Assessment Program's reading test for grade 3. They found, for example, that in a design where 200 items were allocated to two non-overlapping test forms of 100 items each and 10 different students took each form, the measurement–error variance of the group mean was 0.0023. But in a design where the items were allocated to 10 forms and 10 students took each, the error variance was reduced to 0.0006, nearly a fourfold

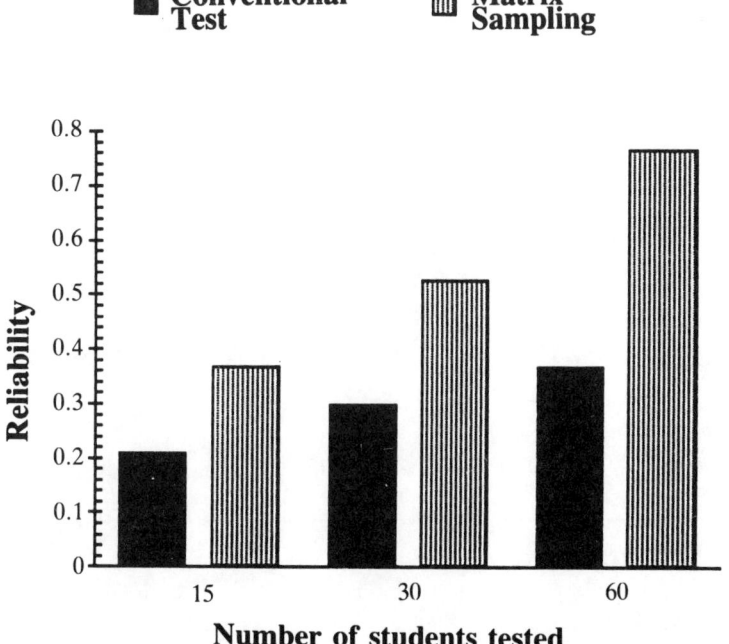

Figure 13.1: Reliability of school mean scores for conventional testing and matrix sampling

reduction. The practical conclusion is that four content areas could have been assessed in the second design with the same precision as one area in the first design. Figure 13.1 shows the stability of test scores for three levels of number of students tested for CAP's grade 6 reading test and a publisher's standardized test; the matrix sampling test required each student to take 8 items, whereas the standardized test required each student to take 60 items. It is to be noted that matrix sampling assessed students on a total of 128 items compared to the publisher's test assessing only 60 items.

However, the gains associated with more items in the pool and more forms will have to be judged in relation to the cost associated in item production and the printing of booklets. Beyond a certain threshold of item pool size, the gains in the precision begin to diminish. The reader may get a feel of relative precision and costs with various item pool sizes in Pandey and Carlson (*ibid.*).

NON-OVERLAPPING ITEM SAMPLING IN THE CALIFORNIA ASSESSMENT PROGRAM

The CAP conducts annual testing in reading, written expression and mathematics in grades 3, 6, 8 and 12. Additionally, science and history/social science are assessed at grade 8. The assessment programme uses a non-overlapping item sampling design for student assessment. Since the assessment programme provides information to all schools – small and large – all students are tested rather than a sample of students. Table 13.1 shows the total number of questions and the number of forms in each of the content areas for each grade tested.

For example, the Survey of Basic Skills: Grade 6 (1984 version) consists of a total of 1260 items – 396 in reading, 396 in written expression and 468 in mathematics – divided into 36 unique test forms. Under the item sampling

Table 13.1: Number of questions and forms of CAP tests

Test	No. of forms	Total No. of items pool	form	Reading No. of items pool	form	Written expression No. of items pool	form	Mathematics No. of items pool	form
Grade 3 (1980)	30	1,020	34	270	9	390	13	360	12
Grade 6 (1982)	40	1,240	31	400	10	360	9	480	12
Grade 8 (1984)	36	1,260	35	396	11	396	11	468	13
Grade 12 (1988)	30	1,050	35	300	10	120	4*	330	11

* Editing questions.

procedure, each test form consists of a total of 35 questions made up of 11 questions in each of reading and written expression and 13 questions in mathematics. Each form of the test is constructed to have an equal number of easy and difficult questions and consists of items from all major skill areas, stratified on difficulty and content. For test administration, the forms are stacked sequentially and are distributed to students in a manner similar to conventional tests. Since each student takes only one of the 36 forms containing 35 questions, testing time is limited to only one class period.

Since CAP administers tests to each student in each school, it allows for aggregating data to produce reports at the level of schools and school districts. Although CAP's procedure could allow reports at the classroom level, no classroom reports are produced.

The report shown in Figure 13.2 is the Skill Area report for a typical school, showing the total score along with the sub-scores useful for programme diagnostic purposes. The sub-scores are shown with a band of 0.67 standard error of measurement around the point estimate to discourage over-interpretation of skill area scores. In general, if the skill area band is below the total score line, it reflects an area of relative weakness; however, if the band is clearly above the total score, it reflects the area of relative strength. If the band overlaps with the total score, it is neither an area of relative weakness, nor an area of relative strength. As many curriculum experts are aware, the interpretation and meaning of these data must be judged professionally before making any curricular changes. The expert will take into consideration the importance of certain skill areas, their interrelationship with other skill areas and the nature and relevance of the questions on the test.

Overlapping BIB designs

Overlapping item sampling designs require that items appear on more than one test form. In actual overlapping item sampling designs, blocks of items rather than single items overlap in all possible combinations. The most popular of these designs is the Balanced Incomplete Block (BIB) design. Compared to the non-overlapping designs, overlapping designs have the advantage of producing correlations among all items in the pool. However, this advantage comes at a considerably higher cost than that for non-overlapping designs. The cost is higher because the number of forms needed to complete the design is considerably larger, even for a modest number of blocks.

The National Assessment of Educational Progress (NAEP) has been using BIB design in their assessments since the 1983–84 assessment cycle. Furthermore, in contrast to student sampling in CAP, NAEP uses a three-stage stratified sampling plan to select students for the sample. The following description of the actual BIB design used in the 1983–84 NAEP reading assessment has been taken from Beaton (1986):

> The booklets in the BIB design each contain the common block and two of the 19 single-length blocks (each requiring 14 minutes). The 19 blocks were assigned to booklets using a cyclic Youden rectangle as described in

School: SHAMROCK ELEMENTARY
District: CALWEST UNIFIED
County: CALIFORNIA
CDS: 99-12345-6789012

The questions on the *Survey* and the reporting of scores reflect a central concern of the *Mathematics Framework* that problem-solving applications serve as an unbrella for all mathematics strands. As shown below, the scores in all skill areas are broken down into skills and applications components. The 'Applications' score under Problem-solving is an aggregation of scores for all application categories.

Interpretive Example
Your total Mathematics score of 250 is expressed below as a bold vertical line, and each skill area score is displayed as a bar. Your score in Counting and Place Value is identified as neither a relative strength nor weakness because the bar overlaps the vertical line.

See Part IV for an illustrative description of the Mathematics skill areas tested.

Mathematics skill areas	Scaled score and standard error	Your total Mathematics score of 250 is represented by the bold vertical line (100 150 200 250 300 350 400)	Relative strength/weakness M2 M3	M3 M4	M4 M5
Counting and place value	242 ± 13	Countin			
Skills	243 ± 16	Skills			
Applications	239 ± 22	Applications		RW	
Operations	258 ± 9	Oper			
Basic facts	235 ± 20	Basic fact	RW	RW	
Addition	244 ± 20	Addition		RW	
Subtraction	248 ± 17	Subtracti	RS	RS	
Multiplication	284 ± 18	Multipli			RS
Applications	270 ± 15	Applica			RS
Basic facts	270 ± 25	Basic facts			
Addition/substraction	263 ± 25	Addition/subt	RS		
Multiplication	279 ± 25	Multiplicati	RW	RW	RS

Figure 13.2: Survey of basic skills – grade 3 (CAP): 1985 (Program Diagnostic Display – Mathematics)

Nature of numbers and properties	252 ± 15			RS
Properties and relationships	191 ± 20	Properties	Nature	RW
Money and fractions	291 ± 27		Money and fr	RS
Applications	276 ± 25	RW	Application	RS
Geometry	214 ± 14			RW
Skills	199 ± 17		Geomet	RW
Applications	243 ± 24	RS	Skills	
			Applications	
Measurement	245 ± 14		Measure	RW
Linear measures	212 ± 21	RW	Linear meas	RS
Other measures	250 ± 23		Other measur	
Applications	288 ± 31		Applications	RS
Patterns and graphs	257 ± 17		Patterns	
Skills	258 ± 23	RS	Skills	
Applications	255 ± 23		Applications	
Problem-solving	262 ± 10		Prob	RS
Analysis and models	256 ± 23		Analysis an	RS
Applications	263 ± 10		Appl	

Figure 13.2, continued

Beall (1971). This procedure required the formation and printing of 57 different booklets. Each block is combined with each other block exactly once in this design, and thus each pair of exercises was assigned to some sample of youths. The block assignments were randomized. There are 57 block triplets, one for each booklet, which were a result of the randomization process.

The design called for each booklet to be given to approximately 289 different students and, since each block was in nine booklets, each block was therefore to be given to about 2600 students at each age/grade combination. The total number of students called for in the sample was 16,467 resulting in approximately 222 students at each age or grade level. Thus, each block was to be administered to 2000 youths resulting in a total age or grade sample of about 12,667.

As mentioned above, the BIB design allows the calculation of covariances among all pairs of items. Furthermore, because BIB spiralling results in many more forms than the non-overlapping design, for NAEP's stratified student sampling, it increases the efficiency by reducing the clustering effect in sampling schools. Hansen *et al.* (1984) have estimated that, given reasonable assumptions, the required sample size to achieve a given standard error is reduced by approx. 20–25 per cent by BIB spiralling, as compared to non-overlapping item sampling; alternatively, the standard errors could be reduced by about 10–15 per cent if the sample size were kept constant.

ESTIMATION OF PARAMETERS IN NON-OVERLAPPING DESIGNS

The design used by NAEP is quite complex because of BIB item sampling followed by a three-stage sampling of students. No theoretically derived equations are available to compute the standard errors associated with the estimated means for various sub-groups of interest to NAEP. NAEP uses Jackknife estimation procedures for estimating the standard errors. Jackknife was initially suggested by Tukey (1958) as a handy statistical tool for interval estimation in a wide variety of situations. Miller (1964, 1968) and others have given Jackknife a firm mathematical justification as a strategy for constructing confidence intervals for a parameter. Although the actual application of the Jackknife by NAEP is complex, and the reader is referred to their 1983–84 Technical Report, the following description of the Jackknife should familiarize the reader with this procedure.

THE JACKKNIFE

The Jackknife can be defined operationally as follows: a set of observations is subdivided into a collection of mutually exclusive and exhaustive groups, parameter estimates are obtained from combinations of these groups, and finally, these preliminary estimates are averaged to construct a final estimate. To be more precise, suppose $X_1, \ldots, X_n$ are N independent and identically distributed random variables, having Θ as an unknown parameter of the common distribution function; furthermore, it is assumed that some method of estimating Θ is available. In the Jackknife, the N observations are first grouped into u groups of v observations each such that $N = uv$:

$$\{X_1, ..., X_v\}, \{X_{v+1}, ..., X_{2v}\}, ..., \{X_{(u-1)v+1}, ..., X_{uv}\}$$

If $\hat{\Theta}_{-0}$ denotes an estimate of Θ based upon all u groups, and $\hat{\Theta}_{-1}$ is an estimate of Θ based upon the $N - v$ observations obtained by the deletion of the ith group, new estimates of Θ, called pseudo-values, are formed by constructing the following combination of $\hat{\Theta}_{-0}$ and $\hat{\Theta}_{-1}$:

$$\hat{\Theta}_{*i} = u\hat{\Theta}_{-0} - (u-1)\,\hat{\Theta}_{-i}, \ 1 \le i \le u$$

The final jackknife estimate of Θ is the mean of the pseudo-values:

$$\hat{\Theta}_{*.} = \frac{1}{u}\sum_{i=1}^{u}\hat{\Theta}_{*i}$$

and an estimate of the standard error of this estimate is given by:

$$s\hat{\Theta}^{*.} = \left[\ \sum_{i=1}^{u}\left(\hat{\Theta}_{*i} - \hat{\Theta}_{*.}\right)^2 / u(u-1)\right]^{\!1/2}$$

The Jackknife estimate of Θ possesses an interesting bias reduction property. Specifically, if Θ_{-0} is biased of order $1/N$, then Θ_*. has a bias of order $1/N^2$. Moreover, Tukey (1958) conjectured that, in many instances, the u pseudo-values could be treated as u independent and identically distributed observations, and an approximate confidence interval for Θ could be constructed from the t-distribution in the standard manner. In other words, Tukey's proposal implies that the quantity:

$$(\Theta - \hat{\Theta}_{*.}) \,/\, s\hat{\Theta}_{*.}$$

is approximately t-distributed with $u - 1$ degrees of freedom and an approximate $1 - \alpha$ confidence interval for Θ is given by:

$$\hat{\Theta}_{*.} - t\left(\frac{\alpha}{2}, u-1\right)s\hat{\Theta}^* . \,/\, \hat{\Theta}_{*.} + t\left(\frac{\alpha}{2}, u-1\right)s\hat{\Theta}^*.$$

Miller has proven that for statistics defined by transformations of means and variances, the pseudo-values are asymptotically normal, and he demonstrated that the Jackknife t-test is a valid competitor to the F-test if the data are normal. Miller's theorem were extended by Arvesen (1969) to U-statistics, or a function of several U-statistics which embrace a large class of statistics including the sample mean, variance and estimates of variance components in ANOVA models.

The foregoing description provides a general application of the Jackknife procedure. For the actual procedure used for the estimation of variability of NAEP estimates the reader is referred to Johnson (1987).

Application of IRT to matrix sampling data

Although application of IRT to matrix-sampled data is beyond the scope of this paper, we will mention that IRT models have been successfully applied to the grouped responses. Bock, Mislevy and Woodson (1982) first demonstrated that IRT models can be adapted to assessments that use the *most efficient* multiple matrix sampling (MMS) designs, that is designs in which each student answers only one question from each skill element. The application of IRT to matrix-sampled data not only adds to the precision of measurement, but unfolds numerous other advantages gained from using IRT, such as linear scale, invariance of test to item selection, content referencing and well-defined standard error. IRT brings added precision to matrix-sampled data because in MMS items are treated as random samples from a pool of indistinguishable items, whereas IRT models allow one to parameterize individual test items in terms of their relationship to the underlying scale of ability.

Assuming that matrix-sampled data meet the assumptions of the IRT model, such as the unidimensionality, local independence and that the regression of item scores on the ability scores follows the general form of the logistic function, one can choose from a number of logistic functions for application to the grouped data, similar to the application of these models for the individual-level data. For example, the proportion of correct responses from school a to item i in a particular skill element can be modelled using the two-parameter logistic function as follows:

$$P_{aj} = \frac{\exp\{(\Theta_a - b_j)\} / s}{1 + \exp\{(\Theta_a - b_j)\} / s}$$

In the above equation, Θ_a indicates the level of attainment of school a and the two parameters that represent item i are b_j, the item difficulty or threshold parameter – the point along the ability scale at which a typical student in the school would have probability of 0.5 of responding to that item correctly – and s_i, the dispersion parameter – the sensitivity of the item to differences in the level of ability or attainment Θ_a. The reader is referred to Mislevy (1983) for the estimation procedures.

Figure 13.2 shows a report of the California Assessment Program using the scale score metric. Each of the skill elements is calibrated and scored independently of other elements and are set to have a state-wide mean of 250 and standard deviation of 50 for the base year 1979–80. Skill elements are aggregated to produce skill area (such as counting and place value) and content area (such as mathematics) scores. In the illustrative report shown in Figure 13.2, the total score of 317 is represented by a heavy line. Skill element and skill area scores and their associated standard errors are shown numerically as well as graphically.

Conclusion

Item sampling procedures have proven to be very powerful assessment tools where the purpose of large-scale assessments is to determine the effectiveness or programmes or to promote curricular goals through testing. Both the non-overlapping and overlapping designs have been used successfully. The item sampling in conjunction with item response theoretic models have proven to be particularly useful in large-scale testing programmes.

References

ARVESEN, J.N. (1969). 'Jackknifing U-statistics', *Annals of Mathematical Statistics*, 40, 2076–100.

BEALL, G. (1971). 'Change-over experiments in practice' (ETS Research Report RB 71-38). Princeton, NJ: Educational Testing Service.

BEATON, A.E. (1986). 'The NAEP reading scale'. Princeton, NJ: Educational Testing Service.

BOCK, R.D., MISLEVY, R. and WOODSON, C. (1982). 'The next stage in educational assessment', *Educational Researcher*, 11, 4–11.

HANSEN, M.H., TEPPING, B.S., LAGO, J.A. and BURKE, J. (1984). *National Assessment of Educational Progress (NAEP) – the sample and data collection design for year 15.* Paper presented at the meeting of the ASA, 1984.

JOHNSON, E.G. (1987). 'Estimation of uncertainty due to sampling variability'. In: BEATON, A.E. (Ed) *Implementing the New Design: The NAEP 1983-84 Technical Report.* National Assessment of Educational Progress Report No. 15-TR-20, Educational Testing Service, Princeton, NJ, 505–512.

LORD, F.M. (1962). 'Estimating norms by item sampling', *Educational and Psychological Measurement*, 22, 259–67.

LORD, F.M. (1980). *Applications of Item Response Theory to Practical Testing Problems.* Hillsdale, NJ: Erlbaum.

LORD, F.M. and NOVICK, M.R. (1968). *Statistical Theories of Mental Test Scores.* Reading, Mass.: Addison-Wesley.

MADOW, W.G. (1972). Multiple Matrix Sampling, with Stratification and Possibly Unequal Sample Sizes from the Strata. Pacific Education Evaluation Systems Monograph (unpublished).

MILLER, R.G., JR. (1964). 'A trustworthy jackknife', *Annals of Mathematical Statistics*, 35, 1594–1605.

MILLER, R.G., JR. (1968). 'Jackknifing variances', *Annals of Mathematical Statistics*, 39, 567–82.

MISLEVY, R. (1983). 'Item response models for grouped data', *Journal of Educational Statistics*, 8, 271–88.

MOSTELLER, F. and TUKEY, J.W. (1968). 'Data analysis, including statistics'. In: LINDZEY, G. and ARONSON, E. (Eds) *Handbook of Social Psychology.* Reading, Mass.: Addison-Wesley.

PANDEY, T.N. (1975). 'Estimating the standard error of the mean in multiple matrix sampling when items are sampled with and without replacement.' Paper presented at Meeting of the American Educational Research Association, Washington, DC.

PANDEY, T.N. and CARLSON D. (1976). 'Assessing payoffs in the estimation of the mean using multiple matrix sampling designs'. In: GRUIJTER, D.N.M. and VAN DER KAMP, L.J.T. (Eds) *Advances in Psychological and Educational Measurement.* New York: Wiley, pp. 265–75.

PANDEY, T.N. and CARLSON, D. (1983). 'Application of item response models to reporting assessment data'. In: HAMBLETON, R.K. (Ed) *Applications of Item Response Theory.* Vancouver, BC: Educational Research Institute of British Columbia, 212–229.

PANDEY, T.N. and HUBERT, L. (1975). 'An empirical comparison of several interval estimation procedures for coefficient alpha', *Psychometrika,* 40, 169–81.

PANDEY, T.N. and SHOEMAKER, D.M. (1975). 'Estimating moments of universe scores and associated standard errors in multiple matrix sampling for all item-scoring procedures', *Educational and Psychological Measurement,* 35, 567–81.

SIROTNIK, K. and WELLINGTON, R. (1977). 'Incidence sampling: an integrated theory for "matrix sampling"'. *Journal of Educational Measurement,* 14, 343–99.

TUKEY, J.W. (1958). 'Bias and confidence in not-quite large samples' (abstract), *Annals of Mathematical Statistics,* 29, 614.

WOMER, F.B. (1980). 'State-level testing: where we have been may not tell us where we are going', *New Directions for Testing and Measurement,* 10, 1–12.

14 Innovative Procedures in the Calibration of Measurement Scales

Theo J.H.M. Eggen

In this paper the procedures for the calibration of the measurement scales in the mathematics assessment of 1987 in the Netherlands are discussed. For detailed information on the general aims of the assessment programme, the instrument construction and the sampling procedures, I refer to Wijnstra's section.

Two major starting-points have been established in preparing the design of the Dutch assessment programme. First, the results of the mathematics assessment will be reported, in terms of the narrowly defined content domains. It is assumed that this is the best way to get curriculum experts and teachers really involved in understanding and discussing the results of the assessment programme. Secondly item response theory provides the methodology for developing the measurement scales. Item response theory for calibrating scales and scoring, if applicable, has proven to have many attractive features, especially the property that it enables us to score responses to different sub-sets of items on the same scale. Furthermore, using item response theory in combination with narrowly defined content domains has some specific advantages, as follows: easier interpretation of the scale score for the practitioner; better chances for model fit; and greater possibilities to deal with possible parameter drift over time.

In this paper, I will give some further details on the design of the project, together with the consequences of the application of item response theory in calibrating the scales. A new item response model and its application in the mathematics assessment will be presented.

Design

For the mathematics assessment at the end of the primary school, the curriculum is sub-divided into 27 topics. Except for one topic, between 16 and 20 items were administered for each of these topics. Together with 32 items on very basic mathematical skills, the total item pool consisted of approx. 500 almost wholly open-ended questions. The design of the assessment programme has two different objectives: estimating item parameters for each topic to calibrate the scales, and estimating the proficiency of relevant sub-groups of the population on these same topics. Although these objectives are, in some sense, conflicting in trying to optimize the design, sampling of students from the population as well as items from the pool (multiple matrix sampling) offer the best possibilities to serve both objectives in an efficient way.

In this paper, I will consider the design on the level of a topic; so on the level at which the calibration of the scales takes place, I refer to Wijnstra's section for details on sampling the schools and students; the distribution of the topics over the test booklets and the items within the booklets; and the allocation of the booklets within schools.

In order to gather information in a more efficient way than the standard multiple matrix sampling design, prior information on the abilities of the students and the difficulty of the items was used in deciding which item sub-sets were administered to which sub-group. For each topic, the items are divided into three sub-sets: A items, intended to be relatively easy; B items, relatively difficult; and AB items, of intermediate difficulty level. Furthermore, on the basis of teacher judgement, two ability-level groups were distinguished: a relatively less able group (group a), and a more able group (group b). The allocation of the items to the students was such that the A and AB items were administered to the group a, while group b did the harder AB and B items. For

Figure 14.1: Allocation of items to students

Item level

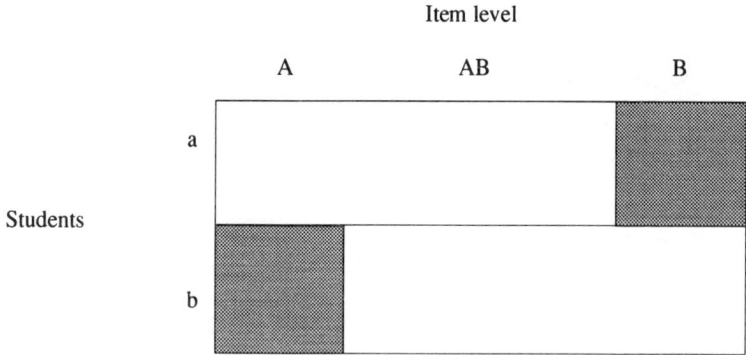

each topic, the general design is given in Figure 14.1.

If we look at the design at this level, we see that we have created two non-equivalent samples of students. We have a relatively able sample that took the more difficult items, and a relatively less able sample that took the easier items. In the next section, I will show that denying this feature and applying item response theory in a standard way can lead to serious systematic errors in the estimates of the item parameters – i.e. in calibration of the scale.

Item response theory

Item response theory is amply discussed in books by Fischer (1974), Hambleton and Swaminathan (1985) and others. Here just some elements of it relevant to the subject of the paper are summarized. In the mathematics assessment it was decided to choose between the one and the two parameter logistic model. In general these models are given by:

$$P(X_{ij} = x_{ij}) = P(X_{ij} \mid \Theta_i, \alpha_j, \beta_j) = \frac{\exp\{\alpha_j (\Theta_i - \beta_j) x_{ij}\}}{1 + \exp\{\alpha_j (\Theta_i - \beta_j)\}} \tag{1}$$

where $x_{ij} = 0, 1; i\varepsilon I; j\varepsilon J$

We have a dichotomous response variable X_{ij} of person i responding to item j, which distribution is given by equation (1) in which Θ_i is the ability parameter of person i and β_j and α_j respectively the difficulty and discrimination parameter of item j. I and J indicate an index set respectively for the persons and items. The model specifies the probability of an individual giving an (in)correct item response. It is completed by the assumption of independence between item responses for every person and so-called local independence – i.e. for given ability, of the item responses over items. If we indicate with **X** the total response pattern for all students on all items and with X_i the response vector of student i we can write this as:

$$P(X) = \Pi_i P(X)_i \mid \Theta, \alpha_j, \beta_j) = \Pi_i \Pi_j P(X_{ij} \mid \Theta_i, \alpha_j, \beta_j) \tag{2}$$

The two-parameter logistic model was introduced by Birnbaum (1968), and is often referred to as the **Birnbaum model**. The one-parameter logistic model, the **Rasch model** (Rasch, 1960), is a special case of the Birnbaum model, with all items having equal and constant discriminations: $\alpha_j = a$ for $j\varepsilon J$. The use of the three-parameter logistic model, which adds a guessing parameter to equation (1) was not considered in the mathematics assessment because almost all questions were open-ended.

Because of its simplicity and its statistical properties, the Rasch model is a very attractive item response model. Two major properties are as follows.

1. The number of items correct $S_i = \sum_J X_{ij}$ is a sufficient statistic for the ability

parameter Θ_i, which means that all the information of a person is contained in this simple statistic. As a consequence, conditional maximum likelihood (CML) estimation of the item parameters is possible (Fischer, 1974). The conditional likelihood function $L(c)$:

$$L(c) = \Pi_j P(X_i \mid S_i) = f(\beta) \tag{3}$$

can be maximized independently of the person parameters because it is only a function of the difficulty parameters. CML estimates have the attractive feature of being consistent and independent of any influence of the ability parameters or an ability distribution.

2. The model belongs to the exponential family of distributions, giving the existence and unicity of the estimates of the item parameters and making several model-fit statistics with known asymptotic properties available. Verhelst and Glas (in preparation) present construction principles for tests of models belonging to the exponential family with exactly known asymptotic properties.

The Birnbaum model does not belong to the exponential family and therefore has no simple sufficient statistic for the ability parameter Θ_i, and for testing model fit we are committed to model-fit statistics for which the asymptotic behaviour is known only approximately. Estimating the item parameters consistently, however, has become possible with Bock and Aitken's (1981) **marginal maximum likelihood method** (MML). Assuming that the persons are a random sample from a population in which the distribution of the ability θ is given by a density $g(\Theta|\gamma)$, the item parameters are estimated simultaneously with the parameter(s) γ of the ability distribution. The marginal likelihood function $L(m)$ is maximized with respect to the parameters

$$L(m) = \Pi_j \int P(X_i \mid \Theta, \alpha_j, \beta_j) \, g(\Theta \mid \gamma) \, d\Theta \tag{4}$$

The MML procedure is implemented in the BILOG computer program (Mislevy and Bock, 1986), by which estimates of the item parameters as well as the Rasch and the Birnbaum model in designs with missing data can be obtained.

Theoretically, the Rasch model has some important advantages over the Birnbaum model. However, on the other hand, the Rasch model is very restrictive and it should be questioned whether it is not too rigid for the scales in the mathematics assessment. It was therefore decided to postpone the final choice of the model depending on the data collected. In the first instance, marginal maximum likelihood methods were used for calibrating the items.

An estimation problem caused by the design

Although we have, in general, a random sample from the population of the students of primary schools, we do not have a random sample at the topic level at which the calibration is performed. We have two non-equivalent samples of students; denying this feature and applying marginal maximum likelihood estimation procedures in a standard way can lead to serious systematic errors in the estimates of the item parameters. The results of a small simulation study will illustrate this problem.

Data were generated according to the following specifications: two non-equivalent samples of 500 students were generated each from two normal distributions, respectively $\Theta \sim N(-0.5,1)$ and $\Theta \sim N(+0.5,1)$. The students considered less able were administered the first ten items out of a pool of 12 items. The more able students took the last ten items. So the anchor consisted of eight

Table 14.1: Input β and estimated $\hat{\beta}$ difficulty parameters (Rasch model)

Item	β	$\hat{\beta}$ (MML)
1	0	0.46
2	0	0.42
3	0	0.02
4	0	−0.01
5	0	0.09
6	0	0.04
7	0	−0.15
8	0	−0.02
9	0	−0.00
10	0	0.04
11	0	−0.41
12	0	−0.48

items. All items have equal difficulty $\beta j = 0$, $j = 1, \ldots, 12$. The responses were generated according to the Rasch model. So, in fact we have a data matrix with the same structure as in the mathematics assessment design.

If we estimate the item parameters ignoring the fact that we have two non-equivalent samples and apply MML estimation in a standard way, we get the results given in Table 14.1, which were computed with the BILOG program (Mislevy and Bock, 1986).

We see a clear bias in the estimates of the parameters that were administered in only one of the two non-equivalent samples. The difficulty parameters of the items only administered in the less able group ($E(\Theta) = -0.5$) are overestimated, and are underestimated in the more able group ($E(\Theta) = +0.5$). This phenomenon is due to the fact that the missing data in our data matrix are not randomly missing, but clearly depend on an external design variable. In such a case, the missing data mechanism is not ignorable if we estimate the item parameters via MML methods. The concept of *ignorability* was introduced by Rubin (1976), who gives a general framework for classifying and handling missing data. Define $Y = (Y_{ij})$ as the total response vector for all persons $i \varepsilon I$ on all items $j \varepsilon J$, and $R = (R_{ij})$ as the design vector, which elements take the value 1 if Y_{ij} is observed and 0 if not observed. Then Y can be partitioned in two parts: $Y = Y_{obs}$ Y_{mis}, consisting of the observed responses Y_{obs} and the responses Y_{mis} that would have been given if these items were administered.

In a statistical analysis we can infer from the design variable (R) and the observed part of the responses Y_{obs}. Ignorability addresses the possibility of only inferring from Y_{obs} and ignoring the design information. A sufficient condition for the ignorability of our design follows from Little and Rubin (1987):

$$P(R = r \mid Y_{obs} = y_{obs}, Y_{mis} = y_{mis}) = P(R = r \mid Y_{obs} = y_{obs}) \tag{5}$$

that is, all the information about the design is in the observed values. Or in other words, the missing data are ignorable if there is no better prediction of the design if we had the possibility to add missing data.

Via simple probability theory, equation (5) can be rewritten as:

$$P\left(Y_{mis} = y_{mis} \mid R = r, Y_{obs} = y_{obs}\right) = P\left(Y_{mis} = y_{mis} \mid Y_{obs} = y_{obs}\right) \tag{6}$$

which allows, perhaps, for a clearer interpretation of ignorability. The design variable is ignorable if the missing answers are equally well predicted by the design and the observed answers as by the observed answers solely. In our situation, which is illustrated by the simulation study, condition (6) is not fulfilled. The design variable is clearly correlated with the observed variables because an external indicator of ability determines the data that we are observing. As a consequence, the events on which is conditioned in equation (6), respectively ($R = r$, $Y_{obs} = y_{obs}$) and ($Y_{obs} = y_{obs}$) are not the same and (6) will not be fulfilled.

Solutions and their performance in the calibration

The non-ignorability of the design seems to restrain us from a standard application of items response theory for calibrating the items, but there are at least two possible solutions to this problem:

1. Add the selection variable, the judgement of the teacher determining the ability group level, as an extra observed variable in the likelihood used for estimating the item parameters. We can consider this as adding an extra item which was wrong for all students in the less able group, and right in the more able group. In that case, all the information about the design is included in the observed values and the events {$R = r, Y_{obs} = y_{obs}$} and {$Y_{obs} = y_{obs}$} coincide, so that condition (6) is fulfilled.

2. Estimate the item parameters with conditional maximum likelihood methods, meaning that the item parameter estimates are free from any influence of the sampling procedure. The non-ignorability of the design causes no problems, if we estimate the item parameters in this way, because in the likelihood function (4) we consider probabilities on responses patterns conditional on the sufficient statistic S_i for the ability parameter Θ_i and this sufficient statistic is a function of the item responses and the design variable. So, in fact we base our reference on both the observed and the design variables.

To show the practical effect of applying these solutions to our problem, we continue our simulation example. The results of adding the selection item and using MML estimation with the BILOG program and of using CML estimation of the item parameters with the RIDA program (Glas, 1988) are presented in Table 14.2. We see that adding the selection variable corrects the bias of item parameter estimates, although the bias does not vanish completely. At this moment, simulation studies are conducted to explore the reasons for this. Estimating the item parameters with the CML-methods gives good results, with none of the estimated parameters deviating significantly from the input (0).

Both solutions were applied in the calibration of the scales in the mathematics assessment. Note that the second solution, estimating the parameters with

Table 14.2: Input β and estimated β̂-MML-sel (adding selection item) and β̂-CML difficulty parameters (Rasch model)

Item	Input	β̂-MML-sel	β̂-CML
1	0	0.27	0.05
2	0	0.24	0.02
3	0	0.02	0.02
4	0	−0.01	−0.01
5	0	0.09	0.09
6	0	0.04	0.04
7	0	−0.16	−0.15
8	0	−0.02	−0.02
9	0	−0.00	0.00
10	0	−0.04	0.04
11	0	−0.23	−0.01
12	0	−0.30	−0.08
sel	−	0.02	−

CML, is only available for the Rasch model. However, in trying to apply the Rasch model to the data in the mathematics assessment the model proved to be too restrictive. Although we have narrowly defined content domains, the Rasch model did not fit the data in any of the scales. Only if we were willing to accept that in a scale about half of the items were deleted, it was possible to obtain Rasch homogeneous scales. Given the generally accepted high quality of the items and the small number of items per scale of 16 to 20, this was not acceptable.

The other solution available, adding a selection item and trying to fit the two-parameter logistic model with the BILOG program also failed. Here the problems were not caused by the estimation procedure, but by the methodology for testing the model fit in this program. The BILOG program has implemented on the item level a test statistic originally introduced by Yen (1981). This test statistic is based on the comparison of expected counts of correct responses to an item under the model with observed correct responses in groups of students whose estimated ability values are similar. The distribution of this test statistic is not known exactly, but it is supposed to be approximately asymptotically chi-squared (χ^2). On the basis of simulation studies, Yen makes plausible that testing with this statistic sometimes gives acceptable results, assuming a χ^2 distribution with as degrees of freedom the number of groups minus the number of estimated parameters.

However, generally, and in particular in our application, it does not. The following example of the analysis of a scale will illustrate this. Consider the analysis of the scale application of ratios in the mathematics assessment. This scale has 16 items and trying to fit the Birnbaum model gave the fit statistics presented in Table 14.3.

Using a significance level of 0.05 the item numbers 2, 3 and 15 can be considered for removal from the scale, but when we do an analysis without these items, in trial 2 we see that five new items are eligible for deletion. This

Table 14.3: P-values of Yen's statistic under the Birnbaum model applied to the scale application of ratios

Item	p trial 1	p trial 2
1	0.12	0.00
2	0.00	–
3	0.00	–
4	0.11	0.60
5	0.06	0.60
6	0.75	0.57
7	0.48	0.21
8	0.06	0.81
9	0.08	0.01
10	0.19	0.03
11	0.11	0.19
12	0.47	0.03
13	0.51	0.04
14	0.25	0.12
15	0.00	–
16	0.23	0.17
sel	0.02	0.00

phenomenon was observed in all scales. This high sensitivity of the fit statistic makes it questionable for use in item analysis. The approximate results for the test statistic appear to be too rough. The asymptotical results cannot be applied in this application, which is possibly also caused by the small number of items in the scales.

A one-parameter model with unequal discrimination indices

In trying to find a model that combines the statistically attractive properties of the Rasch model and the flexibility of the two-parameter logistic model, a new model is proposed by Verhelst and Eggen (in preparation). This model, which in fact is an intermediate form of the one- and two-parameter logistic model, is given by:

$$P(X_{ij} = x_{ij}) = P(X_{ij} \mid \Theta_i, a_j, \beta_j) = \frac{\exp\{a_j (\Theta_i - \beta_j) x_{ij}\}}{1 = \exp\{a_j (\Theta_i - \beta_j)\}} \tag{7}$$

where $x_{ij} = 0, 1$; $i \varepsilon I$; $j \varepsilon J$.

Furthermore, the assumptions given in equation (2) are made again with respect to the independence of the responses. Compared to the Birnbaum model (1), this model has only one change: instead of having free discrimination parameters, α_j, which are to be estimated, we have constant discrimination indices a_j, possible differing between items. The possibility of different discrimination indices between items, makes this model (7) different from the Rasch model. The model, which will be amply discussed in a forthcoming paper by Verhelst and

Eggen (in preparation), has several elegant properties. Some of these properties are:

1. It can be shown that $S_i = \sum_j a_j X_{ij}$, the sum of the item scores weighted with the discrimination indices of the items, is a sufficient statistic for the ability parameters Θ_i. Therefore, conditional maximum likelihood methods can be applied to estimate the item parameters. The CML procedures as, for instance, given by Fischer (1974) for the Rasch model can be applied with some fairly simple modifications. Details are in Verhelst and Eggen (in preparation).

2. Also it can be shown that the model belongs to the exponential family, and for that reason, goodness of fit tests with proven asymptotically χ^2- distributed fit statistics can be deduced along the lines developed by Verhelst and Glas (in preparation).

In fact the model is a more flexible form of the Rasch model, while its major statistical properties are maintained. The flexibility is due to the fact that unlike the Rasch model, item characteristic curves with unequal slopes are allowed. Although, in theory, nothing could prevent us from applying the model with many different discrimination indices, this could cause numerical problems in trying to estimate the item parameters. More important, however, is that there are also very practical reasons to restrict the number of different indices. Tests, especially those that are constructed for limited content domains, will seldom need more than three or four different indices.

Before discussing the way the discrimination indices are to be determined, it is worth noting that the units in which we express the indices are in fact arbitrary and inversely proportionally related to the units of the standard deviation of the distribution of the ability of the population for which the items will be calibrated. This means that the units can be chosen with respect to practical considerations. In estimating the model, only the ratios of the indices are of concern and there are no obstacles for choosing the numerically most attractive values – i.e. whole numbers, for the discrimination indices.

Applying the model in the mathematics assessment

The calibration procedure of the mathematics assessment contained several steps; I will only elaborate on the way the item parameters were estimated, and the way the fit of the model was assessed in the one-parameter model with different discrimination indices. The pre-analyses consisted of:

- sampling checks, for example, assessing the equivalence of the samples across the scales;

- defining the calibration population;

- classical test and item analysis of the scales (p-value, item test correlation) on parts of the design that were complete;

- study of item bias, especially with respect to sex and stratum (see the paper by Wijnstra, in this volume).

All these analyses resulted in a well-defined calibration population and in the detection of a number of items which could cause problems in the calibration of the scales. The parameters of the new model were estimated with a CML procedure, and by that procedure, the non-ignorability of the design does not play a role (for details, see Verhelst and Eggen, in preparation).

The actual calibration of the scales was conducted in two major steps. In the first step, the discrimination indices of the items were determined, and in the second step the calibration was completed given the discrimination indices.

Determining the discrimination indices

If we fit the Rasch model, we estimate the difficulty parameters and test all the assumptions underlying the model. One of these assumptions is that all items have the same discriminating power. If the model is not rejected on statistical grounds, with tests that have sufficient power against undesirable deviations from the model, we work with the model.

In the same way, we could proceed in trying to fit the one-parameter model with unequal discrimination indices. If we have reason to believe that the items have particular different values for the discrimination indices, we could apply a statistical test which has special power against deviations from the hypothesized indices. If this test indicates that there are no statistical reasons for changing the discrimination indices, they are fixed in the model. Alternatively, the hypothesized values are adjusted and tested again.

Working this way, it remains to choose the best starting values of these indices. The best way to choose the item discrimination indices would be to have a theory about every item that could predict the discrimination of the item. Unfortunately, such a theory is not available, so that only empirical data on the items can give first good guesses on the ratios of the indices. Verhelst and Eggen (in preparation) indicate that there are several possibilities to generate these good guesses, but in essence, it does not really matter which one is chosen because the first step is testing on the first good guesses. In the mathematics assessment we used the values of the discrimination parameter estimated in the Birnbaum model. As a first hypothesis, these values were rounded to the nearest integer.

The hypothesis of the discrimination indices are tested in the following way. Because the model belongs to the exponential family, tests with known asymptotic behaviour can be developed along the lines of Verhelst and Glas (in preparation). We constructed a test which has special power against deviations from the discrimination index. The operation of the test resembles a test originally proposed by Molenaar (1983) for the Rasch model. This test, which is sensitive for the steepness of the item characteristic curves, operates as follows.

The basis principle is the same as in Yen's test, described previously. On the basis of the weighted scores, the sufficient statistics for ability, testees are grouped. Within these groups the expected proportion of correct responses according to the model is compared to the actually observed proportion. Next we divide the proportion continuum in two parts: a lower and higher parts, then it can be shown that a statistic M is asymptotically standard normal-distributed. Furthermore, it can be shown that this statistic has a clear interpretation. If M is positive, the hypothesized steepness of the item characteristic curve is overestimated. If the hypothesized discrimination index is too low, M will be negative.

In the actual implementation of the test statistic the groups are formed under the restriction that each group contains at least 30 students and that the expected frequency in each group is at least 5. No more than 9 groups were used. Finally, as cutting points for the division in the lower and high proportions 0.4 and 0.6 were used. The results of a typical application of this methodology to the mathematics assessment is presented in Table 14.4. These results are for the scale fractions, multiplication and division.

In the first trial, we find significant deviations from the first hypothesized values of the discrimination indices for items 3 and 7. The discrimination index of item 3 is overestimated and of item 7 it is underestimated. After adjusting the indices, in the second trial we see that none of the indices significantly deviates

Table 14.4: Hypothesized discrimination indices and values of test statistic M in the scale fractions: multiplication and division

Item	Trial 1		Trial 2	
	inp. 1	M	‑inp. 2	M
1	3	0.341		−0.141
2	2	−0.661		−0.868
3	2	2.942	1	0.538
4	4	−0.110		0.570
5	4	0.391		0.833
6	3	0.743		0.651
7	2	−2.866	3	1.030
8	3	−0.336		−1.265
9	2	1.013		0.243
10	2	−1.250		−0.925
11	3	−0.388		−1.073
12	2	0.135		0.124
13	3	1.935		0.491
14	2	0.864		0.883
15	2	0.198		0.279
16	2	−0.550		−0.680
17	2	−0.159		−0.315
18	2	0.614		0.546

Table 14.5: Discrimination indices (a), estimated difficulties ($\hat\beta$) and p-values in final calibration of scale fractions: multiplication and division

Item	a	Trial 1 $\hat\beta$	p	Trial 2 $\hat\beta$	p
1	3	−0.192	0.517	−0.178	0.517
2	2	−0.546	0.339	−0.533	0.339
3	1	−1.129	0.043	−1.116	0.083
4	4	−0.627	0.669	−0.613	0.670
5	4	−0.458	0.936	−0.445	0.936
6	3	0.143	0.584	0.158	0.326
7	3	−0.591	0.405	−0.579	0.248
8	3	0.434	0.526	0.448	0.783
9	2	0.030	0.818	0.045	0.560
10	2	−0.238	0.433	−0.227	0.141
11	3	−0.219	0.779	−0.206	0.932
12	2	0.152	0.552	0.167	0.106
13	3	−0.427	0.656	−0.415	0.409
14	2	0.240	0.001	−	−
15	2	0.740	0.649	0.757	0.552
16	2	1.025	0.835	1.041	0.992
17	2	1.079	0.749	1.095	0.929
18	2	0.583	0.749	0.600	0.303

from the hypothesized values. Herewith this part of the calibration was completed.

Final calibration of the scale

Given the discrimination indices, the calibration was completed with conditional maximum likelihood estimation of the item-difficulty parameters. The model fit was tested by computing for each item a general statistic constructed along the lines given by Verhelst and Glas (in preparation). It can be shown that the implemented statistic has asymptotically a χ^2 distribution. Because grouping was done as described before, the number of degrees of freedom can vary among items.

The calibration of the same scale on fractions, as above, is given in Table 14.5. Columns 3 and 4 respectively give the estimated item difficulties and the p-values under the model of the test statistic in the first trial. A probability of less than e.g. 0.05 indicates a misfit of the item to the model. Because item 14 seems to misfit the model, the scale was re-analyzed, deleting this item. The results of this second trial are given in the final two columns. We see that after two analyses, all items give good fit and we accept the values in columns 2 and 5 as respectively the discrimination indices and the difficulty parameters of this scale. By this, disregarding the final choice of the units of the scales, the calibration is completed.

With respect to the units in which the item parameters are given, it is worth noting that the scale of the latent variable is arbitrarily fixed, by fixing the mean of the difficulty parameter at 0. This scale can be transformed with any linear transformation. The fixing of the scale in the mathematics assessment was established in such a way that, in the end, the ability of the calibration population has a distribution with a mean of 250 and a standard deviation of 50.

In general, the procedure described above was followed with all scales, and we succeeded in calibrating all 27 scales in the mathematics assessment with the one-parameter model with unequal discrimination indices. For statistical reasons, and content-related reasons, only a few items had to be deleted: 25 out of 492 items, fairly evenly distributed over the 27 scales.

Discussion

The combination of multiple matrix sampling and a rough form of tailored testing, as was applied in the mathematics assessment, not only causes the expected gain in efficiency, but also a non-trivial calibration of the scales. The non-ignorability of the design, in this situation, restrains us from applying a standard maximum marginal likelihood estimation of the parameters. Although, in principle, two solutions are available, they both fail in the mathematics assessment. Working with the Rasch model is far too restrictive and adding the design variable to the estimation procedures in the Birnbaum model fails on methodological grounds.

Item response models are statistical models with nice properties, which only yield if the model is correct. So before using these properties, the validity of the model must be checked. The availability of a test statistic with known asymptotic behaviour seems to be a minimal condition for this. This condition was fulfilled in the application of the one-parameter model with unequal discrimination indices in the mathematics assessment. The properties, theoretically as well as practically, of the new proposed model need further research.

References

BIRNBAUM, A. (1968). 'Some latent trait models and their use in inferring an examinee's ability'. In: LORD, F.M. and NOVICK, M.R. *Statistical Theories of Mental Tests Scores.* Reading, Mass.: Addison-Wesley.

BOCK, R.D. and AITKEN, M. (1981). 'Marginal maximum likelihood estimation of item parameters: an application of an EM algorithm', *Psychometrika*, 46, 443–59.

FISCHER, G.H. (1974). *Einführung in die Theorie psychologischer Tests.* Bern: Huber.

GLAS, C.A.W. (1988). *RIDA: Rasch Incomplete Data Analysis* (computer program). Arnhem: Cito, National Institute for Educational Measurement.

HAMBLETON, R.K. and SWAMINATHAN, H. (1985). *Item Response Theory: Principles and Applications.* Boston: Kluwer-Nijhoff.

LITTLE, R.J.A. and RUBIN, D.B. (1987). *Statistical Analysis with Missing Data.* New York: Wiley.

MISLEVY, R.J. and BOCK, R.D. (1986). 'PC-BILOG: Item Analysis and Test Scoring with Binary Logistic Models (computer program). Mooresville: Scientific Software Inc.

MOLENAAR, I.W. (1983). 'Some improved diagnostics for failure of the Rasch model', *Psychometrika*, 148, 49–72.

RASCH, G. (1960). *Probabilistic Models for Some Intelligence and Attainment Tests*. Copenhagen: Danish Institute for Educational Research.

RUBIN, D.B. (1976). 'Inference and missing data', *Biometrika*, 63, 581–92.

VERHELST, N.D. and EGGEN, T.J.H.M. (in preparation). 'A One-Parameter Latent Trait Model with Unequal Discrimination Indices. Arnhem: Cito, National Institute for Educational Measurement.

VERHELST, N.D. and GLAS, C.A.W. (in preparation). *A Glass of Model Tests for Multinominal Models Belonging to the Exponential Family*. Arnhem: Cito, National Institute for Educational Measurement.

YEN, W.M. (1981). 'Using simulation results to choose a latent trait model', *Applied Psychological Measurement*, 5, 245–62.

15 Comprehensive Educational Assessment for the States: The Duplex Design*

R. Darrell Bock and Robert J. Mislevy

According to a 1985 survey, 47 of the 50 states mandate some form of state-wide testing of student attainment (Winfield, 1986). These testing programmes vary widely in design: some employ tradition every-pupil achievement testing, others are limited to minimum competency testing and still others make use of matrix-sampled assessment at benchmark grade levels.

The most widespread programme is minimum competency testing: 23 states have centrally directed programmes and another 16 allow local options of test content and administration; in 23 of these 39 states satisfactory performance on the test is a requirement for high school graduation. Standards for passing are set variously by state legislatures, state boards of education and local education authorities. Many states have multiple programmes, usually some combination of outcome assessment and individual achievement testing. States that have achievement measurement or minimum competency programmes test every pupil at selected grade levels, but some of those using matrix sampled-assessment test in a sample of schools. Others, such as California, use matrix-sampling methods, but test in all schools.

States that have no centrally directed programme may nevertheless require the districts to conduct periodic achievement testing. In Iowa all districts test annually, and in fact all use the same test. Finally, end of high school tests in specialized subject-matter areas are administered to selected students in some states (New York State Regents Examination, California Golden State examination). Winfield (*ibid.*) and Burstein *et al.* (1985) give detailed accounts of existing and projected state testing programmes.

Considering that the information needed to assess educational productivity must be much the same in all states, the variety of these programmes is, at first glance, surprising. Closer examination reveals, however, that they emphasize different outcomes for which schools should be held responsible. If certification

*We are indebted to Linda Winfield, Leigh Burstein, David Wiley, Zalman Usiskin, Tej Pandey, Pat McCabe, Joan Baron and Mervin Brennan for valuable suggestions. Preparation of this paper was supported in part by the Center for Student Testing, Evaluation and Standards, School of Education, UCLA, and in part by a grant from the Spencer Foundation.

of essential skills and knowledge is the main concern, minimum competency testing is emphasized. If the emphasis is on individual student attainment at all levels, especially when student guidance is required, a commercial achievement testing programme is usually relied upon. If the purpose is to monitor progress towards detailed curricular objectives, a matrix-sampling assessment programme is the only practical approach. To the extent that mandated testing is committed to these disparate goals, the multiplicity of the existing state programmes would seem to be inevitable.

We will argue, however, that with a suitable measurement design, a single, comprehensive assessment programme can serve all of these purposes. We base this conclusion on an analysis of the information needs of the main users of educational test results within the states. The design we propose meets their needs directly and efficiently.

Educational information users

Anyone concerned with the conduct of education is conscious of the need for regular appraisals of student progress. Without such information, there can be no objective basis for guiding the student, for planning instruction, for evaluating schools, school systems and programmes or for correcting deficiencies or rewarding progress. It is not as well understood, however, that different forms of information about educational outcomes are required in these different applications. The first step in formulating the design must be an analysis of the anticipated uses of the results. These uses depend, of course, upon the *users* of the information, among which we delineate the following seven main categories.

Teachers, school counsellors, parents and the student

Standardized individual achievement tests, independent of particular teachers or courses, are widely relied upon as aids to informed and fair decisions on student advancement and placement. In this role, the tests must have three important properties: (1) they must cover content that is relevant to the coursework for which the student is responsible; (2) they must be sufficiently reliable that scores on alternative forms of the same test will, with high probability, lead to the same recommendations on individual advancement or placement; and (3) the results must be presented in a form readily understandable to the parties involved.

To construct achievement test forms capable of this kind of consistent differential measurement is technically demanding. The problem is that decisions about students are made at all levels of the score distribution: low-ranking students may be kept back or sent to remedial programmes; high-ranking students may be put ahead of their grade or assigned to honours programmes; and students in the middle range may be assigned to tracked classrooms differentially. To be accurate over the entire range, an achievement test must have a sufficient number of items to measure accurately at widely differing difficulty levels. To span this wide a range, an individual achievement test must be rather long.

As a result, the testing time available usually restricts the separate proficiencies that can be tested to a relatively small number. A test that reliably estimates achievement in six areas, for example, may require three to four hours to administer. A major challenge in comprehensive assessment is to reduce the time required for dependable measurement of individual student achievement while serving the needs of all users. Fortunately, new methods of adaptive testing and conjoint scoring, described below, make such savings possible.

In communicating achievement test results to students, parents and teachers, we depend upon the normative nature of guidance-oriented use of test information. Teachers rarely make decisions about the student on an absolute basis; they can single out for special treatment only those students who deviate from the local standard. Because only rank-order information is required for such decisions, any form of reporting that indicates the student's standing in a reference group is suitable. In other words, **norm-referenced** reporting is quite adequate for guidance purposes.

Designers of curricula and planners of instruction

In designing curricula or developing instructional methods and materials for the classroom, it is not the individual student that is to be evaluated, but the overall performance of students taught under alternative conditions. Although the classroom teacher has an interest in the outcome of such evaluations, it is primarily the school department head and principal, the professional curriculum specialist and the textbook and workbook writer who will make direct use of these results. Because measures of broad content areas provided by achievement tests tend to be insensitive to differential curricular effects, these workers need much more detailed information about student attainment than is available in traditional achievement test scores. Although not often mentioned in the evaluation literature, this fact has been amply demonstrated in empirical studies of alternative curricula. Walker and Schaffarzick (1974), in a lengthy review of research on science and mathematics curricula from 1956 to 1972, found that any given curriculum tends to be superior to others only in respect to material that is distinctive to it. Differential outcomes are thus seen primarily in detailed score profiles, not in overall performance. A corollary to this finding is that the tests employed in such comparisons must be capable of measuring accurately separate outcomes for distinctive parts of the curricula. An instrument used to evaluate 'new' mathematics and 'traditional' mathematics, for example, would have to produce reliable scores for both of these types of content.

By the same token, instructional planners need to examine student performance in units of content that can be manipulated in instruction. To write lesson plans for mathematics, for example, the instructors need to know the specific units – computation, number systems, problem-solving, applications, etc. – that need attention. These units are almost always tested formatively, but time restrictions prevent their separate evaluation during summative testing of individual achievement.

To be broadly useful, an evaluation instrument may need to distinguish perhaps 20–40 curricular objectives at a given grade level. Fortunately, individual achievement testing of these many topics is not necessary in programme evaluation: only the average performance of classroom or other experimental units need be assessed for this purpose. Thus it is not the reliability of individual test scores, but the generalizability of the group mean scores, that is the important consideration.

It has been known for some time that to obtain adequate generalizability in estimating programme effects, evaluation should not be based on the traditional achievement test, but on an instrument in which each student responds to only a few items sampled from each of a number of content domains, while different students respond to different samples of items. This approach assures good generalizability of the group mean for each domain with minimal demands on testing time. In these so-called **matrix-sampling designs**, the test instrument is constructed in many forms, 15–20 or sometimes more, with a small number of items assigned randomly to each form from the pool representing each curricular objective. Lord (1962) has shown that the most efficient matrix sample is one in which each student in the group is assigned one distinct item from each objective. In that case, the number of curricular objectives that can be assessed in one form is then equal to the number of items that the student can respond to during the testing period, usually 30–50. This number is quite adequate for a highly detailed curricular evaluation.

The scoring of matrix-sampled instruments is also different from that of achievement tests. In Lord's formulation (*ibid.*) of matrix sampling the scores are not presented with reference to any norm, but simply as average percentages correct for each content domain. Classrooms, groups of students, instructional programmes, schools and other aggregations are then compared with respect to the strengths and weaknesses revealed in the profile of average percentage correct scores over the curricular objectives. Since these objectives usually correspond to units or topics of instruction, definite recommendations about teaching practices or emphasis can be made from the results.

More recently, Bock, Mislevy and Woodson (1982) have shown how matrix-sampled data can also be analysed and scored by use of scaling techniques based on item response theory (IRT). According to this theory, the probability that a student will respond correctly to a given test item is a function of the student's location on the proficiency dimension and of properties of the item such as its difficulty and validity. The properties of each item in a test can be estimated from large samples of responses and then used to estimate a 'scale score' for the student indicating his/her proficiency level.

Average percentage correct scoring and IRT scale scoring both retain the detail necessary for curricular evaluation and instructional planning, but scale scores have the advantage of remaining comparable as items are added to or retired from the instrument from time to time. This consistency of interpretation as the item content is updated is essential if educational progress is to be followed over long periods of time. Recently developed IRT test maintenance systems provide for the detection and correction of drift in the relative difficulties of items that may occur over time (Bock, Muraki and Pfeiffenberger, 1988).

Local school system managers, officers and boards

In making decision on personnel, resource allocation and policy, school officials must be able to support their actions with data on educational outcomes in the schools for which they are responsible. In addition to such operational statistics as number of students in school, number of hours of schooling, teacher–student ratio, etc., they need measures of outcomes in the relevant subject-matter areas at a number of grade levels. The detail required depends somewhat on the style of administration or supervision of the persons involved. Superintendents and boards that have considerable experience with education and instruction probably will be interested in more detail than is available from achievement testing, although perhaps not to the same extent as the curriculum specialist. They will not, however, be interested in a level of score reporting below that of the classroom or school. Because their concern is with group-level rather than individual outcomes, they can make profitable use of the matrix-sampling methods of programme evaluation. The only difference is that classrooms or schools rather than programmes are being evaluated, a distinction that is conveyed by describing the activity as 'assessment' rather than 'evaluation'.

Assessment procedures based on matrix-sampling designs have the advantage of providing a detailed profile of aggregate outcomes without intruding excessively on classroom time. Equally advantageous, however, is their resistance to effects of 'teaching to the test items'. Because there are so many items in the forms that make up assessment instruments, it is difficult for a teacher to discuss enough of the items to have any great effect on the school outcome. Indeed, if the assessment represents the full range of curricular objectives, an attempt to teach a majority of the items would be virtually equivalent to teaching the subject-matter of the course. In addition, if scale-scoring is used, a proportion of items can be replaced periodically to protect further the integrity of the test.

Achievement tests, in contrast, typically exist in only a few forms and are not always updated regularly. If school districts use the same achievement tests from year to year, the items tend to become known to the teachers, who may then consciously or unconsciously teach the specific information required to answer particular items. If so, the tests will tend to show year-to-year average gains that do not reflect increased general knowledge of the subject-matter on the part of the student. The more pressure the teachers are under to improve student outcomes, the greater the probability that these teaching-to-the-test-item effects will appear.

Whether or not the information on student progress comes from achievement tests or assessment, it is important to school officials that the scores be reported on a scale with fixed origin and unit, so that gains or losses in each subject-matter area can be compared over a period of years. The sort of rank-order information that is acceptable for comparing individual students is not suitable for monitoring the progress of schools and school systems. Average number correct scores in assessment results have this property, but they have the disadvantage of losing their comparability if some items are retired from or added to the content areas assessed. As Lord (1980) has discussed, IRT scoring of tests facilitates both the equating of test forms and the updating of item content within forms. This theory also allows accurate calculation of measurement error standard deviations at all points on the scale. These standard deviations are required for assessment results in the form of confidence intervals that convey uncertainty due to the sampling of both students and items (see Figures 15.1 and 15.2).

State departments of education

The activities of most state departments of education are sufficiently varied to benefit from all of the outcome measures described above. Departments that formulate curricula or set objectives need feedback from the assessment of detailed curricular objectives. For these activities most states employ professional specialists whose work depends critically on this type of information. At the same time, most departments of education are also concerned with the performance of schools as measured by numbers of students reaching or exceeding defined levels of achievement, whether basic, intermediate, advanced or outstanding. For these purposes, individual achievement measures in broad subject-matter areas are required. This is the reason that many states operate assessment programmes simultaneously with conventional, in many cases commercial, achievement testing.

Some states have limited assessment programmes based on sampling of schools and of students within schools. If the state also has a policy of accountability of school districts for levels of student attainment, however, this type of sampling is not sufficient, and a complete census based on every-pupil testing in the benchmark grades is preferable. The effort can be well repaid: because the census provides accurate information at the level of the individual schools, results can be reported in a form that is interesting and informative locally, and schools with exceptional outcome patterns can be identified throughout the state.

An additional problem with a sampling assessment is that the schools have no immediate pay-off. Motivation for co-operation on the part of both staff and students is minimal, and levels of performance may suffer as a result. Apart from the lower cost of sampling assessment, there is little to recommend it over an every-pupil programme.

State legislators and officials.

At the state level, legislators not exclusively involved in education can attend only to rather general indices of educational outcomes. They cannot go into the detail that would interest the curriculum specialist, or even the more limited achievement profiles required for student counselling. Their concern is primarily with the main subject-matter areas measured at transition grade levels – e.g. 4, 8 and 12. Typically, year-to-year gains and losses are of more interest than absolute levels of attainment. The statistics necessary for these general summaries of educational progress can readily be obtained by aggregating the more detailed assessment figures at the school or district level. The precision and generalizability of these statistics will be so high that the confidence intervals required at lower levels of aggregation will seldom be necessary, although they can be calculated if required. If reported in the form of scale scores, the results will remain comparable over extended periods of time, and long-run changes in the average performance of students in the state can be followed.

By examining year-to-year data, state officials may be able to infer the impact of current social trends on student performance (e.g. television viewing or microcomputer use). They may then be able to anticipate educational problems that will eventually influence public policy or legislation. Long-term stability and consistency of a state's assessment programme and procedures are essential to such inferences.

The media and the public

Communicating school performance data to the general public is a challenging task for the educational evaluator. The key to success is making the findings understandable to the journalists who must report such information in the newspapers and on radio and television. Reporting of average percentages correct for a content area, which provides only relative information and varies in level from one content area to another, is not very useful for this purpose because the audience has to keep in mind that the scales are not comparable. A much better practice is to employ scale-scoring, defining a scale with a common origin and unit for all subject-matter areas, and employing it uniformly until its characteristics become known. Comparisons between schools or groups of students can then be expressed in familiar numbers, and year-to-year gains or declines in student performance can be followed in units that have an accepted meaning. Certain achievement scales, such as that used to report Scholastic Aptitude Test (SAT) scores, have achieved this status.

An even more comprehensible form of reporting, however, is to state the percentage of students who fall above or below certain thresholds on the attainment scale. If these points correspond to administrative cutting points (e.g. for graduation, special honours, admission to college, etc.), their practical implication is entirely clear. If these objective criteria do not exist, the item content typical of selected score levels can be exhibited to convey the nature of the tasks that students at these levels can typically perform. The reading scale of the National Assessment of Educational Progress (NAEP), for example, is characterized for reporting purposes by displays of items that students at the 150, 200, 250, 300 and 350 points on the scale have an 80 per cent chance of answering correctly.

Another possibility is to take a normative approach and to designate certain arbitrary percentile points in the population of students. The 25, 50 and 75 percentage points, for example, might be referred to as the 'basic', 'intermediate' and 'advanced' mastery levels. In this connection, it must be mentioned that achievement testing and assessment are quite different when it comes to estimating the percentage of student above a specified performance threshold. In achievement data it is a simple matter to obtain these percentages by enumerating students whose individual scores fall in the defined intervals. But from matrix-sampled assessment data, individual scores are not available, and the percentage of students above some point on the group means scale can be estimated only if the distribution of proficiencies within the group can be described. Up to now, the information necessary to estimate these within-group distributions has not been part of assessment results; it has had to come separately from conventional achievement tests rather than matrix-sampled assessment designs. One of the main strengths of the duplex design is that the proportions of students exceeding specified mastery levels can be estimated in the same manner as in achievement testing. This enables the proportion of students at specified levels to be estimated directly.

Educational research specialists

A constituency independent of school systems, yet having an interest in the information generated by state testing programmes comprises the academic and professional research workers engaged in the study of education and the schools. In principle, they can use information from either achievement testing or assessment. But like the curriculum specialists, they are also often interested in detailed areas of attainment, not just the broad skill areas measured by individual achievement tests. The data from assessment programmes may be more relevant to them than traditional test scores. Assessment data will also typically have higher generalizability indices, and thus clearer relationships with other variables.

The effect of matrix sampling on generalizability is demonstrated by the estimated correlation coefficients shown in Table 15.1. The data are reading score means in California schools measured in two successive years. Note that the sizes of the correlations increase (the school means become more accurate) as the sizes of the samples of students increase from row 1 to row 3. Similarly, the correlations increase when student sample size remains fixed, but the numbers of items sampled increase from 85 in a single test form to 128 in 16 forms, to 400 in 40 forms. This latter effect arises from the increased generalizability due to item sampling. It would be even more pronounced if different items were sampled each year. It would then maximally suppress the effects of item heterogeneity that attenuate relationships between student attainment and the background variables.

Table 15.1: Effect of sampling of students and sampling of items on year-to-year correlations of sixth-grade mean reading attainment scores of California schools

| | | Number of items in matrix sample | | |
		85	128	400
No. of students	50	0.59	0.73	0.79
sampled	100	0.67	0.78	0.88
per grade	200	0.76	0.81	0.93

Because most standard computer packages require scores for individual re-spondents, however, matrix-sampled assessment data can present something of a dilemma to research workers. Only more advanced investigators currently know how to use matrix-sampled data directly by hierarchical methods (see Mislevy, 1985). Until computer packages become available for analysing scores that exist only at the group level, the data obtained from matrix-sampling de-signs will not be convenient for secondary analysis. In this respect, the duplex design proposed in this paper has a marked advantage: it supports scoring of the item response data at both the individual and the group level. Research workers can thus make use of either of these types of data, depending on their statistical resources.

Table 15.2: Summary of uses of assessment information and type of data required in each

Use	Test instrument	Reporting level	Reporting detail
Guidance			
Counselling, placement, promotion and certification	Standardized achievement tests	Individual student	Profile of 5–10 subject-matter areas or sub-areas
Evaluation			
Judging alternative curricular, instructional methods and materials	Multiple matrix sampling	Classroom, school or programme	20–40 curricular objectives
Management			
Monitoring student attainment in schools, programmes and districts	Achievement tests and matrix sampling	Classroom, school, programme or district	Distribution of student scores and results for curricular objectives; trend measures
Policy			
Judging overall attainment in the student population, or important sub-populations, for the purpose of formulating legislation or allocating resources	Achievement tests or matrix sampling	State or county	Numbers of students at defined levels of achievement in main subject-matters; trend measures
Research			
Secondary studies of conditions and back-ground variables that influence student attainment	Achievement tests or matrix sampling	Student records or classroom and school summaries	Varies, but typically limited to main subject-matter areas and sub-areas

The *uses* of information on student attainment associated with the above users are summarized in Table 15.2.

Combining student achievement testing and assessment of curricular objectives: a duplex design

It should be clear from the preceding discussion that traditional individual achievement testing differs in important ways from assessment of the success of schools or programmes in attaining specific curricular objectives. Up to now, these two types of educational measurement have been conducted in separate testing programmes using different instruments. Because the item content of these instruments is much the same, however, substantial duplication of cost, effort and demand on classroom time is incurred to obtain the same information in different forms.

We suggest that with a suitably designed assessment instrument, both of these forms of information can be obtained in a single-test administration requiring no more classroom time than conventional achievement testing. The instrument we propose for this purpose, which we call a **duplex design**, has multiple stratified random test forms like those used in assessment. But the items are assigned to forms in such a way that a student's response to a particular form can be scored in broad skill and content areas, while responses over forms can be aggregated to provide scores for detailed curricular objectives at the school or other group level. An example of the layout of an instrument of this type in eighth grade mathematics is shown in Table 15.3.

The arrangement in Table 15.3 is referred to as a 'content by process' classification of tasks or test items that might be presented to the student. The rows represent content, and the columns, cognitive processes. We call the content and process intersections 'curricular elements'. Not all of the intersections are necessarily occupied; some may define tasks that cannot be realized.

The design in Table 15.3 is based on the assumption that the main processes in performing mathematical tasks are expressed in three broad categories of behaviour, called **proficiencies**. These proficiencies are derived from cognitive distinctions between procedural knowledge, semantic knowledge and problem-solving. The mathematical substance of the proficiencies is classified in the content categories of the discipline as reflected in current curricula and textbooks at this grade level.

A profile of the scores for individual students can be calculated within forms by **conjoint** scoring of items in rows and columns of the table. In this procedure scores for each of the three proficiencies are obtained by aggregating over content. Then diagnostic scores in the main content categories (Number, Algebra, Geometry, Measurement, and Probability and Statistics) are obtained by aggregating over the proficiencies and over the sub-topics within the main content categories. In addition, an overall score for mathematics is computed by aggregating over all items.

At the same time, scores for *groups* of students can be calculated for each of the 57 elements in the table by aggregating over test forms. When the scoring methods described in Mislevy and Bock (1989) or Bock, Muraki and

Table 15.3: A grade 8 mathematics duplex design

Content categories	Proficiencies		
	(a) Procedural skills*	(b) Knowledge of facts and concepts**	(c) Higher-level thinking***
10 Numbers			
Integers	11	11	11
Fractions	12	12	12
Percentages	13	13	13
Decimals	14	14	14
Irrationals	15	15	15
20 Algebra			
Expressions	21	21	21
Equations	22	22	22
Inequalities	23	23	23
Functions	24	24	24
30 Geometry			
Figures	31	31	31
Relations and	32	32	32
transformations	33	33	33
Coordinates			
40 Measurement			
English and metric units	41	41	41
Length, area and volume	42	42	42
Angular measure	43	43	43
Other systems (time, etc.)	44	44	44
50 Probability and statistics			
Probability	51	51	51
Experiments and surveys	52	52	52
Descriptive statistics	53	53	53

* Calculating, rewriting, constructing, estimating, executing algorithms.
** Terms, definitions, concepts, principles.
***Proof, reasoning, problem-solving, real-world applications.

Pfeiffenberger (1988) are used for this purpose, the mean of the proficiency or of the content area scores at the student level when averaged over students will equal the mean of the school-level, curricular-element scores for that school. Thus the several types of information extracted from the duplex design are expressed in the same units on the same scale of measurement.

Depending on the item pool, not all of the curricular elements may be included when the design is implemented. In a prototype of the grade 8 mathematics design based on items from the California and Illinois Assessments, certain content categories (irrationals, inequalities, other systems of measurement, experiments and surveys) were not represented. In the prototype instrument the included elements were replicated in 24 booklets containing a total of 888 distinct items. The items in any given form were chosen randomly from the pools representing each of the curricular elements.

In the administration of this type of instrument, the booklets are distributed in rotation within classrooms. The fact that different students may be responding to different forms and items does not typically present any difficulty. The experience of the California Assessment shows that when expendable test forms are used, group testing with this type of instrument can be carried out as early as the third grade.

The contribution of modern item response theory (IRT)

Efficient estimation of comparable scores for all students, regardless of which test form they are assigned, requires the use of modern IRT methods of item scaling. Because the item content of each of the scales is balanced in the duplex design, the scoring is robust in the presence of minor departures from the conditional independence assumed in conventional IRT methods. In the implementation of these methods the instrument is administered initially to a probability sample of students at the selected grade level. The test items are then calibrated, preferably by the marginal maximum likelihood method (Bock and Aitkin, 1981), with the unit and origin of measurement chosen such that the mean and standard deviation in the population of students is the same for all scales in the base year. The resulting item parameters are then used to compute students' scores by maximum likelihood or Bayes methods, and each score is accompanied by a standard error or posterior standard deviation. Scores computed in succeeding years with these item parameters have constant origin and unit and are suitable for measuring growth and change in the population from the base year onward.

Scores for schools or other groups of students can be estimated by IRT methods using the models for group data described by Mislevy (1983). These methods provide scores for the curricular elements on the assumption that each pupil responds to one item from each element, a condition which the duplex design satisfies. This type of scoring is especially easy to carry out because it uses, as statistics, the number of students who attempt each item within the classroom or school and, among those, the number who respond correctly. Thus the calculations require only a classroom or school summary file rather than the much larger file of individual item responses required for the scoring of students in the skill areas.

Because IRT methods are used, it is possible to add and retire items from the test without altering the initial definition of the scale. This updating can be done as part of the operational administration of the test without additional field trials. This armamentarium of IRT techniques, along with provisions for writing and critiquing new items, constitutes the item maintenance system that supports the comprehensive assessment programme.

Adaptive testing

With the aid of IRT scoring methods, it is possible to minimize testing time by using some form of adaptive test administration. If the item domain is strictly unidimensional, one would prefer individual, fully adaptive, computerized test administration in which each item presented to the examinee is most informative, given the provisional estimate of the examinee's proficiency. But almost equal gains in efficiency can be obtained by a much more robust, group-administered, two-stage testing (Lord, 1980). In this form of testing, each student takes a short pre-test of general knowledge in the subject-matter area. This pre-test is then scored by the teacher prior to the main test, and the student is assigned the appropriate second-stage form according to the result. A feasibility trial of a two-stage form of the duplex design for eighth-grade mathematics described above is presently being conducted in Illinois and California as a project of the OERI Center for Student Testing, Evaluation and Standards. The assessment instrument for this study consists of a 15-item pre-test and 8 second-stage forms, each consisting of three test booklets at 'easy', 'intermediate' and 'hard' levels of difficulty respectively. At the student level, the instrument tests three mathematics proficiencies and five main content areas; at the classroom and school level, it evaluates 45 distinct curricular elements.

Performance anchoring of proficiency scales

Although cost considerations make it difficult to include performance tests in a census assessment, the interpretability of assessment results will be greatly enhanced by a collateral programme of performance testing in a limited sample of students from the population. Performance tasks, which require the student to respond or produce a result in a real-world context, give much more direct evidence of a student's usable skills than do the discriminations among the alternative answers of multiple-choice items typically used in large-scale testing.

Despite the considerable cost of the expert administration and scoring required in performance testing, state testing programmes could certainly afford to present such tests to a sample of some hundreds of students who have also participated in the regular assessment. If the two sets of scores are then matched for those students in the sub-sample, graded levels of accomplishment on the performance task could be located statistically on a corresponding proficiency scale. For example, the performance task might be for the student to find a certain item in a mail-order catalogue and to order it by phone. Assuming this behaviour could best be predicted from the student's score on the Reading scale, one could estimate by IRT methods the score on the Reading scale where a 50 or 80 per cent success rate on the performance task would be expected. The result would make the scale interpretable in the neighbourhood of that point, and similar tasks could be devised to 'anchor' the scale at other points. Not only would this method of criterion-referencing the assessment scales enhance their external validity, but the tests themselves would call attention to performance as the proximate objective of instruction rather than mere passing of scholastic tests.

Reporting

To be most broadly useful, a comprehensive assessment should produce reports for a variety of audiences. Computer-generated reports, with explanatory comments, should be supplied to students, classroom teachers, school department heads and principals, district supervisors, the state department of education and the media. Possible content and reporting forms for this purpose are suggested in this section and illustrated for the duplex design of Table 15.3. The results presented in these illustrations are drawn from the California and Illinois field trials of the duplex design; the names of the student and school have been changed.

Students

A report to individual students, to be shared with their parents, and a similar copy supplied to the student's classroom teacher, might take the form shown in Figure 15.1. The student's profile of scale scores in the main skill and content areas is presented both graphically and numerically. In the graph the score value is repressented by a small diamond bracketed by a 66 per cent confidence interval on the true score. The numerical value of the score is also shown at the right.

The origin and unit of the scale scores are assigned in the first year of the assessment and remain fixed thereafter. In Figure 15.1 a scale similar to that used by the California Assessment Program and by NAEP is shown: the mean for the state is set at 250 and the standard deviation at 50; the range of the scale is 0 to 500.

To aid in the normative interpretation of the scale, percentile points of various score distributions are shown for selected points on the scale. The student reports include percentiles for the classroom to which the student is assigned for the subject-matter, and for the state. Percentiles for the state are the same on all forms and can be printed beforehand; those for the school and classroom are overprinted by computer along with the information pertaining to the particular student.

In addition, the scale is referenced to certain mastery levels, defined here normatively as *basic*, *intermediate* and *advanced*. The implication is that students who fall in the basic range are candidates for some form of additional instruction or remediation, those in the intermediate range are progressing at the normal pace and those in the advanced range should be given opportunities for special instruction or activities in the relevant subject-matter.

In the display, the heavy vertical line indicates the student's overall mathematics scale score. The deviation of the confidence bands about this line to the right indicates areas of relative strength, and to the left areas of relative weakness. In the display of a student showing uniform progress (not requiring additional work in any skill or topic), all confidence bands would overlap the heavy vertical line.

Figure 15.1: A report of individual achievement intended for guidance purposes
Survey Test of Grade 8 Mathematics (NORC, University of Chicago)

Student report

Student: David Taylor
Teacher: Mary Jones
Class: Math 8G
School: Dos Robles
Date of Testing: 12 October 1987

YOUR PERSONAL MATHEMATICS ACHIEVEMENT PROFILE

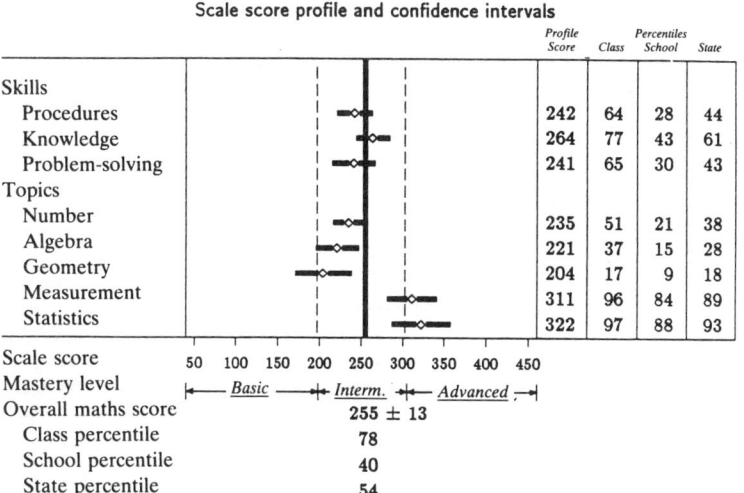

Scale score profile and confidence intervals

	Profile Score	Class	Percentiles School	State
Skills				
Procedures	242	64	28	44
Knowledge	264	77	43	61
Problem-solving	241	65	30	43
Topics				
Number	235	51	21	38
Algebra	221	37	15	28
Geometry	204	17	9	18
Measurement	311	96	84	89
Statistics	322	97	88	93

Scale score   50 100 150 200 250 300 350 400 450
Mastery level |—— *Basic* ——|—|— *Interm.* —|—|— *Advanced* ;—|
Overall maths score   255 ± 13
Class percentile   78
School percentile   40
State percentile   54

EXPLANATION

Your scores for eight areas of mathematics are shown in the graph above. Each bar on the graph has a 2/3 chance of including your true score. The diamond marks the best estimate of your true score. Scores to the right-hand side of the graph indicate relative strength in the mathematics skill or topic. Scores to the left indicate relative weakness. The heavy black verticle line marks your overall average score in mathematics. The overall mathematics score, and the class, school and state percentiles corresponding to it, are shown below the graph.

School

The school report is designed for teachers, school principals and district superintendents. The school report takes two forms: the first, shown in Figure 15.2 (a) summarizes the student reports for the school. The distribution of student scores is depicted as a histogram, and the percentage of students in each of the mastery levels is indicated for proficiencies and main content areas. The mean scale scores and corresponding state percentiles are shown at the right. The heavy vertical line in the display represents the average overall mathematics score for the school. As a further aid to teachers, these results could also be presented in the form of a class roster giving the student scale scores, percentile ranks and mastery levels.

The second part of the school report, shown in Figure 15.2 (b) and (c), gives the scale scores for each of the 45 curricular elements of the duplex design in Table 15.2. Results are again presented in graphic form, as confidence bands and diamonds, and in score values and percentiles on the right. The heavy vertical line, which is at the same point as in Figure 15.2 (a), shows the overall mathematics score for the school. Specific units in which instruction is relatively strong are indicated by bars to the right, and those units where instruction is relatively weak (and possibly requiring attention) to the left.

Emulating the reports of the California Assessment Program, the school report for curricular objectives also includes a rectangular box or 'comparison band' for each element. The band represents the range of scale scores for the element that would be expected on the basis of the resources and community background of the school. (In the Illinois study these school characteristics were (1) size of enrolment, (2) urban or rural, (3) percentage minority enrolment, (4) north or south location in state, and (5) median income of district.) From data for the state as a whole, relationships are empirically determined to best predict the performance of the school from these characteristics. The relationships give a range of scores that would reasonably be expected from knowledge of the school background alone. For each curricular element, they permit the actual performance of the school to be compared with schools in districts with characteristics similar to its own. If the diamond marking the scale score of a school lies to the right of this band, then the effectiveness of its instruction for the curricular element is better than might have been expected. If it lies to the left of the comparison band, the effectiveness of the school's instruction in the curricular element is poorer than might have been expected. Comparison of scale scores with these bands thus reveals *relative* strengths and weaknesses of the school's programme.

District

Reports to the district superintendents, not illustrated here, take the same form as the school reports, but they aggregate over all students and all schools in the district. These reports are shared with the local school board, and copies would be forwarded to the state department or board of education.

Figure 15.2(a): School report showing distributions of individual student scores

School Report

School: Sanderson
Date of Testing: 11-11-86
Number of Students Tested: 72

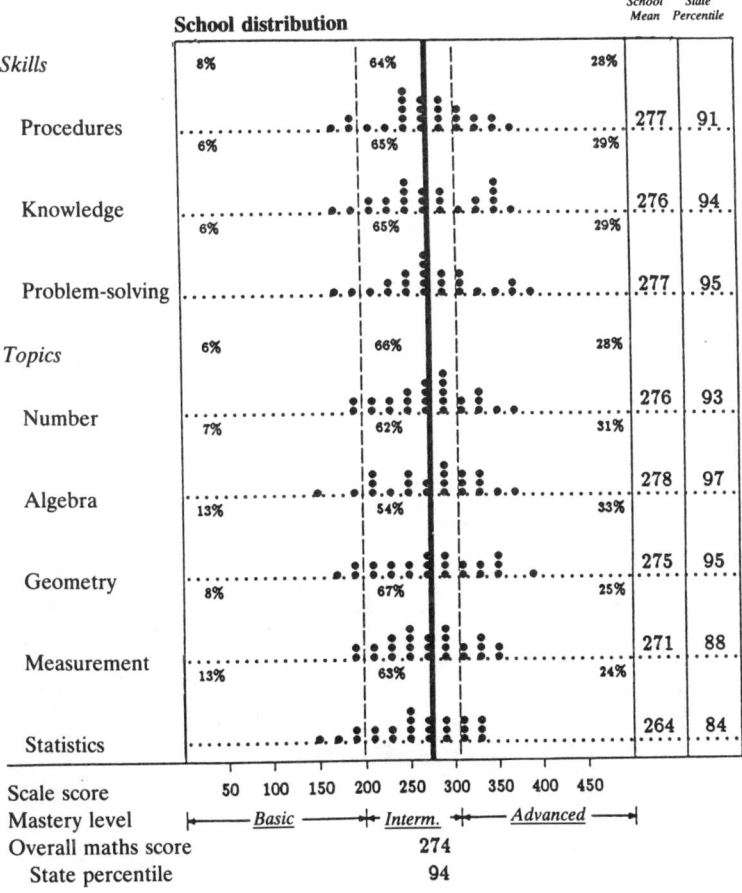

EXPLANATION

Each • represents about three students. The heavy black vertical line marks the overall average score of the school in mathematics.

Figure 15.2(b): Report of scores for detailed curricular elements estimated at school level

School performance on curricular objectives

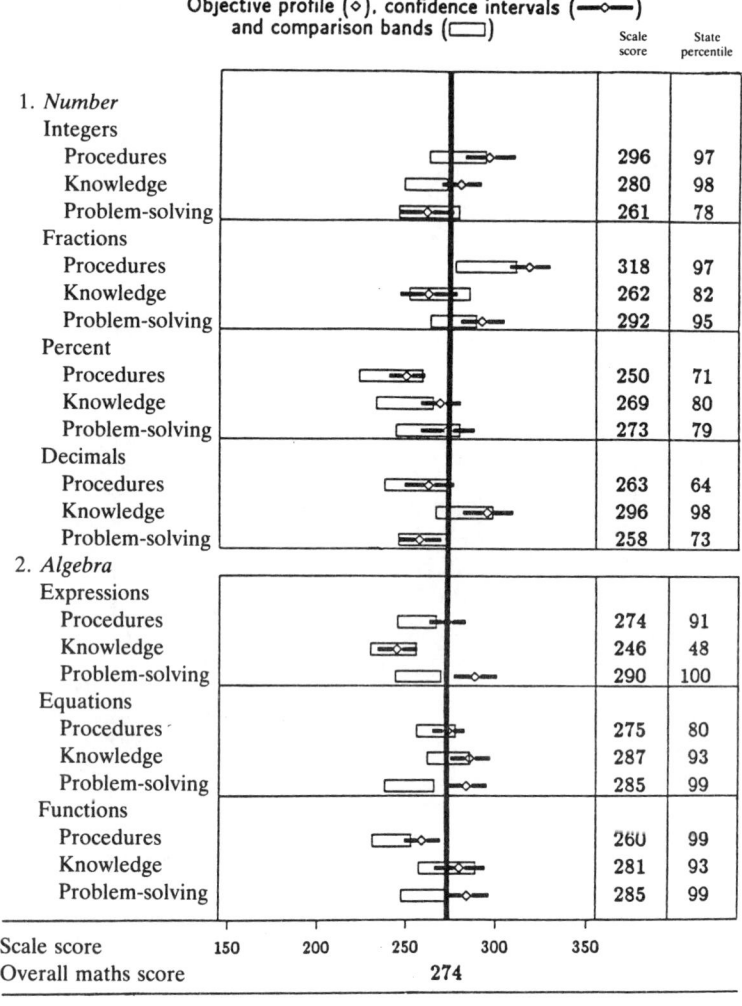

Objective profile (◇), confidence intervals (—◇—) and comparison bands (▭)

			Scale score	State percentile
1. *Number*				
Integers				
Procedures			296	97
Knowledge			280	98
Problem-solving			261	78
Fractions				
Procedures			318	97
Knowledge			262	82
Problem-solving			292	95
Percent				
Procedures			250	71
Knowledge			269	80
Problem-solving			273	79
Decimals				
Procedures			263	64
Knowledge			296	98
Problem-solving			258	73
2. *Algebra*				
Expressions				
Procedures			274	91
Knowledge			246	48
Problem-solving			290	100
Equations				
Procedures			275	80
Knowledge			287	93
Problem-solving			285	99
Functions				
Procedures			260	99
Knowledge			281	93
Problem-solving			285	99

Scale score   150   200   250   300   350
Overall maths score   274

Procedures: Calculating, rewriting, constructing, estimating.
Knowledge: Terms, definitions, concepts, principles.
Problem-solving: Proof, reasoning, real-world applications.

Figure 15.2(b) contd

Objective profile (◇), confidence intervals (—◇—)
and comparison bands (☐)

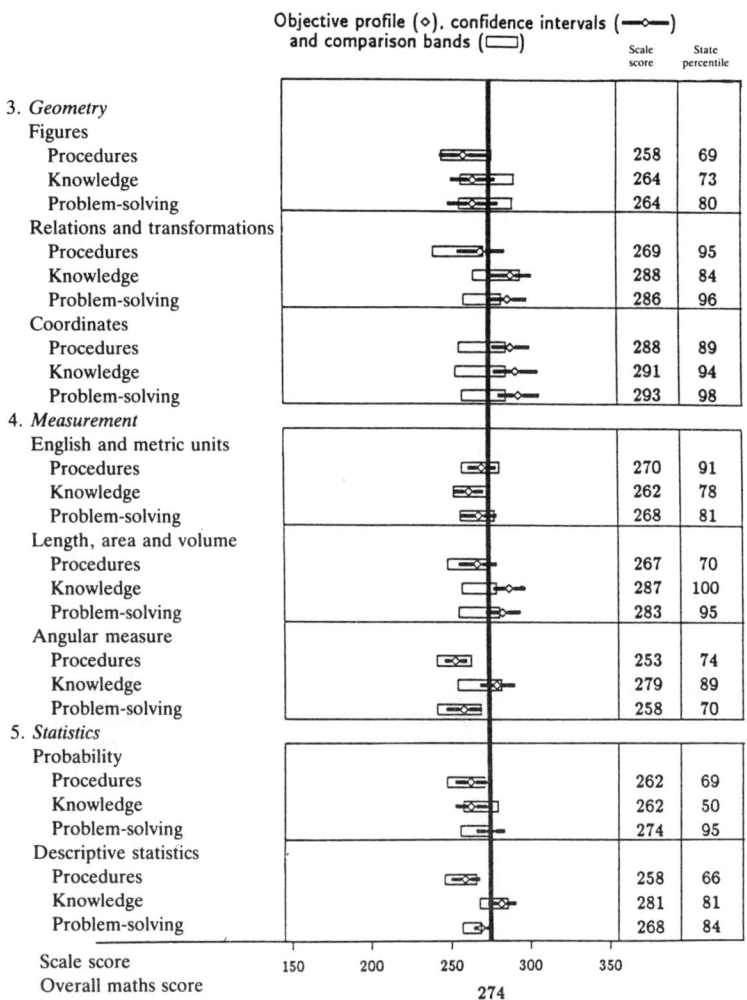

	Scale score	State percentile
3. *Geometry*		
Figures		
Procedures	258	69
Knowledge	264	73
Problem-solving	264	80
Relations and transformations		
Procedures	269	95
Knowledge	288	84
Problem-solving	286	96
Coordinates		
Procedures	288	89
Knowledge	291	94
Problem-solving	293	98
4. *Measurement*		
English and metric units		
Procedures	270	91
Knowledge	262	78
Problem-solving	268	81
Length, area and volume		
Procedures	267	70
Knowledge	287	100
Problem-solving	283	95
Angular measure		
Procedures	253	74
Knowledge	279	89
Problem-solving	258	70
5. *Statistics*		
Probability		
Procedures	262	69
Knowledge	262	50
Problem-solving	274	95
Descriptive statistics		
Procedures	258	66
Knowledge	281	81
Problem-solving	268	84

Scale score   150   200   250   300   350

Overall maths score   274

State

For state level summaries of the performance of eighth grade students and their schools, the displays in Figure 15.3 (a) and (b) are informative and easily understood by the general public. The state-level information is summarized in terms of overall mathematics achievement and is not broken down into scores for proficiencies, content or curricular elements. Figure 15.3 (a) shows the distribution of overall mathematics scores for all students in the state. Data for the current year and the previous year are presented in order to show the direction of change. In this figure the data for 1986 is real, but that for 1985 has been simulated for purposes of this example. The median score of students in the state is shown as a heavy line, and the percentage of students in each of the mastery levels is also given. The graphs thus convey both the numbers and the percentages of students who are achieving in eighth-grade mathematics at defined levels of mastery. This is the form of data that is of most interest to state officials, legislators and the public.

Figure 15.3 (b), showing both the absolute and relative performance of schools with respect to overall eighth-grade mathematics scores, would be of special interest to state departments of education as well as to the media. By the use of code numbers for the school, the display shows the mathematics achievement scale score for each school relative to the score that would be predicted on the basis of the school's characteristics and resources. The heavier diagonal black line on the graph shows the expected score, and the vertical distance of the school location from that line indicates relative performance. If this distance is greater than the two-standard deviation interval indicated by the upper light diagonal line, the school is performing better than expected from community characteristics; if it is below the lower light diagonal line, the school is performing significantly poorer than would be expected on these grounds. Anyone privileged to view the list of schools and school codes can see immediately on this graph those schools that are relatively effective in teaching eighth-grade mathematics, and those that are relatively less effective. In addition, the absolute performance of the schools is conveyed by the position of the school with respect to the observed outcome scale on the left. The chart is a basis for discussing school performance in terms that are fairer to the school districts than a report of outcome scores alone.

Media

Any of the foregoing reports from the school level upwards could be released to the media. A considerable amount of descriptive material and comment may have to accompany the quantitative reports in order to make the material understandable to reporters and the public. As an aid to interpretation of the results, it is standard practice to display actual items from the test. The pre-test items of the two-stage testing serve this purpose admirably. Because of the high level of exposure of these items, they should be replaced annually and are thus available for release to the public immediately following the testing. Having been chosen from among items of high discriminating power and covering a wide range of

Figure 15.3(a): Estimated state distributions of overall mathematics attainment scores

State summary

MATHEMATICS SCORES OF 8TH GRADE STUDENTS IN 1985 (SIMULATED) AND 1986 (ACTUAL)

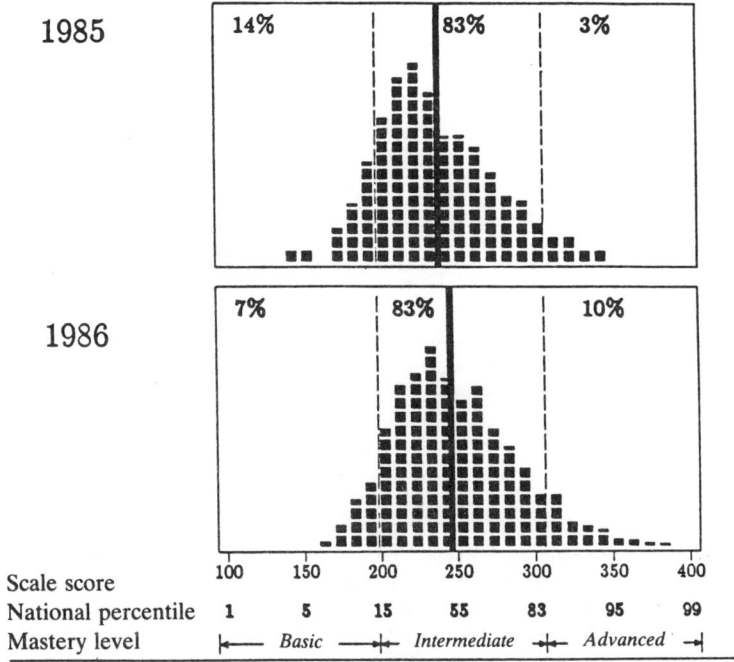

EXPLANATION

Overall mathematics attainment of 8th grade students in December of 1985 and 1986. Each box (■) represents 1,000 students. The heavy line (▌) is the median score for each year.

general mathematics proficiency, they are among the most powerful indicators of overall attainment in the subject-matter. The locations of their threshold on the scale score continuum can be presented graphically as a means of content-referencing various levels on the scale.

Figure 15.3(b): Observed overall mathematics scores for each school in the sample plotted against expected score

SCHOOL PERFORMANCE CHART

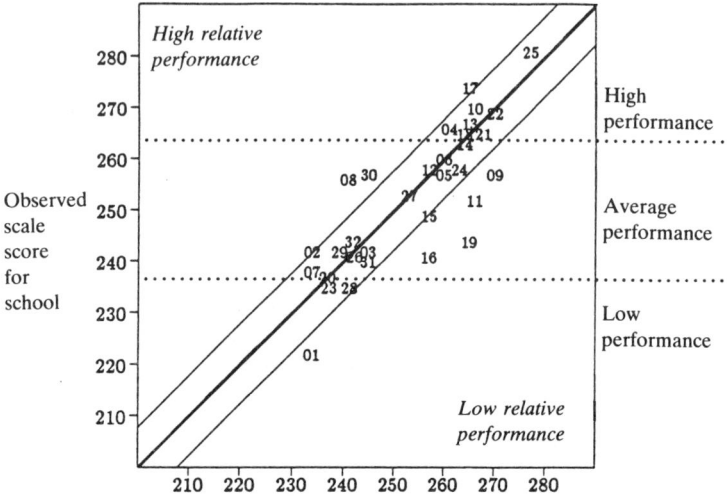

Scale score expected for school based on community characteristics and resources.

EXPLANATION

The location of schools on the performance chart is indicated by their identification codes. *Absolute* performance levels are given by the positions of the schools on the scale on the left. Performance *relative* to other schools with the same community characteristics and resources is indicated by the vertical distance of the school code from the heavy diagonal line. Schools located above the upper light diagonal line are performing better than expected. Those below the lower light diagonal line are performing less well than expected.

Between-state comparisons

The utility of state assessments can be further enhanced by expressing the results in terms of a common scale, preferably one for which national norms exist. State can then be compared with state, and state with nation, for purposes of evaluating educational programmes and promoting economic development. National norms could, of course, be obtained by administering the state test in a nation-wide sample of schools, but the prospect of all, or most, of the 50 states undertaking such surveys is not pleasant to contemplate. By use of equating methods, a much more efficient and less intrusive approach is possible. All that is needed is to administer, to a sample of students who have taken the state test, a nationally normed test covering approximately the same content as part or all of the assessment instrument. Statistical methods could then be used to obtain the best unbiased prediction of the national test scores from the scores on the state test. The predicted national test scores could then be aggregated to the school district or state level for purposes of comparing educational performance in one state with the national norm or with any other state using a similar procedure to express its assessment results.

From the normative score distribution of the national test the predicted scores could be interpreted in terms of percentiles of the national population in the same way that the student scores are interpreted in local and state percentiles. This method has already been used to express the reading comprehension scale of the California Assessment Program in the units of the Degrees of Reading Power test at the eighth grade level (Bock, Sykes and Schilling, 1987). As a source of national test scales in terms of which state assessment results could be expressed, the National Assessment of Educational Progress is an obvious candidate, provided it could produce scores at the pupil level suitable for this purpose.

Conclusion

Our analysis of the potential users of data on educational outcomes – students, parents, teachers, school counsellors, school administrators, boards and officials, curriculum experts, textbook writers, state legislators and departments of education and educational research specialists – leads us to conclude that currently existing programmes for evaluating educational productivity should, and can, be re-designed to serve the needs of this varied community. We propose for this purpose the duplex design, which supplies achievement scores for individual students in the main areas of proficiency and content while, at the same time, evaluating the progress of schools in attaining the detailed objectives of the instructional programme and curriculum. Based on new developments in educational statistics and measurement, including item response theory, matrix sampling and two-stage testing, the duplex design is capable of delivering this range of information with no greater demand on testing resources and classroom time than is now required in conventional every-pupil achievement testing.

References

BOCK, R.D. and AITKIN, M. (1981). 'Marginal maximum likelihood estimation of item parameters: an application of an EM algorithm', *Psychometrika*, 46, 443–59.

BOCK, R.D. and ZIMOWSKI, M.F. (1989). *The Duplex Design: Giving Students a Stake in Educational Assessment*. Chicago: NORC.

BOCK, R.D., MISLEVY, R.J. and WOODSON, C.E. (1982). 'The next stage in educational assessment', *Educational Researcher*, 11, 4–11, 16.

BOCK, R.D., MURAKI, E. and PFEIFFENBERGER, W. (1988). 'Item pool maintenance in the presence of item parameter drift', *Journal of Educational Measurement*, 25, 275–85.

BOCK, R.D., SYKES, R. and SCHILLING, S. (1987). *CAP Reading Comprehension Skill expresses in units of the Degrees of Reading Power test*, NORC technical report to the California Assessment Program, Chicago.

BURSTEIN, L., BAKER, E.L., ASCHBACHER, P. and KEESLING, J.W. (1985). *Using State Test Data for National Indicators of Educational Quality: A Feasibility Study*. Los Angeles, Calif.: Center for the Study of Evaluation, UCLA Graduate School of Education.

LORD, F.M. (1962). 'Estimating norms by item sampling', *Educational and Psychological Measurement*, 22, 259–67.

LORD, F.M. (1980). *Applications of Item Response Theory to Practical Testing Problems*. Hillsdale, NJ: Erlbaum.

MISLEVY, R.J. (1983). 'Item response models for grouped data', *Journal of Educational Statistics*, 8, 271–88.

MISLEVY, R.J. (1985). *Inferences about Latent Populations from Complex Samples*. (NAEP Research Report No. 85-41). Princeton: Educational Testing Service.

MISLEVY, R.J. and BOCK, R.D. (1989). 'A hierarchical item-response model for educational testing'. In: BOCK, R.D. (Ed) *Multilevel Analysis of Educational Data*. New York: Academic Press.

WALKER, D. and SCHAFFARZICK, J. (1974). 'Comparing curricula', *Review of Educational Research*, 44, 83–111.

WINFIELD, L.F. (1986). The relationship between minimum competency testing and students' reading proficiency: implications for NAEP. Unpublished.

International Roundtable: Methodological Aspects of Large-scale Assessments

Chair and minutes:
Professor Dr R.S. Jäger, Zentrum für Empirische Pädagogische Forschung der EWH Rheinland-Pfalz, Landau (FRG).

Participants
Professor Dr R.D. Bock, The University of Chicago (USA).
Professor Dr R.K. Hambleton, University of Massachusetts (USA).
Professor Dr K.J. Klauer, Rheinisch-Westfälische Technische Hochschule, Aachen (FRG).
Professor Dr U. Raatz, Universität Duisburg (FRG).

The chairman compared the papers and comments made during the past two days with elements of diagnostic processes, aspects of social and educational background being the first step of large-scale assessments. One further step could be seen in the operationalization of school achievement and other intended educational goals. A third step covered questions raised in connection with data collection. Such data could serve as feedback to parents, students, teachers and administrators about the achievement in the educational setting. With this background in mind, the last round of discussion could begin, now the methodological basis of large-scale assessments could be discussed. Theoretical aspects, data collection and measurement problems could be focused upon.

The chairman, Professor Jäger, phrased the first question: which theoretical basis must be given to collect data, which can be used as a basis for feedback to parents, teachers and students? Can one rely upon a sound theoretical basis or do methodological aspects dominate research questions?

Professor Hambleton picked up this question. The clarity about the goals of educational assessment is very important. It is essential to decide what is to be measured, and how. For various large-scale assessments, the needs will be very different. From criterion-oriented assessment we have learned a great deal about how to write objectives. When we ask how to measure, we can focus upon the well-known principle of multiple-choice items. The principles of measurement should be orientated at the skills that one wants to measure.

Professor Klauer answered that educational measurement must be representative for the educational objectives: 'Here content validity must be central: two matters must be differentiated – i.e. trait and a set of tasks. The latter form of conceptionalization of objectives is especially important for testing devices. On the basis of a representative set of tasks as the foundation for test-instruments, it seems to me that items, that do not fit the model should not be deleted for any reason whatsoever. If this becomes necessary, these models are not appropriate for this testing problem.'

Professor Hambleton replied that measurement people should not be dictating to the curriculum people on what to do, rather they should help them to get the job done.

Professor Bock said that removing items which are too easy or too difficult in no way biases the content classification.

Professor Raatz felt uneasy about the models: 'We must begin with a theory, then we collect the data and then we look for a model to prove the theory.'

Professor Bock felt unhappy with the way the discussion was going: 'On one hand, there are well-elaborated, test-theoretical models. There are also procedures for item sampling. On the other hand, it is necessary to get valid and reliable measurements. These are the necessary conditions to establish large-scale assessments.'

He compared the situation with what Winston Churchill once said about democracy, that it is not the best form of government – but what are the alternatives? With the IRT, invariant scales can be established. For ten years ETS (Educational Testing Service) has used the same tests and researched the invariance of scales. One of the advantages of IRT is that it allows such comparisons to be made over time, between sub-populations of students, even if items are replaced. Under those conditions, percent-correct scores could not be used.

Professor Nenniger asked for the relationship between cognitive theories and test-theoretical models: 'Well elaborated cognitive theories do exist, though these have not found any equivalent test-theoretical models.'

Professor Hambleton responded that he did not care what he was measuring: 'Policy-makers will have to decide what they want to know and which measures they need. They have the responsibility to get such data which allow us to answer the questions. The persons that deal with measurement, on the other hand, have the responsibility to make sure that the questions can be answered with the data at hand. Increasingly, people reflect about the connection between IRT and cognitive theory. This is the reason why more and more test-theoretical models are provided, especially since the 1960s, which can be applied to questions that the measurement-specialists are faced with.'

Professor Raatz addressed the responsibility of psychometricians concerning the data collection: 'In the case of low test scores the question of what should happen to the respective students arises. When advice is asked for, it should be necessary to have other data at hand. A certain theory must always be given.' He asked how a psychometrician would react when a school system is changed: 'Can an item-pool be constructed, which is sensitive to such changes?'

Professor Bock replied that such experiences did exist; it was very important to apply dynamic measurement models to such changes.

Professor Klauer referred to his own experiences and confirmed that one should primarily have a theory concerning the subject-matter that is to be measured: 'Without such a theory, it is not possible to measure adequately. But this is only a question for the field of psychometrics, not the field of education. Those involved in this will have to declare what is to be measured. Another question is the item selection; one could select items that represent certain objectives. This is the background for the necessity of a theory.'

Item response theory makes strong assumptions which cannot always be checked on. Among other things, whether the necessary psychometric conditions also apply at the individual level is not tested. One alternative is the binomial model which is based upon weaker assumptions. Other theoretical positions are within the generalizability theory of Cronbach *et al.* and multidimensional scaling.

Mr Eggen returned to the discussion regarding theory. He saw great use in the IRT for large-scale assessments: 'IRT works much better than the other alternatives. This theory provides a fit for many areas of research.'

The chairman, Professor Jäger, introduced the next question. He asked if national or international experiences with rule-oriented item construction could be reported.

Professor Hambleton replied first. He mentioned the case of California, where certain variations of this procedure had been established: 'There the objectives have been clearly defined which are to be the basis of research. The following points could be considered to be relevant: (1) the clearer the objectives are defined, the clearer the measures that can be interpreted; (2) the clearer the definitions, the more valid the test items constructed; and (3) the clearer such definitions, the clearer the test scores that can be interpreted. Therefore, teachers who write items can also construct good items.'

Professor Ingenkamp asked if besides the IRT-models, other models exist which are better in principle – e.g. the binomial model.

Professor Hambleton replied that the binomial model possesses certain properties; but only on the basis of empirical data could the decision be made whether the binomial model fits or not.

Professor Bock added that, in his view, it was not easy to apply the binomial model. Professor Klauer responded that one must differentiate between two aspects: 'First, testing an individual, and secondly, the position a person has reached with reference to a group. Concerning the first matter it is obviously unnecessary to make assumptions about the distribution. In applying the binomial model, it is necessary to have a large sample. For individual testing, IRT-models are not useful; in this case, the necessary conditions for testing are not given.'

Professor Jäger introduced the question of feedback: 'What can be learned from large-scale assessments with respect to feedback mechanisms? Are there experiences in the USA concerning progress in achievement?'

Professor Hambleton referred to existing programmes in the USA which had realized such feedback mechanisms: 'It is only a matter of the sophistication of testing procedures to provide the data which can answer the questions asked by teachers.'

Professor Klauer expressed his doubts that on the basis of large-scale assessments, it was possible at all to address the individual level: 'If a teacher only gets the information towards the end of a school year, this information is not very helpful. On the other hand, is information comparing the performance of different classes very helpful for teachers. Those data are necessary at the school level. On that basis, schools can learn whether good work has been done or whether deficiencies exist, as compared to other schools.' Mr Hambleton added that all those questions can be answered by means of large-scale assessments: 'It is only necessary to adjust the measurement to the questions asked – e.g. to provide the information desired on the basis of appropriate models.'

Professor Tietze referred to the situation in Germany: 'One can, of course, debate about the best model. What is of primary importance is whether the information is provided or not. Especially in the period of introducing large-scale assessments, it is necessary ultimately to rely upon weaker models, conditions which are not as well founded theoretically, but have at least some information which can act as screening instruments.'

Professor Klauer agreed with Professor Tietze. The availability of such information can serve as a better basis for teachers than is the case now. Professor Raatz also agreed: 'Some information is better than no information. But it is necessary to provide such information at the beginning of a school year rather than towards the end. It is also necessary to combine information from large-scale assessments with the teacher's information from the class setting. Only the combination of both sources can provide the optimal basis for the individual student.'

Dr Sandbergen stressed the point that for a psychometrician it is highly risky to try to answer any given question on the basis of large-scale assessments: 'The main problem is to get politicians to formulate their needs. It is also necessary to learn something about the effects upon the school system: what are the effects of learning in schools?'

Professor Ingenkamp closed by warning against getting all questions answered by large-scale assessments. He called for a 'pragmatic access': 'The experiences of other countries have clearly indicated that the necessary foundations have been laid to start with large-scale assessments in Germany now.'

Appendix

Presenters and Partners*

Archie E. Lapointe,
Director,
National Assessment of Educational
Progress (NAEP),
PO Box 2923, Princeton, NJ 08541,
USA.

Professor Dr Horst Dichanz,
FB Erziehungs- und Sozialwissen-
schaften Fernuniversität GH Hagen,
Postfach 940,
D-5800, Hagen.

Dr Roy M. Forbes,
HuCo Associates,
PO Box 325, Kure Beach, NC 28449,
USA.

Dipl-Päd. Walter H. Schreiber, M.A.
Zentrum für empirische pädagogische
Forschung der EWH Rheinland-
Pfalz,
Im Fort 7,
D-6740 Landau.

Dr Ramsay W. Selden,
Director,
State Education Assessment Center
(CCSSOC),
379 Hall of the States,
400 N. Capitol Str., NW
Washington, DC 20008,
USA.

Professor Dr Helmut Lukesch,
Fakultät für Pädagogik und Psycho-
logie,
Universität Regensburg
Universitätsstr. 31
D-8400, Regensburg.

HMI Mr Peter Silvester,
APU,
Department of Education and
Science,
Elizabeth House,
York Road,
London SE1 7PH.

Dr Günter Trost,
Direktor,
Institut für Test- und Begabungsfor-
schung der Studienstiftung des Deut-
schen Volkes,
Koblenzer Str. 77,
D-5300, Bonn 2.

Dr Sjaak Sandbergen,
Ministerie van Onderwijs en Weten-
schapen (BO/SP),
Postbus 25000,
NL-2700 LZ, Zoetermeer.

Professor Dr Karlheinz Ingenkamp,
Zentrum für empirische pädagogische
Forschung der EWH Rheinland-
Pfalz,
Im Fort 7,
D-6740, Landau.

*The presenters are listed in the left-hand column, the respective partners in the right. The order is according to the sequence in this volume. The partners have done invaluable work in briefing the presenters on the state of knowledge in the field in Germany and given information on what would be especially interesting for the audience.

Dr Dale Carlson,
Director,
California Assessment Program
(CAP),
California State Department of Education,
PO Box 944 272,
Sacramento, Calif. 94224-2720,
USA.

Professor Dr Wolfgang Tietze,
FB 9 Erziehungswissenschaft Westfälische Wilhelms-Universität,
Georgskommende 33,
D-4400, Münster.

Professor Ingemar Wedman,
Umea Universitetet, Pedagogiska Institutionen,
PO Box S-901 87, Umea.

Professor Dr Kurt Aurin,
Lehrstuhl Erziehungswiss. II
Albert-Ludwigs-Universität
Rempartstraße 11/III,
D-7800, Freiburg.

Dr Paul D. Sandifer,
Director, Office of Research,
State Department of Education,
Columbia, SC 29201, USA.

Dr Jürgen Baumert,
Max-Planck-Institut für Bildungsforschung,
Lentzealle 94,
D-1000, Berlin 33.

Dr Clare Burstall,
Director,
National Foundation for Educational
Research (NFER),
The Mere, Upton Park,
Slough, Berks SL1 2DQ, England.

Dr Jürgen van Buer,
Universität-GHS Siegen FB II –
Erziehungswiss,
Adolf-Reichwein-Str. 2
D-5900, Siegen 21.

Dr Johan M. Wijnstra,
Project Director,
Dutch National Assessment Program
(PPON),
CITO,
PO Box 1034,
NL-6801 MG, Arnhem.

Dr Andreas Helmke
Max-Planck-Institut für psychologische Forschung,
Leopoldstr, 24
D-8000, München 40.

Professor Dr Helga Thomas,
Technische Universität Berlin,
FB 22 – Erziehungs- und Unterrichtswissenschaften Franklinstr, 28/29
D-1000, Berlin 10.

Professor Ron K. Hambleton,
University of Massachusetts,
Hills South, Room 152,
Amherst, Mass. 01003, USA.

Professor Dr Karl Josef Klauer
Institut für Erziehungswiss,
RWTH Aachen,
Eilfschornsteinstr, 7
D-5100, Aachen.

Dr Tej Pandey,
California Assessment Program
(CAP),
California State Department of Education,
PO Box 944 272,
Sacramento, 94224-2720,
USA.

Professor Dr Ulrich Raatz,
FB 2 – Erziehungswiss.
Universität GH Duisburg,
Postfach 101 629
D-4100, Duisburg.

Mr Theo Eggen,
Dutch National Assessment Program
(PPON),
PO Box 1034,
NL-6801 MG, Arnhem.

Professor Dr Peter Nenniger,
Christian-Albrechts-Universität Kiel
Institut für Pädagogik
Olshausenstr, 40
D-2300, Kiel.

Professor R. Darrell Bock,
The University of Chicago,
Department of Behavioral Sciences,
5848 South University Avenue,
Chicago, Ill. 60637, USA.

Professor Dr Heinrich Wottawa,
Fakultät für Psychologie,
Ruhr Universität,
Postfach 10 21 48
D-4630, Bochum 1.

Additional participants in the International Roundtable

Dr W. Ebert,
President,
Verband Bildung und Erziehung,
Dreizehnmorgenweg 36
D-5300, Bonn 2.

Professor Dr Reinhold S. Jäger,
Zentrum für empirische pädagogische Forschung der
EWH Rheinland-Pfalz,
Im Fort 7,
D-6740, Landau/Pfalz.

Dr E. Thürmann,
Gewerkschaft Erziehung und Wissenschaft,
Deventerweg 40,
D-4770, Soest.

The NFER-NELSON Assessment Library

Edited by Dr J Beech and Dr L Harding

The *NFER-NELSON Assessment Library* is a major new initiative which will gradually build up to form the UK's definitive test reference collection.

It is designed to improve the knowledge and expertise of existing test users, as well as to introduce other professionals to the possible use of assessments in their work.

The first three books in the series are: **Testing: A Statistical Introduction to Psychometrics; Educational Assessment of the Primary School Child; Assessment of the Elderly.**

Further titles are in preparation, including books on neuropsychological assessment, assessment in the secondary school and assessments for speech therapists.

Testing has long been seen as the province of psychologists. The *NFER-NELSON Assessment Library* takes a multidisciplinary approach by drawing on authors from a wide range of professions, avoiding specialist vocabulary and showing how a number of different approaches can contribute to a particular problem or area.

Each volume comprises two basic elements:

1. a series of chapters discussing basic assessment issues within the area

2. a collection of critical, evaluative reviews of the main tests within the area

The chapters and reviews are backed up by diagrams, glossaries, bibliographies and full indexes. Each chapter is written by a leading authority in that area.

The *NFER-NELSON Assessment Library* will be invaluable reading for initial and in-service students as well as a useful reference for busy professionals who want to refresh their knowledge or learn more about their colleagues' work.

If you would like to receive further information about
any of the above books please write in to our
Customer Support Department,
NFER-NELSON,
Darville House,
2 Oxford Road East,
Windsor SL4 1DF

and we will send you ordering details and
prices as soon as they are available.